Realize Enterprise Architecture with AWS and SAFe

A comprehensive, hands-on guide to AWS with Agile and TOGAF

Rajnish Harjika

BIRMINGHAM—MUMBAI

Realize Enterprise Architecture with AWS and SAFe

Copyright © 2022 Packt Publishing

Group Product Manager: Rahul Nair
Publishing Product Manager: Yashashree Hardikar
Content Development Editor: Nihar Kapadia
Technical Editor: Shruthi Shetty
Copy Editor: Safis Editing
Project Coordinator: Ashwin Dinesh Kharwa
Proofreader: Safis Editing
Indexer: Rekha Nair
Production Designer: Sinhayna Bais
Marketing Coordinator: Nimisha Dua
Senior Marketing Coordinator: Sanjana Gupta

First published: September 2022

Production reference: 1190822

Published by Packt Publishing Ltd.
Livery Place
35 Livery Street
Birmingham
B3 2PB, UK.

ISBN 978-1-80181-207-8

www.packt.com

To my mother, Mrs. Sulochna Harjika; my wife, Naveen Nav; and my colleagues at NETSOL Technologies, especially AG and Furrukh Sohail, who have motivated and supported me throughout the process.

Also, I would like to thank Naila Afsheen, the editor who worked with me to ensure high-quality content.

Contributors

About the author

Rajnish Harjika is a technologically sophisticated, goal-oriented IT leader and a TOGAF 9.1 practitioner with 25+ years' success, driving high-performance teams to architect and build cutting-edge solutions from inception to delivery. He has a strong history of delivering digital and cloud transformation efforts that substantially enhance efficiency and technological excellence. He has a demonstrated ability to mitigate and significantly reduce risks by comparing current and target architecture, monitoring compliance, and implementing key security measures. Rajnish has great expertise in providing strategic consulting for business transformation, digital transformation, and cloud transformation.

About the reviewer

Vibhu Kuchhal is an enterprise architect who loves assisting stakeholders to solve business problems, utilizing a variety of architectural tools and technology. He often assists customers to make sense of existing business, technology, and capability investments and helps to optimize desired transformations. Vibhu has extensive experience working with several implementation paradigms and technologies, and he has led teams to deliver large-scale transformations for his customers.

Vibhu Kuchhal is currently working as a managing consultant with Telstra Purple, an organization that puts people at the center of solving real problems for organizations, enabling the delivery of great digital transformation with purpose.

I'd like to thank the author, Rajnish, and the team at Packt for giving me the opportunity to do something that has been wholly enjoyable; reviewing this great book presented an interesting perspective. Most thanks, however, go to my wife, Shilpi, and my kids, Vishishth and Atharv, for supporting me in reviewing this book alongside my busy professional life.

Table of Contents

2

Defining Core Foundation and How to Get It Right

3

Applying Enterprise Architecture to the AWS Cloud

Part 2 – Enterprise Architecture Frameworks

4

Available Frameworks for an Enterprise Architecture

5

AWS Prescriptive Guidance Frameworks

TOGAF Framework in Action with AWS

Part 3 – SAFe in EA and the Cloud

7

Align and Scale Agile Framework with Enterprise Architecture

8

SAFe Implementation for AWS Cloud Migrations

Part 4 – Setting Up an EA

9

Setting Up an Enterprise Architecture Practice

10

Conclusion

Index

Other Books You May Enjoy

Preface

In order to build cloud-based systems, you must understand the pros and cons of your decisions. You can use the AWS Well-Architected Framework to help you maintain a balance between the pros and cons. Using the Framework's six pillars and SAFe strategies, you will learn how to design and operate systems that are reliable, secure, efficient, cost-effective, and sustainable. This book sheds light on the importance of enterprise architecture, how it fits into AWS, and its relation with SAFe. By the end of this book, you will understand how to apply SAFe with enterprise architecture principles on the AWS cloud and achieve/apply the best practices with an EA setup, in conjunction with the cloud and SAFe.

Who this book is for

This book is a reference for both experienced and non-experienced IT architects who seek to understand the real-world application of EA with SAFe methodologies in the AWS cloud. If you are an IT professional who is interested in learning how to apply EA principles to the AWS cloud, especially with an agile approach, then this book will prove to be extremely useful.

What this book covers

Chapter 1, *Core Foundation for Building an Enterprise IT Architecture*, provides a basic understanding of the EA core foundation and the need for it. It looks at how a core foundation can help to realize business value and how organizations can achieve the highest business agility and a core foundation role. We will further explain the building blocks of an architecture to derive solutions building blocks. By the end of this chapter, you will have an insight into achieving operational efficiency with core EA components.

Chapter 2, *Defining Core Foundation and How to Get It Right*, delves into the basics of EA ownership, roles, and responsibilities, paired with a leadership principle overview that derives the EA practice. The ways to manifest an ineffective core foundation, building, optimizing, and executing the right core foundations for your enterprise. IT engagement model, setting up the EA goals, and priority. Lastly, we will understand what is involved in realizing business value from EA assets.

Chapter 3, *Applying Enterprise Architecture to the AWS Cloud*, looks at the role of EA in the cloud and its alignment with AWS. It can have a positive impact on cloud adoption and any project related to cloud adoption. This chapter is about the EA principles applicable to cloud and architecture domains and how to proceed in setting up AWS services in support of EA and what roles and responsibilities of EA play a major role in AWS..

Chapter 4, Available Frameworks for an Enterprise Architecture, focuses on the importance of knowing where and how EA can be implemented, which frameworks are available today, and when to use them. In what ways does EA contribute to the industry, and what are its objectives? We will discuss the tools and software used by EAs, including application portfolio management and EA tools. The identification of the current, targeted, and transit state of architecture will be followed by an explanation of EA in the context of digital transformation.

Chapter 5, AWS Prescriptive Guidance Frameworks, covers prescribing the frameworks for enterprise to ensure that EA is kicked off and moves in the right direction, and we will identify the EA areas of weakness. This chapter focuses on understanding AWS prescriptive guidance frameworks, including MRA, CAF, and WAR, and aligning with frameworks such as TOGAF. The readiness assessment process, the prerequisites, and the next steps are also discussed.

Chapter 6, TOGAF Framework in Action with AWS, explores TOGAF architecture domains and cloud ecosystems in the context of AWS, along with a review of reference architecture and models. This chapter looks deeply into the ways to approach each phase of TOGAF ADM in AWS cloud transformation. We will determine non-functional aspects of the system, including security, reliability, operational excellence, performance efficiency, and cost optimization.

Chapter 7, Align and Scale Agile Framework with Enterprise Architecture, examines selecting an IT initiative across your enterprise and digging deeper into a strategy that drives your architecture building blocks and solution building blocks. This chapter discusses and explains approaches to infrastructure, including on-premises, cloud, and hybrid implementation and application. Furthermore, we will talk about SAFe as a good fit in EA, aligning EA and SAFe for any business, and how it caters to AWS cloud customers.

Chapter 8, SAFe Implementation for AWS Cloud Migrations, takes a deeper look into cloud migration and where an organization should start its journey from. We will look at the meaning of the cloud with respect to a specific industry and figure out whether it would be the right choice or strategy to adopt. When it comes to cloud transformation, how does adopting agile or SAFe help? This chapter further narrows down to steps that can ensure cloud migration is a success with SAFe agility.

Chapter 9, Setting up an Enterprise Architecture Practice, focuses primarily on EA enablement readiness. This chapter is about understanding the process and flow to establish EA practices. Furthermore, owners are identified, and a workflow is determined for each of the owners along with roles and responsibilities. This part of the book also explains EA modeling languages and gives more details about ArchiMate, along with the best practices and architecture principles that will drive an EA roadmap for a business.

Chapter 10, Conclusion, targets to summarize all previous chapters. It relates the flow of chapters in the sequence and aligns it all together. This chapter also highlights key AWS Framework, TOGAF 9. x overview with ADM and how SaFe aligns with TOGAF and AWS.

Download the color images

We also provide a PDF file that has color images of the screenshots and diagrams used in this book. You can download it here: `https://packt.link/F31q9`.

Conventions used

The following convention is used throughout this book.

> **Tips or Important Notes**
> Appear like this.

Get in touch

Feedback from our readers is always welcome.

General feedback: If you have questions about any aspect of this book, email us at `customercare@packtpub.com` and mention the book title in the subject of your message.

Errata: Although we have taken every care to ensure the accuracy of our content, mistakes do happen. If you have found a mistake in this book, we would be grateful if you would report this to us. Please visit `www.packtpub.com/support/errata` and fill in the form.

Piracy: If you come across any illegal copies of our works in any form on the internet, we would be grateful if you would provide us with the location address or website name. Please contact us at `copyright@packt.com` with a link to the material.

If you are interested in becoming an author: If there is a topic that you have expertise in and you are interested in either writing or contributing to a book, please visit `authors.packtpub.com`.

Share Your Thoughts

Once you've read *Realize Enterprise Architecture with AWS and SAFe*, we'd love to hear your thoughts! Scan the QR code below to go straight to the Amazon review page for this book and share your feedback.

https://packt.link/r/1801812071

Your review is important to us and the tech community and will help us make sure we're delivering excellent quality content.

Part 1 –
Enterprise Architecture
Foundation and Implementation

In this first part, you will learn about the critical core foundation components of **enterprise architecture** (**EA**) and how to relate them to the AWS cloud. This part of the book will assist you in applying EA architecture principles and domains to the AWS cloud by building the right core foundation.

If you need help with the basic concepts of the EA core foundation or are looking to learn more about its importance, the first three chapters about the core foundation will help you to make decisions and realize business values. With this, you will learn how to achieve business agility. You'll be in a better place to explain the building blocks of architecture to derive solutions driven by both architecture and solution building blocks.

The EA foundation and implementation help you to achieve operational efficiency and help you define the success of the core foundation.

Organizations often struggle to keep up with ever-evolving technology. Hence, innovation and growth process slows down a notch. The way forward is by implementing EA that navigates an organization through business processes for desired business outcomes. Hence, a well-structured and thought-through business agility model is needed now more than ever.

By the end of these chapters, you will be able to execute an EA strategy by building a core foundation. You will be more capable of handling the constant need to adapt to continuous advancements within a system. Plus, some background on the core foundation of an execution strategy comes in handy.

You'll know more about the EA leadership principle of business dynamics and the ways to set up the right core foundation.

This part of the book comprises the following chapters:

- *Chapter 1, Core Foundation for Building an Enterprise IT Architecture*
- *Chapter 2, Defining Core Foundation and How to Get It Right*
- *Chapter 3, Applying Enterprise Architecture to the AWS Cloud*

1

Core Foundation for Building an Enterprise IT Architecture

Many efforts toward creating and maintaining an ideal digital work environment with a smooth and seamless workflow go to waste. Even when stakeholders are equally involved, departments' actions are aligned, finances are managed efficiently, and research teams are monitoring the latest trends in the industry unless the execution is backed by a mature **enterprise architecture** (**EA**). A mature IT EA is often based on a solid EA foundation, strategically aligned, and tailored to the business needs.

In this chapter, we will cover areas that contribute to an effective foundation for execution. Therefore, we will cover the following topics:

- The EA strategy begins with building a core foundation
- The core foundation for execution strategies
- Building a business-specific core foundation
- EA domains
- Business dynamics versus IT complexity in businesses and IT systems

The EA strategy begins with building a core foundation

The EA strategy is the process of translating the business's vision and strategy into effective enterprise change by creating, communicating, and improving the key requirements, principles, and models that describe the enterprise's future state and enable its evolution. If we compare EA with its strategy, we can identify EA as a discipline for proactively and holistically leading enterprise responses to disruptive forces. It does this by identifying and analyzing the execution of change toward desired business vision and outcomes.

We live in a digitalized world where everything is automated. The need for an up-to-date IT infrastructure is more crucial than ever. Each aspect of modern life is in some way directly or indirectly associated with the use of technology. To keep technology running smoothly, being able to execute the core operations reliably is the top priority.

Business architecture is fundamentally about configuring IT resources in support of a company's business strategy. It brings together certain aspects, such as a company's strategic goals, its workflow, and the information it creates, as well as the infrastructure that underpins it. As part of its technology blueprint, EA determines not only what technology it currently possesses, but how future technology upgrades can be used to complement or enhance its current technology.

EA helps companies structure IT projects and policies to achieve the desired outcome. It employs architectural principles to keep up with industry practices, often known as EA planning.

However, apart from providing a strategic and business context to systems, the EA strategy provides an improved approach to looking at them holistically. It has been described as more of a management process that helps businesses with organization, resource allocation, and implementation. Organizations benefit from EA strategies in many ways. It allows them to review their IT status and IT goals in a comprehensive manner:

- Stability is improved as a result of standardizing processes and applications. Simplifying processes allows businesses to be more efficient and reduce the risk of problems.

- As an organization expects from EA, it reduces the complexity of systems. The right tools simplify system administration and management.

- By allowing the causes of problems to be identified quickly, organizations have been able to prevent bigger issues.

- Organizations are more agile thanks to EA. This allows them to analyze changes in the industry and respond to them promptly.

- Keeping an eye out for weak points in the system can prevent threats from entering the system. Cyber security breaches today are being addressed using systematized measures determined by EA.

In today's competitive marketplace, innovation rules the day, and opportunities to innovate are virtually endless, especially when it comes to applying technology to modernize processes, products, and services. Global market leaders, such as Dell, Capital One, and Walmart, have taken over their industries at a massive scale. While this development seems encouraging for the global economy, other companies with comparatively slower growth ratios must reconsider their plans of action.

In a survey of 103 US and European companies, 34% have a digitized core infrastructure and leverage modern technologies for a higher profit, faster time to market, and a better value from their IT investments. Such a core infrastructure ultimately leads to a 25% lower operational cost, better customer experience, lower risk of system failure and data loss, and higher satisfaction among stakeholders regarding technological advancements.

This chapter is based on insights into the stats, tools, strategies, and fundamentals applied by 500 US, European, and Asian companies for an effective foundation for execution. These elements provide the right substratum for large, medium, and small businesses to set their operations in the right direction by digitizing them. We will deep dive into their strategies and learn how they exploit their foundation for execution to achieve business agility, which leads to noticeable growth.

Automating routine tasks in an organization from top to bottom is the way to move forward in the coming years. This means minimizing or even eliminating human involvement in repetitive, manual work, such as food processing, supply and delivery operations, invoice generation, and payment processing. Building an effective core foundation for execution requires a capable infrastructure to handle this automated and digitized workflow without any chances of errors occurring. Organizations that maintain a reliable network and predictability in routine operations set organizations apart from their competitors.

We like information to be at our fingertips, just a click away from execution. In light of that, the food processing industry requires a transparent flow of information across the board, from customer orders to shipping, maintaining inventory, and delivering products and services.

7-ELEVEN Japan is the eighth largest retailer in the world. Climbing this ladder of success, the company's team leveraged the foundation of execution for their 10,000 stores to capably manage all of their inventory. The company's digitized process of collecting data at the point of sale using 70,000 computers allows users to place orders online and connect with the manufacturers for direct and effective communication. This automated and centralized mode of conducting business makes it possible for companies to develop new products each year.

A common misconception about the digitization of core business operations is that organizations must focus their energy on competitive capabilities. However, success lies in the strategy, where, every day, mundane processes are combined with complex tasks. This begins the digitization process with common services such as recruiting, investments, and telecommunication and then moves toward more bespoke components. With a smooth and seamless workflow for employees who use these systems every day, management has the freedom to let go of low-value tasks and focus on revenue, innovation, and growth.

The elements of the core foundation

Whether the goal is cloud computing, **robotic process automation (RPA)**, or **machine learning (ML)**, organizations must constantly evaluate new technologies and the ways they can or should be incorporated into their business strategies. Continuous innovation requires an EA that is well designed and documented, with clear processes for achieving the desired business outcomes. By definition, a well-designed EA is an architecture model that draws a big picture of the entire organization, with a long-term view. This blueprint explains the business processes, hierarchical structure, information systems, and technologies. It also allows modern innovations to be adopted. Let's take a look:

- **Architecture management**

  Setting up and implementing a single model is one thing while ensuring productivity across the board is another. A team must keep track of every move within the organization to ensure the business goals align with the IT infrastructure.

- **Architecture framework**

  The framework provides the foundation for the architectural model, along with basic guidelines and principles. These practices are defined for all stakeholders under this framework so that they can align their work ethics with the system.

- **Implementation of the development methodology**

  There are ways to implement methodology smoothly across the board while making sure that critical business operations are not disrupted. However, ensuring there's a seamless and effective implementation may take longer than expected.

- **Effective governance**

  This ensures that an EA program is managed properly to produce artifacts and plans that are truly representative of the organization's goals and needs. EA governance also ensures that business and technical decisions become aligned with the EA from initiation to implementation.

- **Documentation artifacts**

  One of the core elements of business models is to document every move for future reference. In an EA, plans, strategies, implementations, and workflows are documented and consistently maintained.

- **Architecture repository**

  The repository defines and documents the resourcefulness of the organization during the implementation process. It also contains the tools that are essential for accomplishing the goals defined by the framework.

- **Best practices**

  A set of best practices and guidelines are used to guide a sturdy workflow and review the existing architecture. These practices ensure transparency and productivity. This can have a trickle-down effect that can help establish a better understanding of the drivers of growth and innovation.

The core foundation for execution strategies

The need for an agile business model has never been more crucial. Especially with the COVID-19 pandemic, many industries have suffered irreparable losses that can only be recovered or avoided in the future with a more adaptable business strategy and innovation model.

> *"Rapid transformational changes are required when it comes to innovation in new digital products and services and an immense improvement in customer experience."*
>
> *Analyst firm Forrester*

Companies that had already embraced cloud infrastructure and an agile workflow adapted to the pandemic more quickly than digital laggards, who struggled with the remote work model and keeping customers happy.

EA maturity models are a way to assess the maturity of functional domains. They distinguish different maturity levels that an organization successively progresses through. As such, they can be used as a guideline for balanced incremental improvement of a functional domain.

EA is all about providing direction to IT regarding where to invest – that is, how to make the right technology choices to deliver business value. When it comes to predicting the impact on business value and outcomes, EA management tools provide crucial guiding elements for the process.

Now, let's look at some of the typical initiatives to ensure that an EA program is being tracked correctly.

Leadership and vision

A company's short-term tactical steps and long-term enterprise architectural vision must be aligned. To ensure EA success, leadership must take steps to ensure teams are educated on relevant initiatives, focused on business values, and equipped to do their part in moving the organization and processes toward the common end goal.

Early buy-in

It is especially helpful to get early alignment with every individual involved in the decision-making process for an organization to quickly move toward the common end goal. Buy-in across the business makes it easier to avoid unspoken concerns, uncover potential issues, or manage other factors that can derail an EA program.

Governance

Strong leadership paired with the right stakeholders in place across the board is essential to ensure tasks, milestones, and performance are moving in the right direction. Aligning the vision and interests of all stakeholders with a properly designed network is a huge challenge that will require processes to ensure teams and processes are operating as designed and intended.

Future-first design

Driving toward a future-centric approach that is in sync with leading technological advancements is imperative. EA should prepare an organization to confront known challenges and be flexible enough to leverage emerging technology. Indulging in current issues and struggles between legacy systems and innovation can be devastating when you're trying to achieve EA business goals and values.

CIO and business leader harmony

Stakeholder leaders must work together to ensure divergent viewpoints can be heard and addressed harmoniously. When the EA infrastructure is not sturdy enough, diverse opinions can make it tricky to resolve issues that come down to technology versus business.

Balance business and technology

Some may let the technical aspects of an EA operation take over an entire business environment. A more balanced approach is better, where business and technology requirements and the strategy are considered and information is shared to ensure effective operational processes.

Balanced team

There is a world of business opportunities out there, but finding the right team that is skilled and motivated to seize this opportunity can be a struggle. Organizations should strive to assemble a team that reflects a diverse blend of individuals who, among them, possess deep business acumen, technical understanding, and enthusiasm for the vision.

Goal-oriented vision

Technical input, business process, and performance measurement come together to form the basis for gauging the benefits of EA. Leaders must establish goals that focus beyond short-term achievements and strive for long-lasting impacts for each **key performance indicator (KPI)** associated with the EA vision.

Interoperability and integration

In our constantly evolving digital world, a team's ability to adapt to new changes is essential. To ensure this, the sustainability and a credible EA must be as future-proof as possible, with easy integration and operational flexibility that is supported and enforced across the board.

Solid communication

The right communication design can make or break the success of an EA organization, so this aspect of the work must not be taken lightly. Every stakeholder must be on the same page strategically speaking, and teams must be aware of the latest EA advancements within the organization. It is important to communicate the layout, benefits, and scope of the architecture.

Customer focus

Internal processes are important, but the most important stakeholder is the customer. The ultimate EA objective, business plan, and KPIs should be centered around the needs of the customer.

Resilience – the key to EA

Before and during the pandemic, EA experts have been in great demand to assist with the immediate and future migration of business applications to the cloud. They have also been engaged in multiple facets of transformation, depending on their business roadmap, risk assessment, feasibility, security, budget, development strategies, and other factors. EA teams have influenced the hastening of transformation and related processes.

EA translates company strategy into identified objectives to enable business capabilities. When executed well, EA translates business objectives into clearly defined transformation initiatives that analysts, portfolio owners, IT solution architects, and others across the business can move forward in their areas of focus.

In times of crisis, EA facilitates business continuity by focusing resources on the company's critical capabilities and accelerating recovery once the crisis has passed by, making the most of the new environment. EA supports resiliency, which can help a business not only survive a crisis but thrive post-crisis.

The following diagram shows the process of establishing a *knowledge-oriented* mentality in a firm, analyzing the current knowledge, and planning the knowledge that will be needed in the future. However, the *strategic level* portrays identifying the existing knowledge and how to effectively and efficiently allocate that knowledge within a firm.

The *operational level* is about ensuring that knowledge is used in everyday practices by those who need access to the right knowledge, at the right time, at the right location:

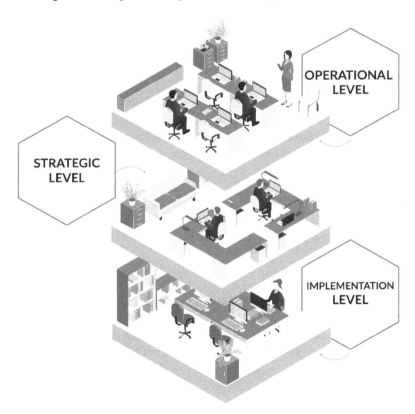

Figure 1.1 – Scope of EA

The following table categorizes the different EA values:

Category of EA Value	Value Description
Strategic and Political	Business and IT alignment
	Governance and compliance management enablement
	Management of IT and business capabilities
	IT investment decisions and the development of new infrastructures and capabilities
Transformational	Navigate from the strategy to delivering projects and portfolio management
Communication	Intentional, strategic communication
	Channels that connect business and IT professionals
Economic	IT costs lowered
	Operational efficiency, including operational cost
Flexibility and Agility	IT adaptability
	Responsiveness and time to market
Integration and Interoperability	Business processes across the supply chain
	IT resources across the enterprise
	IT and human dimensions
Inter-Organizational	Acquisition management improvements
	External relationship management
Knowledge Management	Knowledge sharing between IT and business professionals
	Knowledge source
Others	End-to-end security with a complete overview
	Client satisfaction
	Service availability analysis
	Increased spending on innovation
	Limited information duplication

Table 1.1 – The category of EA value is supported by evidence from the literature

Building a business-specific core foundation

An organization aligned with EA principles must have EA leaders who are thinking ahead about certain elements of the process to keep the workflow smooth and seamless. The size of the team, infrastructure model, and organizational structure are at the top of the list. Individuals or teams that are working together on a project with a common goal may have a different approach, but the work ethic and EA model must be aligned to maintain an effective workflow and ensure the agility of operations:

- **Understanding EA stakeholders**

  Attracting and identifying the set of stakeholders, including customers, that meet certain criteria is the top priority for an organization looking to transform its EA model. Each stakeholder holds a position with specific needs that can be fulfilled by the credible EA structure. For instance, while setting the foundation for the business value from technology, a CIO is likely to have a set of queries about the application roadmap, investments, and cost structure. Referring to the application life cycle map, financial matrix, and cost heatmap can help find answers.

- **Involving EA stakeholders**

  Getting the right team and having them on board is likely an easier task than keeping them all aligned and providing continuous support and effective communication. A stakeholder engagement initiative will vary based on an organization's structure and EA program scope, but it typically involves the following progressive levels:

  - **Develop a strategy**: Plan the approach, keeping in mind the ongoing processes that must be maintained, to retain key stakeholder support

  - **Understand the organization**: A firm grasp of the organization's history, culture, and key stakeholders makes it easier to assess and identify best institutional practices

  - **Assess current competencies**: Use analytics, organizational insights, and data to scope steps for desired outcomes

  - **Operate and evolve**: Set up EA operations based on organizational guidelines and continuously evolve the effort amid industry and organizational developments to generate and maintain stakeholder support

- **Choosing an operating model**

  It is important to build a model that fortifies the organization and can deal with arising internal or external issues efficiently. It is the first step toward the foundation for execution in EA.

  Each model is different from another, based on the organization's core values, goals, and program size. Here are the most common EA operating models:

- **Coordination Operating Model**: Autonomous business units control the business process design and adapt to its operations.

- **Unification Operating Model**: A matrix approach is used to integrate a global set of business processes with centralized management. Under this model, higher management stays focused on standardizing business processes across all units.

- **Diversification Operating Model**: Every business unit is unique, with a set of independent transactions. Apart from a minimal business process standardization, most IT decisions and business choices are made independently using a set of shared services.

- **Replication Operating Model**: Business units leverage a federated approach for integration and standardization. The workflow is centrally managed, but data is locally owned, with some aggregation and sharing with the enterprise.

- **Defining the structure of the EA team**

How to structure the EA team is sometimes a constantly echoing question within an organization that is planning to build an in-house EA structure. Any decision that's made in the beginning will have a long-term impact, and it is easier at this stage to garner organizational buy-in.

Despite having small teams, limited budgets, and little decision-making power, most enterprise architects are expected to implement powerful strategic technology programs. EAs can be distributed among leadership across an organization to strive for better alignment and a better workflow.

"The key to the success of any EA lies within a strategic allocation of architects. They can either be based in one department or spread across various groups reporting to a different manager. Hence, no two EA teams look identical."

Forrester

- **Building an EA ecosystem**

Building a network wider and wider by garnering buy-in from major stakeholders will ultimately achieve the maximum good. The core EA team should keep exploring the ways it works with the wider team and make improvements along the way.

The core EA team owns the overall EA structure, defines standards, and develops the business-aligned strategy. According to *Marcus Blosch*, research vice president at Gartner, instead of focusing on standards, structure, and control, organizations must widen their strategy toward driving business outcomes and work flexibly and creatively to define the future and how to get there. By adopting these traits, EA teams can develop a new group of talent to support digital business and digital transformation. They will establish competencies in developing a business strategy, designing new services and experiences, pursuing innovation, orchestrating collaboration across the organization, and navigating to the future.

Conversely, wider EA teams that consist of the solution, technical, and business architects are an extension of the core team. They work with other stakeholders in a constantly evolving, chaotic environment. A smooth and consistent flow of information among the core team and the wider team ensures a sturdier infrastructure and better outcomes.

- **Size teams accurately**

    A large EA team may have 50+ individuals focusing on different architecture domains or EA overall, a medium team that consists of between 15-50 people, and a small team that consists of fewer than 15 people. Here is a list of factors that can help EA leaders determine the appropriate size for their team:

    - Number of products and services within an organization

    - Timing for revenue and profit calculations

    - Maturity of the business process in an organization

    - How efficiently accounts and finances are managed

    - Organizational resources and the IT budget for advancements

    - The rate at which an organization adapts to the EA

Overall, there is no set standard for the right size when it comes to an EA team since it is based on certain factors within the organization.

EA domains for building a core foundation

Stephen Spewak's Enterprise Architecture Planning contributed greatly to the current popularity of dividing EA into four domains. While his approach was published in 1993, it is still in use today by most EA project teams.

Let's look at the four domains of EA work.

Business architecture

This domain defines organizational structure while addressing who will be involved and what they will do within the company's functional capabilities. Let's look at some example questions that must be answered to represent this domain. In general, a business architecture includes business processes, business capabilities, services, operating models, and value streams. What are the business vision, strategy, and objectives? Who is responsible for driving toward and achieving the anticipated goals?

Application architecture

This domain considers the relationships between specific applications and the core business processes of the organization while asking the question, how have current business capabilities been implemented? The process of tailoring software solutions based on evolving needs is addressed in this phase. When the software an organization is using cannot fulfill customer needs, feature updates are crucial. Redesigning software is the final resort but is necessary in cases where it fails to adapt to modern advancements.

Data architecture

This domain involves structuring an organization's data assets and management resources. An insight into business analytics lets businesses evolve along with customer needs. Data that's collected from users is stored in the database so that it can be managed and maintained for future reference. A strategic architecture makes processing complex data much easier.

Technology architecture

Resources, including software and hardware, are required to implement the application services. Modern technology is essential to building a functional network. This includes devices, routers, software, and storage. Adapting to changes is the key to success, and these changes will come in the form of a dynamic marketplace and changing user behavior.

A common practice of combining data and application domains into a single information system component works well for many EA frameworks. Moreover, all of the data that's collected from customers can take up quite a lot of space. Putting it in the cloud is the safest, most advanced way to keep things rolling seamlessly.

What role does the core foundation play in the business?

Every business has an inbuilt EA helping it achieve certain goals. In some organizations, it's thoughtfully designed to support teams of highly skilled professionals, who get together and form strategic guidelines. Based on these guidelines, the EA is implemented. With other organizations, the EA may simply be an underlying process for designing, improving, and maintaining an IT network that goes on without proper infrastructure.

Applying innovative technologies, such as blockchain, **artificial intelligence** (**AI**), and cognitive computing seems tempting. But you can never underestimate the potential and power of rock-solid EA since it can transform an organization. In each framework, EA represents a comprehensive methodology for an organization to be visualized, described, and adopted. It is one of the ways to associate your infrastructure with a slew of proven benefits.

Here are the benefits of establishing a core EA foundation:

- **Comprehensive strategy**

  EA can safely be considered a bridge between the business values and IT infrastructure of an organization. Providing teams with the direction for IT processing and a technical roadmap, EA is an essential strategic tool that offers the comprehensive insights that are required for effective communication across the board. EA provides the blueprint for delivering concrete products, services, processes, and other structural elements.

- **Reduced complexity**

  The purpose of modern advancements, tools, and IT solutions is to make processes simpler. EA can be a game-changer when an organization pairs a proactive, results-oriented approach with a streamlined workflow. Businesses with data-driven core values that are striving for strategic changes are most likely to benefit from this optimal setup.

- **Minimized costs**

  Budget allocation and accountability are the driving forces behind smoothly executed business operations. When costs are poorly managed, an EA team's efforts can go awry in the blink of an eye, and the problems they see will just be the tip of the iceberg since worse outcomes are likely to follow. A thoughtful EA strategy can be the impetus for more efficient resource allocation, which will lead to significant savings. These benefits go beyond resource investments that have an impact on stability, profits, and the time to market. A streamlined finance structure reduces friction for EA teams and greatly increases the likelihood of achieving the desired outcomes.

- **Standardization and flexibility**

  Every stakeholder across the technical, sales, marketing, research, and development teams must be aligned on the strategy for EA values to achieve maximum productivity. Done well, an EA initiative will ensure this. In addition to creating multiple business units that can be managed hassle-free, EA can offer better software support and guidance than ever before.

  By harnessing the power of EA, an organization can strengthen and streamline its working environment by integrating services and applications.

- **Robust security**

  EA can be the guiding force behind data protection and cybersecurity processes in general. With constantly rising security concerns across digital networks, an effective EA blueprint is crucial to mounting a robust defense against the burgeoning risks of cybersecurity threats. This doesn't even include the additional security risks that stem from internal IT missteps, such as shadow IT and redundant applications. EA, in that area, holds the key to protection and ensuring better use of your digital assets.

- **Analytical adaptability**

   EA empowers teams with quick reaction capabilities, adaptability to embrace modern advancements, and greater agility to adapt to sudden shifts in the industry. Nothing beats the ability to assess a situation and do away with outdated and potentially harmful practices. An organization can use these data-driven insights to improve the business model and its strategies. The perks that follow include a noticeable decrease in business risks.

These benefits of establishing a core foundation speak volumes about the usability of an EA. For an organization juggling innovation, growth, and strategy, EA can act like the glue that holds the company's vision and operations together. That is why consultants who work with organizations on their EA development often encourage them to abandon legacy systems and establish EA as an ongoing project – success hinges on effective planning and implementation over time.

One such consulting firm, *NetSol Technologies*, has worked with companies to accelerate the reinvention of their applications and data for a cloud-native world. With the benefit of having experience with hundreds of engagements on EA projects, the team has found that the reality of effective IT infrastructure is being able to elegantly orchestrate interconnected elements within a multi-level organization. Complexities are often associated with unpleasant events. Simplicity and adaptability are the names of the game.

Business dynamics versus IT complexity in businesses and IT systems

Something that the thriving leaders of the digital world must consider is that such systems can be complicated to understand but not necessarily bad. On the contrary, they have proven to offer a massive turnover. In dynamic and uncertain environments, complexity confers critical benefits.

It's time to dive deep into the business dynamics to reflect on the nature, benefits, and costs of complexity. We will offer guidance and insights into the best practices on how to manage complexity in a business organization.

What good does complexity bring?

As far as business circumstances are concerned, complexity can be defined as multiple elements, including technological infrastructure, raw materials, products, services, and other organizational units. They are interconnected and are codependent and equally prone to offering advantages and disadvantages, depending on the way they're managed.

Some notable advantages include an increase in the resilience of the business architecture. There is no second thought about the fact that companies that adapt to modern technologies and equip their employees with industry best practices are in a better position to cater to any unforeseen unpleasant situation. Adaptability is the most natural phenomenon when dealing with human matters, including business and technology. Shuffling and reshuffling existing elements can ensure sustainable learning mechanisms. This approach has helped leading fashion retailers, such as *Zara*, create a tailored selection for customers and adapt to ever-evolving trends. Closely correlated and interconnected elements ensure effective coordination. Shared behavioral protocols and a similar wavelength with which their movement is enabled ensure foolproof collective security.

Above all other benefits, inimitability caused by complexity can be an unbeatable element for competitors. The challenge of replicating the interrelationship between each element requires unmatched skill. The same happened with *Apple* when they tried their luck with the Map application. The results were devastating and struggled to gain acceptance with consumers.

The costs of complexity

A phenomenon that offers a plethora of benefits to taking your organization to new heights is bound to cost a fortune. Creating and maintaining multiple elements is not only complex and beneficial but expensive as well, especially compared to other standard approaches that bring down a company's productivity.

The inability to manage regular operations gets difficult with increased complexity, which is rooted in the system's decreased understandability. Things can get hard for the leaders within an organization as they will have no clue about where and how to intervene to manage performance in case of a system glitch.

When combined, the whole situation that's ingrained in complexity can cause extreme uncertainty. The organization works tirelessly to set up a system with responses based on predictable behavior. This is taken over by unpredictability if it's not managed effectively and promptly. Catering to this situation of uncertainty demands high levels of reliability through strategic investment in time and resources.

Losing sight of business matters

History is loaded with examples that showcase diverse impacts of excessive complexity. At top of the list, *Three Mile Island Nuclear Reactor* was the result of a complex control panel. The team failed to interpret the crazy alarms and layers of notifications, resulting in catastrophic confusion. A fixable rudimentary issue of the stuck coolant draining valve turned into something horrific – courtesy of complexity.

Why complexity gets out of hand

The ever-so-evolving internet has exposed the inflexibility of many technologies and business processes. The inability to adapt to new channels comes complimentary with it. This inflexibility is rooted in complex systems, where developing and testing new capabilities is time-consuming, and every change becomes an expensive adventure. In major banks, the systems are often so complex that even the bare minimum operations result in rigidity and high expenses.

Inefficient and non-value-adding variations of complexity make it difficult for the system to maintain the culture of innovation and growth, resulting in strategic disadvantages. Implementing a standard centralized digital process may sound boring but is the right approach in many cases.

Going beyond anecdotes for dealing with quantifiable results and a larger sample led us to two major findings:

- Conventional wisdom may consider agility-borne benefits to be contradictory – that is, efficiency at the cost of employee engagement. However, our results show otherwise. Smooth and seamless agile transformations delivered 30% higher customer satisfaction, employee engagement, and operational performance, leading to a turbocharged innovation model. Organizations with a successful agile transformation are more likely to be top-quartile performers among their counterparts.

- Management and organization leaders must take charge of the operations, rather than sitting back and waiting for this to happen bottom-up. Four elements stood out in our logistic regression model when we compared around 300 highly successful transformations with the 580 less successful ones to see the difference in their course of action. The results of this analysis are the secret behind a higher success average of around 75%:

  - To ensure a trickle-down impact, ensure that the team at a higher level within an organization has these concepts at their fingertips. They should be in a position to lead by example and enable change.

  - Among all the efforts toward agility, do not forget to set clear organizational values and ensure that the top team follows them in a structured manner.

  - There is more to an agile infrastructure than just the top team. Focus on building connective tissue among strategy, business process, people, and technical aspects.

  - Slow and sturdy wins the race, but do not let the organization exhaust itself with unnecessarily extended processes. Commit by picking high-priority areas.

Based on this analysis and findings, organizations that improve customer satisfaction and boost operational turnover can rely on agile transformation.

Significant performance improvements with agile transformations

An agile transformation sure has bundles of benefits, but does it work as well in reality as it does in a theory? With this new model, you welcome a team with a new highly motivated mindset, effective strategy, and state-of-the-art technology. The scope to take risks and investments will follow. An agile working environment where employees are an essential part of the decision-making process and have the opportunity to master their craft drives innovation.

Business agility depends on the foundation for execution

Modern business approaches, where there is a need for a hands-on strategy and extraordinary decision-making skills to enable change, have made business agility an absolute necessity. Accurate predictions are often a long shot but are quite effective when it comes to digitizing consistent business elements. Setting your eyes on constantly evolving factors ultimately makes a foundation for execution turn into a foundation for agility.

Among various types of agility, there could be multiple explanations for different outcomes from a similar agile setup. However, the takeaway is simple: a digitized foundation for execution enables managers to focus on what products would succeed and then bring those products to market within an industry.

National/political environments and business discipline

With increased revenue comes great responsibilities and accountability. Many companies with complex and unsorted financial and operational matters get stuck with legal obligations. Some organizations face complicated rules and regulations within the same country and end up having massive expenditures with no added value. On the other hand, a solid foundation for execution and transparent processes makes it easy to access data in no time. New laws and business regulations may affect a business process but with a well-structured system, data can easily be accumulated.

Building a foundation is safe and cheap

It's time to shake off the outdated idea that making improvements is risky and can rip off your business financially. The foundation of execution can be implemented on a single ongoing project within a company. It can be a pilot project to understand how it works and how much it costs. A massive decrease in processing costs and enhanced efficiency is a done deal.

Creating business value with a foundation for execution

Knowing where to defend and where to attack can go a long way when mapping business strategies, tactics, and capabilities. However, organizations need to approach business agility in terms of the dynamics of the business strategy. EA not only enables agility but can play a major role in increasing the flexibility and viability of an organization.

Business agility is facilitated by sufficient resources that are required to react to a certain improvisation. Although the need for a balance between efficiency and flexibility helps execute the process, increased requisite variety and fewer constraints for implementing strategic change are guaranteed. There could be a manual agility process or an automated one; the main factor that sets these apart is the process's ability to replicate the improvements in the latter. Moreover, business agility management is as crucial as the transformation itself. This new and specialized business capacity is event-driven and consistent.

EA principles for business agility

The ability of a business to react to a certain change in the industry that affects customer behavior is what agility is all about. Apart from enabling more innovation and improved value proposition, a noticeable decrease in system risks makes the business stronger from the core. However, before putting business processes on the path of agility, leaders must consider some fundamental principles of EA for business agility.

At the top of the list, we must reduce bureaucracy and constraints to avoid multiple approaches. No matter which industry we are dealing with, a system should put the customer first and keep up with their journey to make relevant up-sales. In every business structure, effective communication paired with data-driven processes enables fast decision-making, which is an essential ingredient for business agility.

The value a business agility model brings along is worth giving a shot. Not only does it offer greater freedom of choice for management but also to the teams at an individual level. With an appropriate and timely flow of information, an organization can do wonders, and that is what business agility offers – the knowledge of change followed by immediate action capabilities.

Implementing change is without a doubt an essential pillar of the business process, but being able to unlearn certain trends and legacy is equally important. Moving fast in response to customers' needs and gaining critical advantages allows organizations to switch resources quicker and faster than their competitors.

Successful business agility management factors

To determine the positive impact that improvisation has on business agility management capabilities, we must cross the following factors off our checklist:

- Ensure there are measurable aims for stakeholders and create a business model that is updated regularly
- Stay atop all the potential risks and equip the team to deal with dependencies, costs, return on investment, and cultural issues
- Stakeholders must be updated about the change, the reason behind it, and the cost and benefits that follow a particular implementation through effective communication
- Ensure there are training programs and skill polishing sessions across the board for personal counseling that help alleviate any change-related fears

Combined, these factors work effectively toward the success of business agility management.

What challenges may follow business agility management?

Apart from the undeniable benefits, business agility management may encounter multiple challenges that can only be catered to through proper skill development. The constant need for the adaptation of continuous advancements within the system might be exhausting for some stakeholders. With constant change follows constant risk and unpredictability. To be able to deal with such fears, uncertainty and doubts can often get a bit difficult.

Designing a business model and setting the right foundation for viable outcomes is essential for agility management. Setting realistic goals and maintaining the balance between decision-making speed and efficiency is one of the biggest challenges for highly motivated leaders. However, by continuously scanning the market trends and customer behavior, organizations are likely to grab game-changing investment opportunities.

Summary

Putting business operations on the right track in today's digital world is essential. One of the smoothest and most seamless ways to ensure this is by adapting to modern tools and techniques that enable effective communication, as well as help the company land impactful investments and stay atop modern industry trends and customer behavior. It helps keep a balance between IT technologies and business processes.

All these elements set the right foundation when it comes to building an EA. Organizations often struggle to keep up with the ever-evolving technology, so the innovation and growth process slows down a notch. The way forward is by implementing an EA that navigates the organization through business processes for desired business outcomes. With visionary leadership, a skilled team, and a future-centric approach, along with a guide for best industry practices, an organization is in a better position to execute a seamless transmission based on EA.

This chapter focused on developing management and implementation skills within an EA while following industry best practices. Furthermore, an organization based on EA principles needs to have EA leaders that are ahead of certain elements to keep the workflow smooth and seamless. The size of the team, infrastructure model, and organizational structure are at the top of the list.

However, the thriving industry leaders of the digital world must consider the complications and challenges that come with the package. Only a well-structured and thought-through business agility model is capable of handling the constant need to adapt to continuous advancements within the system. This might be exhausting for some stakeholders because with constant change, there are constant risks and unpredictability. In the next chapter, we will evaluate the core foundation and the most efficient ways to achieve the desired outcome in our first attempt.

References

- https://www.gartner.com/smarterwithgartner/5-talents-needed-for-a-successful-enterprise-architecture-team
- https://www.gartner.com/smarterwithgartner/cios-need-to-help-scale-the-digital-business
- https://blog.prabasiva.com/2008/10/18/enterprise-architecture-team-size-analysis/
- https://www.trendmicro.com/vinfo/us/security/news/cyber-attacks/data-breach-101
- https://www.gdpr.associates/data-breach-penalties/
- https://www.sciencedirect.com/science/article/pii/S0268401217305492#bib0270

2

Defining Core Foundation and How to Get It Right

To achieve strategic digital goals, **Enterprise Architecture** (**EA**) requires the involvement and integration of people, processes, and technology. Architectural flaws are exposed every time a negative interaction occurs with your application, website, phone call, or service provider. Without resolving these issues, great organizations can be destroyed. The issues, their solutions, and related aspects will be covered in this chapter, where we will be explaining the following aspects:

- Owning EA and the manifestation of an effective Core Foundation framework
- Business agility and IT value realization are complex
- Steps for getting it right the first time – core foundation
- Leadership principles and how they relate to enterprise architects

Owning EA and the manifestation of an effective core foundation framework

Even financially thriving organizations have faced massive challenges because they did not pay close attention to customer dissatisfaction and negative feedback related to interactions with customer service.

These architectural gaps have had a devastating impact on prominent companies in the past. One of the primary reasons for such inadequacies lies in the fact that their digital economic model is based on an integrated solution; however, most businesses operate around product verticals. Companies tend to define customer experience based on a certain product or service, not the overall experience with the business. These are effective approaches for creating an infrastructure that delivers a top-notch experience for target audiences:

- **EA and the business must align**

  After careful consideration, an EA team proposes changes within the business landscape. They conduct thorough research on how a particular implementation will affect the business and to what extent it will provide capabilities that can enhance the overall system and processing workflow. Another approach to make this system effective is to divide responsibilities among various business units. EA is the bridge between functional groups; therefore, a centralized EA is the preferred option.

  It is not recommended that you implement an independent EA department for every business unit. This approach is more likely to result in misalignment, inefficiencies, and potentially devastating outcomes. EA encourages organizations to engage with various stakeholders or EA that are not just technology-focused, such as application consultants or data specialists, but also business stakeholders, financial people, and risk people, and really try to involve them in the process model which would benefit the business and IT alignment far better.

- **Who is accountable for EA decisions?**

  When plans work out well, everyone is ready to take the credit, but with a failed IT venture, everyone tends to pass the responsibility onto someone else. To avoid such a situation, where a disagreement turns into finger-pointing, companies must establish clear accountability for the issues related to business architecture. Accountability problems begin in a conference room filled with IT and strategy teams, finance departments, and software development groups. With every stakeholder on the table, differences of opinion are bound to surface. Transparency is important, but with an ineffective accountability system, things can get out of hand. In general, the EA Governance committee should be held responsible for any EA decisions across the organization, but keep in mind the collaborative efforts of architects from different lines of businesses and domains.

- **The collaboration of EA with the business and organization**

  Communication is the key to success for any organization, and meaningful collaboration among various teams within a company ensures a positive outcome. Often, the EA department limits itself to creating comprehensive system maps with critical information that addresses all the requirements. However, with limited or no discussion with and among the departments affected by those plans, it is impossible for the business to interpret the EA's recommendations.

  Across the EA effort, other teams are held responsible and accountable for their areas of expertise – for example, software developers are held responsible for designing complex technology frameworks. Typically, the EA team works with more conceptual tasks, such as business processes, the time and talent required for the delivery of software and services, the overall business objectives, and the scope of individual IT projects. To ensure the maximum productivity and advancement of target goals within an organization, close collaboration is imperative. To increase the likelihood that IT and other internal teams will embrace and support the new architecture, EA must guide team leaders across the business, interpret complex ideas, gather feedback, and involve other teams within the design process.

- **Keep strategy and operation tasks separate**

  The EA team is responsible for conceptual tasks such as strategy, analysis, and facilitating the implementation of prescribed changes. However, in many organizations, their duties are not limited to just these tasks. Often, they are pulled in to manage or provide direction on key issues or initiatives. For example, building the business case for a large IT transformation project or assisting the IT team with a systems-migration project.

  The EA team's extended knowledge of every department and ongoing projects, along with the problem-solving skills within an organization, are leveraged to make the right business decisions. Instead, the team's primary focus should be on strategy building, lending a helping hand on other projects, and assisting with day-to-day business affairs as they relate to the work of the EA team. As long as operational and strategic tasks are managed efficiently without the duplication of work, the EA team will be most productive.

- **Approval rights for the EA team**

  Organizations underestimate the power and capabilities of EA teams, and this can be seen when the leadership fails to understand how EA works or they do not give the EA team credit for achieving positive outcomes. Other departments, such as IT, marketing, and sales, tend to have bigger budgets at their disposal and are often provided room to take risks.

  When leadership provides equal opportunities for the EA team to be involved in decision-making, policy change, and other processes, EA can turn out to be the most valuable asset in an organization. They have visibility to issues across the organization and can think ahead to potential issues that the business might encounter in the future. They can attract high-potential management talent that can help the organization rethink tailored IT systems. Being recognized and acknowledged as a valuable stakeholder is meaningful and motivates EA leaders and team members to continue great work.

- **EA elements for accountability**

  A centralized system for communication, collaboration, and accountability is absolutely essential for maintaining a seamless workflow. In an organization, if each group uniquely interprets a piece of information, communication issues are bound to occur. The EA team should have full control over all IT decision-making processes while also ceding responsibility for particular elements to other business units. Teams can avoid communication errors and ensure maximum productivity by assigning an individual on the team to be accountable for the work of the EA team.

- **Measure EA's effects on the business**

  The need to pursue an EA approach has never been greater. EA supports a digital-forward approach with a flatter leadership hierarchy. Minor glitches and operational issues can be addressed easier and faster with this Enterprise Architecture model.

Analyzing and measuring the overall impact an EA approach has on a business is a very complex task, due to the operational methodology behind EA's day-to-day processes. The team's everyday affairs are dependent on individual business units, external service providers, and many interdependencies. The nature of their tasks is conceptual, which makes it nearly impossible to measure an absolute impact. However, the best way to critically analyze it is to base judgments on a single project.

For example, consider how application features overlap, the capabilities that might be required for integration testing, or the complexity or cost-effectiveness of overall management tasks.

The organization's overarching EA strategy can be mapped using **key performance indicators (KPIs)** upon which each stakeholder has agreed. While the organization evolves, these strategies can be adjusted accordingly.

Having said that, EA cannot be leveraged to redesign operations when there are fewer than 50 team members. In that case, the first step is to digitize the business and pursue appropriate courses of innovation. The following diagram illustrates the transitional processes of architectural modules and the relationships between security, data, applications, and technology:

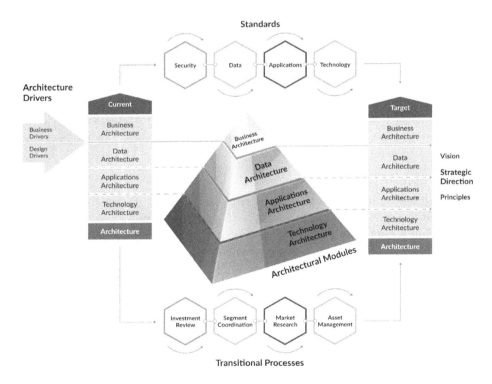

Figure 2.1 – The standards and transitional processes within an architecture model

Business design influences business strategy. That's why it's important to take a clear stand on responsibilities and accountability and enable teams to engage in cross-communication to ensure smooth and effective processes.

Three principles for organizational redesign

Three organizational design principles can be applied to ease the process of establishing an EA approach, support seamless implementation, and promote the achievement of maximum positive outcomes.

The following sections describe the three principles of organizational redesign.

Principle 1 – componentization – designating clear responsibilities and accountability

In light of today's fast-paced technological advancements, every organization must be continually upgrading and revising the EA program. This is achieved by breaking down multiple elements of an organization into different components. For example, an organization might choose to focus particular attention on products, customer experience, and core enterprise processes.

It's critical to designate clear responsibilities and accountabilities among those groups. An organization's ability to adapt to a given change is directly related to how well the EA team can map a quick and effective redesign of the EA process to incorporate the change.

For example, typically, payment processing is built into many different products within a single organization. The resulting dependencies require building technology capabilities that transform payment processing into reusable methodologies. Payment processing is a good example of the kind of system that can be updated easily to incorporate modern advancements, which results in meeting or exceeding customer needs with minimum effort. Such an infrastructure might apply componentization (*breaking software down into identifiable pieces*) to leverage data strategically, and can drive additional opportunities for innovation.

In the past, EA meant redesigning whole systems, strategies, and operational processes. IT specialists and enterprise architects helped management to set goals and map business processes. However, this approach is now obsolete, as it does not support componentization. Each new component that arises from the EA process adds value when it is implemented, and an incremental approach ensures steady, reliable progress toward organizational goals.

Principle 2 – functional diversity – ensure team members reflect a wide range of perspectives

At this stage, the role of leadership defines the overall business strategy. Leaders must assemble productive teams and provide skill-developing sessions that help each member set realistic individual performance goals that map appropriately to ensure the team, as a whole, will achieve the company's goals. Along the same lines, one of the most important aspects of embracing people, process, and technology opportunities is to empower cross-functional teams along with their clear responsibilities and accountability measures.

This approach might seem like a drastic and sudden shift from the traditional way of dealing with management matters, and initially, that might upset the smooth flow of operations. To mitigate the negative effects of such circumstances, leaders must allocate appropriate processes and technology within each component. Every individual on each team must feel empowered to speak up and be supported by leadership when it comes to processes and technology related to their functional areas of the business.

Research shows that diverse teams perform better than homogenous teams. From data scientists and software engineers to lawyers and finance experts, every team member must bring unique skill sets. Diverse talent means more than cultural diversity; it can include worldview, educational background, family responsibility, neurodiversity, and more.

Each member should stand out with diverse capabilities to boost creativity and ensure better critical thinking. Functional skills, such as product expertise, development capabilities, and user design experience, add great value to the team, too. When a diverse team of experts comes together to ensure excellent cross-functional operations within an organization, a maximum outcome is virtually guaranteed by the EA.

Principle 3 – user focus – creating a culture of continuous feedback and redesign

EA can have a significant positive influence on the overall operational strategy of the organization. When teams are equipped with the right kind of information, resources, and technological capabilities, innovation and growth make their way into the company. Leaders play a major role in shuffling the existing teams or creating new ones to make the most out of their opportunities.

In setting the foundation for EA, it's imperative to identify new investments based on end user behavior and feedback. A redesign of the strategy is made possible based on the objectives and goals leveraging digital technologies, which advance quickly and may offer capabilities that were previously not possible.

For example, the music-streaming, audio-streaming, and media services provider service Spotify took an unconventional step, given its own opportunity in the marketplace. Its leadership team decided to bet on employees by investing in teams rather than focusing their approach strictly on strategic initiatives.

Spotify embraced a people-driven, autonomous approach for scaling the agile methodology that emphasized the importance of culture and network. This approach helped the company increase innovation and productivity by providing team members with autonomy, communication, and accountability.

The results far exceeded their expectations, and even those of industry analysts, and today, the company is an industry leader in entertainment.

Identifying the need for a foundation for execution

Every company needs an efficient operational system from top to bottom, and EA must set the foundation for execution. For some organizations, the need is critically time-sensitive, while others are less pressed and can take things slow to plan for a smooth transition.

Let's dive into some of the risks that leaders must take, the reasons behind them, and metrics to assess the key factors in those situations. We will explore how to recognize the need to take quick and effective steps that will allow continued work on the foundation for execution.

Here are nine risks to EA to avoid, identify, and resolve.

Risk 1 – single customer queries elicit different answers

Think like a customer and imagine how frustrated you would be if individuals and departments gave you different answers to the same question. The same is true with EA. When an organization doesn't have the infrastructure to share accurate information across functional areas, the result can be extremely damaging.

The need for a foundation of execution is absolutely urgent if customer-related matters that should have been done in one project cycle are being attempted again and again. The higher the percentage of employees' total time spent on rework, the greater the need for action.

Risk 2 – new regulations require a major effort

The organization must comply with ever-evolving government regulations. Companies listed on the New York Stock Exchange underwent major processing and operational strategy upgrades in response to the Sarbanes-Oxley Act of 2002 (`https://thehill.com/blogs/congress-blog/technology/531781-why-a-sarbanes-oxley-update-is-needed-to-protect-our-financial/`), a US law that mandates financial reporting and record-keeping practices for corporations.

The legislation was a trigger for many companies to implement the foundation for execution to streamline financial management. In 2005, large companies spent 15% of their IT budget on measures related to Sarbanes-Oxley compliance.

The cost of regulatory compliance can be reduced with an EA foundation for execution by creating a capability to access data on a recurring basis. A company is in urgent need of action if more than 15% of its IT budget has been allocated to fulfill regulations.

Risk 3 – agility challenges and unprofitable growth initiatives

The operational processes within an organization have a certain workflow that is difficult to change after a merger. Developing new capabilities might take longer than expected when the team cannot leverage an existing business strategy.

Using an outdated system instead of digitizing the infrastructure delays profitable outcomes. So, if an organization applies existing capabilities for a new strategic initiative and those initiatives are profitable, there's no urgent need for action.

Risk 4 – IT is consistently a bottleneck

Usually, companies follow the traditional method of implementing IT processes that are carried out through a two-step exercise:

1. Communicating a business strategy
2. Building the IT infrastructure accordingly

In such environments, IT is a point of congestion, rather than a strategic asset, and the implementation of a new system to facilitate a strategic initiative can take up to 2 years. By that time, there would be dozens of new innovations within the same industry. Therefore, tasking IT with the entire EA initiative will, almost certainly, lead to unnecessary delays in implementation and challenges in keeping up with the modernization of IT infrastructure happening both within and outside the organization.

Transportation and logistics company UPS creates new customer service updates using information and feedback from current stakeholders to ensure added value every 90 days. The need for urgent action in an organization is crucial if it takes longer than 12 months for projects to deliver in an efficient manner.

Risk 5 – different platforms for the same task

Would you pay for 20 different platforms that perform the same function, or work toward enhancing the capabilities of a single platform that integrates with every other system? The latter approach is more realistic and practical, so it's clearly the right way to proceed.

Yet, there are hundreds of companies that operate on multiple order-entry systems, and still, others have more than 30 different ways to pay customer benefits. Not only are the operational costs huge in these situations, but the time and effort that goes into keeping these platforms going are not worth the outcome.

The high cost of redundant systems and the risk of inaccurate data for compliance regulation and reporting lead to damaging outcomes. The desire for a variety of systems simply doesn't justify the expense that follows. So, if an organization is running multiple platforms to execute the same task, it doesn't add value. In fact, it will undermine the foundation for execution, and at some point, there will be an urgent need for action.

Risk 6 – critical information for decision-making is unavailable

No matter how big your warehouse is, or how extensive and comprehensive your data management system is, unless they are effective, they are useless. There are companies that have developed million-dollar software to streamline their everyday business affairs, but either the right information is unavailable or the facts and figures are not accurate.

The role of the EA decision-maker is extremely important here, along with a strong foundation for execution. They can use the right data to make the appropriate decisions while leveraging standardized processes. Your case for action is urgent if the decision-makers within your organization are unable to make effective choices on the same set of data every day.

Risk 7 – employees move data from one system to another

When a company pays a fortune to set up hardware and software to ensure maximum efficiency, what's the point of it if employees are manually moving data between systems? After all, this is why organizations spend millions of dollars on technology and software.

Above all, in such cases, the risk of error is extremely high, and employees' valuable time is wasted. Most leading companies have transitioned to **artificial intelligence (AI)**, **Internet of Things (IoT)**, and **robotic process automation (RPA)** systems that require little to no human interaction. These systems perform security measures, data compiling, storing and analyzing, inventory management, centralizing the whole purchasing process, and more.

As an example, Hewlett-Packard printers can reorder cartridges automatically when the toner runs low. That process is IoT, and it doesn't require human intervention at any level. Most digital-forward companies execute half of their sales electronically. An organization can compare its processing with the existing percentage to see whether its system might require action.

Risk 8 – senior management dreads discussing IT agenda items

Almost all large, multi-department organizations have committees that look into issues related to their assigned area (e.g., finance, resource allocation, IT, hardware, and hiring).

Risks can be spotted here when only the senior executive committee deals with IT governance, setting the foundation for principles and investment priorities. The problem here is a lack of understanding and interest among executives regarding IT matters. When this risk is in play, these meetings might appear to be boring to these leaders, and/or they might not understand the IT needs of an organization. Growth initiatives are at risk when these problems are present in an organization.

On the other hand, companies with effective CIOs who exhibit a dedicated commitment to these agendas thrive because they are focused on strategic matters. An organization is in urgent need of action when the senior committee responsible for IT-related decision-making is ineffective.

Risk 9 – uncertainty about positive outcomes from IT investments

If you have to think about whether or not IT is offering good value, it's likely the answer is no. While investing money, effort, and valuable resources in a project, leaders must make sure to set measurable goals. By the end of a quarter or a year, if they are unable to measure the outcome, the whole effort may have been a waste.

It is important to devote attention to ongoing projects to ensure they are on track and are delivering positive outcomes and value for the business. Part of that effort to recognize value is being aware of all internal matters related to IT and finance.

To cater to the previously mentioned risks and smooth flow of processes, clarity of the requirements and the consistent analysis of the results of architecture initiatives help ensure strategic value from IT. A company where senior-level management can describe the EA is in safe hands. However, an ineffective core foundation can lead to devastating consequences. In such circumstances, EA plays a major role in acting as a bridge between business groups. An organizational redesign could be an option, but a few principles should be considered, as mentioned previously. Before becoming invested in infrastructure, setting measurable goals and working toward them can generate a huge positive impact.

Complex business agility and IT value realization

The need for business agility can never be overestimated, as agility makes it possible to respond to any type of enterprise change as quickly as it happens. Being able to adapt to market changes by opting for modern technology sets the right foundation for an agile organizational process.

For some, this process can be slow and steady; however, other organizations believe in rapid transition. This adaptation is facilitated by modern tools and digital solutions that help decision-makers take the right steps. The accurate and readily available data is reported and analyzed so that it can be leveraged for the business agility process.

Digitally mature companies are 23% more profitable than their less mature peers. Depending on the size of an organization, the ratio between the extent of digital transformation and the outcome could vary.

The following list of business agility statistics as derived from a thorough analysis and demonstrates the percentage of businesses that embraced the agility model and the true value of the process. Moreover, the statistics reflect the challenges that companies encounter during the transition:

- The majority (71%) of businesses have opted for the business agility model. However, 45% indicate that breaking down the silos between business and IT has been the driving force for their shift toward agility. The process is impactful to a great extent but can be a bit challenging when it comes to abandoning traditional practices.

- Some decision-makers are so accustomed to their legacy procedures of conducting business affairs that any kind of change seems uncomfortable to them. A survey of employees found that, in 35% of cases, the most common obstacle to digital transformation was the CEO. The advancement of technology and growth initiative suggestions simply do not mean anything to these leaders. However, 56% of CEOs who welcome modern shifts in technology report that digital improvements have led to increased revenue.

- An organization's culture defines the pace at which growth initiatives are executed. Most (59%) professionals find it difficult to facilitate any kind of advancement. According to them, culture and performance management are the key challenges in their shift toward agility:

  - 81% of organizations started their agile transformation within the last 3 years.
  - 70% of businesses want to integrate both business- and IT-enabled agile transformation in the next 3 years.

Organizational agility is not just an essential element to keep moving forward toward increased revenue and customer satisfaction. Another undeniable aspect of this transformation is the capability to withstand turbulent markets, competition, and other forces. The companies that have a weak EA find it difficult to stand tall when the ground shakes. Conversely, the ones that are able to predict new market trends and customer behavior can plan their strategies accordingly. They are prepared for the worst system shocks and use these tough times to their advantage.

Transitions leading to a future state can be overwhelming for the business and IT departments of many organizations. However, the decision-makers can make the whole process bearable by prioritizing excess spending. The focus must be on satisfying customer expectations and advancements that position a company well for long periods of growth.

To ensure optimal outcomes from this infrastructure, business leaders can improve collaboration inside and outside their enterprise, and align interdepartmental objectives and performance measures with the overall strategy. Following the establishment of an effective and seamless flow of information across the organization, teams should put in place an automated knowledge-sharing platform to operationalize processes to share that knowledge.

The importance of realizing value

What's the journey all about if there is no end goal? Similarly, when an initiative is implemented and investments are made to achieve a strategic mission, the possible outcomes are measured.

The role of the leadership is to set the target and expectation of a certain implementation; then, the project is handed over to the team assigned to implement it. The team works to deliver while following the set schedule and allocated cost. Their primary focus is to maintain the flow without the day-to-day concerns regarding the larger business outcomes their work will enable. Leaders can educate teams about the business benefits of their work. When teams don't understand how their work fits into the larger picture, this results in multiple challenges that could interrupt the success of the process.

Poor governance, ineffective communication, the failure of teams to collaborate, and poor adoption are some of the leading challenges that teams face. Moreover, delays in mastering operational efficiencies are, typically, rooted in processes, roles, and strategies that are out of sync.

The third parties who provide an organization with tools or solutions can have insightful opinions on how to utilize them. Not engaging with them to leverage their expertise on a particular matter can have negative outcomes. Companies that are unable to adopt modern work cultures and change resources based on new market trends will suffer from poor operational readiness. To garner maximum outcomes from business initiatives, value realization is crucial.

How can teams support the realization of value in their investments?

An impactful organizational and governance structure sets the foundation for the effective coordination of stakeholders to align their common business goals. The realization of goals is the first step in making efforts toward success. How these goals are managed largely depends on how well the business vision is in sync with the investment, and both have a huge impact on the outcome. A clear direction on measurable achievements, how each stakeholder executes their assigned tasks, and appropriate and timely steps in the case of a deviation define the realization of the goal for any project.

These key elements come together to boost the capabilities of business infrastructure to lead the team effectively by making correct and timely decisions. A performance management system then leverages these elements to measure and monitor investment outcomes.

Within an organization, the focus must be on the efficiency with which services are delivered. Being productive with available resources enables teams to pursue initiatives that add value. The effectiveness of these services is measured at the business level, where the focus is on user experience. At the strategic level, the priority must be identifying and adapting to changing business needs based on market trends. It measures how sensibly the growth opportunities have been leveraged.

Companies run on data and statistics to calculate potential outcomes that can be compared with past achievements. However, when goals are set based on that data, without any measurable figures, the business operations won't have a clear direction or management. This is the kind of compromised infrastructure that can lead to devastating results.

Adapting to unique models, tools, and strategies requires a hands-on grasp of each and every IT solution. A fast-paced, complex business transformation requires the proper guidance and management aid that comes from EA.

In general, there is a lack of awareness about EA benefits realization. The value this offers to organizations and the ease of transformation that follows are huge contributions. Developing an EA value realization model using the EA conversion process, the EA use process, and the EA competitive process can help realize the benefits. It will lead to the identification of factors that could influence the value realization process, too.

EA value realization model

The EA value realization model eliminates the perception that EA funding will always prove to be profitable no matter how an EA initiative is handled. Organizational performance is a huge factor that influences the overall process. It sheds light on the complex relationship between EA and organizational performance. Furthermore, assessing the organizational conditions that facilitate EA business value realization can be accomplished using this model.

A number of elements within an organizational structure have a strong impact on the effectiveness of the conversion process, such as the faith of management within the system, effective communication, EA goals, vision, and governance. The way EA assets are represented and integrated with the existing practices has a major influence on how these assets are utilized.

To better understand the process of EA value creation, we are separating it into interrelated categories and smaller, more manageable pieces. This research puts us on the right path but is simply a stepping stone toward a more extensive exploration. More specific and in-depth research is required to learn about EA funding, activity details in the EA conversion process, issues, and the interactions between the conversion factors.

With the study of EA outcomes and value, not only will teams be less likely to experience a massive failure, but the risks and potential outcomes will be easier to anticipate. Keeping track of all of the actions taken by decision-makers based on the project plan and holding them accountable is an effective way to move forward. That way, all missed milestones will be clearly reflected in the action plan.

Value realization management

The urgent need for efficient value realization management is often understated when it comes to the program structures of most businesses. Value mapping is an absolutely essential step, and it offers a simple, convenient, and powerful infrastructure for result-oriented management. The following steps make the process adaptable for teams:

1. Involve stakeholders in each and every aspect of the business development process. It makes them feel empowered enough to be motivated. Apart from that, they can be held accountable for the vision. Stakeholders' commitment should be taken into consideration as potential savings drivers and socialized objectives. Involving stakeholders is one vital way to ensure extraordinary business outcomes. Moreover, a value map is an essential part of the contracting process.

2. Align and link the value map with the project plan prior to the beginning of the process. Without proper collaboration on business goals and the value map, the realization of value is unlikely. Value realization proceedings go on for a set period and increase the chances that every stakeholder will be satisfied with the project. Toward the end, a team gathers to analyze whether the transformation was worth all of the effort and to determine whether the company achieved a valuable outcome.

Failure can have varied causes depending on multiple factors, but the most common reason could be the inability of the team to adapt to new technologies in a timely manner. If the business requirements and development delivery are poles apart, the results are most likely going to be catastrophic. The constant evolution of business ideologies and market trends makes it hard for most organizations to catch up, which leads to them no longer being relevant.

Incremental updates and changes in products and services should be part of the investment cycle for the continued management of business benefits. If the initiative turns out as expected, it's a win-win for all parties; however, for partial success, the plan can be revised with the changes based on data.

Role of enterprise architects in the transformation process

Being the biggest stakeholders of an IT landscape, enterprise architects have insight into all aspects of the business. Hence, they play a major role in the transformation process. The ability to anticipate and predict the possible outcome of implementation is essential for tailoring the decision-making process. EA recognizes the true value of the IT landscape that leads to a business's success or failure. Business trends and customer behavior constantly change, and based on these innovations, the everyday operations, customer experiences, and direction in which the business grows also change. Enterprise architects can analyze and assess the impact that these changes have on any business in the long run to improve the transformation process.

Let's go through a few important roles EA plays when it comes to a business transformation process:

Strategy	Enterprise Architecture	EA Roadmap	EA Governance	Design Assurance	Compliance	Performance Monitoring
Business Strategy Support & Alignment (future)	Current State EA Model	Business Capabilities	Architecture Governance Board	Design Assurance services to programmes & projects (internal and external)	Compliance Assessments against future state EA Model	Collection of Performance Measures
ICT Strategy development (Future)	Future State EA Model	Capability Increments	Governance Decisions		Managing divergence and Exceptions	Progress Tracking
Business Change Events (Current and in-flight)	Production of Diagrams, Catalogues & Matrices to ensure quality and to answer questions	Business Change Initiatives	Mandates for programmes & projects created from approved Capability Increments provide	Architecture Reviews	Issuing temporary Waivers	Dashboards, Charts and Graphs for MI/BI about EA
Business Motivation, Goals, Objectives	Provision of Information, Advice and Guidance	Business and IT capability Increments aligned to Risks, Priorities, Funding	High level Solution Models delivered to programmes & projects	Formal EA approval at Quality Gates	EA Approval to continue to next phase	Capability Maturity assessment against Strategies, Goals and Objectives
Metrics & Measures (KPIs/CSFs)	Conduct Gap, Traceability and Impact Analysis	Key Inputs to investment Proposals and Investment Board		Informal Design Assurance support for Solution Architects	EA intervention in projects to ensure remediation and to resolve issues and ensure future compliance	
Architecture Vision Model	Produce Recommendations	Supports Business Engagement	Formal EA Approval Guidelines required for projects to proceed to next stage in the change lifecycle	Policies & Guidelines		
Support for Strategic Planning	Create Position papers on business and IT trends	Key Inputs to Programme/Project Portfolio Planning	Standards	Standards Technical Design Authority		
Support for Executive Board queries			Governance Process	Evaluation of Vendors & Suppliers		

Figure 2.2 – The role of EA in business transformation

Extraordinary customer experiences

Today is a modern age of digital innovation, where the customer is the ultimate decision-maker. EA can help organizations analyze the path customers take to interact with them, what they find interesting, and where they abandon their contact. Mapping the customer journey is one of the most common methods by which to see an organization from the customer's perspective. Designing a strategy that will engage customers and lead them to make a purchase can only be done by being intrigued with their journey. Customer experience can be improved by redesigning the strategy, enabling new services based on customers' choices, and adopting modern technology to communicate with customers. Automation is a key element to ensure a better customer experience. Technology can help organizations meet customer needs in a much more convenient and hassle-free manner. Enterprise architects within a company can come up with a plan to take things to a new level by helping people with an adaptability mindset about innovation. Their business understanding and analysis of the data can be leveraged to speed up the process of business transformation.

Improved agility to speed up time-to-market

Agile processes lead to an effective flow of work and smooth internal and external operations. Not only does this lead to a productive work culture, but it provides more time for the decision-makers to indulge in more important matters such as strategy, innovation, and growth.

Based on that, a major chunk of the managerial lot of leading companies aims to change or expand their agile processes in technology and process improvements in the near future. The less time a company spends on marketing new products, the greater the window they have for coming up with ideal customer-focused initiatives based on data and analytics. It's a critical step in today's nonstop, ever-evolving digital world.

No matter how efficient and customer-centric their approaches are, organization leaders need to be alert at all times to become aware of and consider the organization's responses to modern trends. The changes in the industry are almost instant, and sometimes, they might take leaders by surprise; however, those who can predict changes and adapt their strategy accordingly will be equipped to handle these matters brilliantly.

Modern industry leaders who plan for the future have based their processes on agile development, as it is the only practical and powerful way to increase delivery speed. Above all, the agile methodologies of operating businesses offer great flexibility in how a company responds to fast-paced changes and how each and every stakeholder embraces the transformation. Enterprise architects set the foundation for these changes by offering a strategic view, operational guidelines, and functional methods to development teams that work in silos. Often, these teams adapt to and rely on their own best practices and capabilities to lead the way for the ongoing evolution of the industry.

Investing in advanced technologies

The EA plays a primary role in facilitating a seamless process to assess the need and adoption of new technologies. Organizations that embrace transformation by adapting to new, sophisticated, and progressive models are likely to do better than those who do not, and they are likely to win on the competitive front, too.

By leveraging a successful digital transition, companies that aim for a leadership role within their industry go for disruptive technologies, such as IoT and machine learning techniques. Adapting to modern tools and techniques plays a vital role in ensuring an organization retains resourceful employees with diverse sets of skills.

With constantly evolving digital devices, software, and trends, companies must continuously evaluate opportunities to work smarter, not harder. It's the only way for an organization to create and maintain a competitive advantage over other industry leaders, as the impact of emerging technologies on businesses can create massive opportunities. Leveraging next-generation tools and technologies can offer organizations an advantage when considering future strategies, too. Technology can improve more than products and services – it can enhance an organization.

Compliance with data privacy regulations

The digital world runs on data that has been collected directly or indirectly in the course of everyday business. Organizations leveraging opportunities with data while complying with regulations is essential for running smooth and legal operations.

In today's modern digital world, data is undoubtedly an organization's most valuable asset. The importance of its potential cannot be underestimated, as it can facilitate seamless operations and surface new opportunities, too. It allows companies to take advantage of emerging technologies that can accelerate the process of digital transformation and improve customer experience on a wider scale. While establishing the importance of data, it is crucial to consider regulatory compliance requirements and data governance aspects.

Cyber security incidents are on the rise, and they put any kind of data at continuous risk of being stolen, lost, or used for illegal purposes. To address these issues, governments around the world have justifiably imposed restrictive regulations to protect individuals' data privacy and security. As a result, every organization must plan its IT roadmaps and build its strategies around these regulations to protect the individual's identity.

EA works toward improving each and every aspect of the business; however, there are certain areas that top the list. The business strategy that is focused on enhancing the customer service and technological capabilities of the organization delivers the best outcomes. Let's go through each of these factors and determine their importance, their role in the operational workflow, and the possible outcomes they facilitate.

Improving customer experience, digitizing processes, and achieving operational excellence

Customer experience is tightly interwoven with digital capabilities. Companies with a state-of-the-art, modern setup and streamlined IT infrastructure are likely to offer a better customer experience.

Consumers face an overwhelming number of options when it comes to products and services and the platforms where they can purchase them. A company's digital experience must be extraordinary to engage and win over a visitor. The relationship with the customer doesn't end when they make a purchase; customers remain in an organization's database.

Companies can use data to inform and entertain customers on topics related to their products of interest. Keeping customers engaged after a sale by leveraging digital capabilities to offer communications, such as email newsletters, online surveys, and product review opportunities, can enhance customer experiences and improve sales. It's important to always be mindful that an unhappy customer can easily damage a company's reputation through social media and can conveniently switch to another provider.

Customer experience is the highest priority when building a business strategy, but operational excellence, implementation, the execution of initiatives, and increased productivity are the next priorities. In cases where an employee is managing a complex query, dealing with a frustrated customer, or handling a large returned order, having the tools and processes to take the best approach can make or break a brand's reputation.

Mapping the current IT environment to create a better future strategy

Every company has technology applications that departments rely on to maintain smooth day-to-day operations. Every aspect of an organization is dependent on network technology, so creating a comprehensive inventory of applications is one important way to assess capabilities and plan for future strategic initiatives. Multiple frameworks and tools can be used to assess, maintain, and analyze this inventory, while considering factors including application life cycles, costs, deployments, exchange flows, and impacts on the business.

IT specialists and other stakeholders must be able to access this data and understand it for better decision-making. One way to support better decisions is to design the inventory to be as comprehensive as possible, including roles, processes, locations, business capabilities, vendors, and other key factors.

Operational gaps can be filled using these inventory maps that reflect the business capabilities of the organization. This is the data used by enterprise architects to conduct objective and subjective analyses via automated questionnaires for stakeholders, who provide information to help assess the value, technical efficiency, and business fit of the applications they use. By the end of these analyzing exercises, enterprise architects are able to list all the applications that are consuming an organization's resources and rank them according to their importance and value, consolidating scores and cross-referencing KPIs. The result helps determine which resources have been the most fruitful in the past, what should be included in the future strategy, and how the IT team should approach applications that are in use.

Digital transformation works hand-in-hand with innovation, so for organizations that are lagging behind, it is the best way to catch up. Often, there is a conflict between industry leaders when it comes to IT systems and strategic business initiatives. Every company has its unique objectives, so each plan must also be unique. Too often, organizations fail to understand the impact of changes on the project scope, time, or budget, especially in agile environments. The resources that the team leverages to reach the ultimate goals should be well aligned with the business strategy. If not, the teams will not be able to respond to the needs that require innovation.

To avoid such drastic situations, EA provides the right approach for thriving businesses. Getting a clear understanding of the business objectives is the first step toward an efficient business architecture. Enterprise architects evaluate current business capabilities based on their engagement with business teams to map and understand how they can change over a course of time. This exercise helps them determine which capabilities the organization should work on in the coming years and which customer segments need a revised strategy.

Enterprise architects define the course of action for the future while ensuring that the IT infrastructure is in sync with the business capabilities. Mapping the current IT environment and setting the foundation for new IT architecture is how they do that. The map helps make it clear which IT resources are crucial for the business development as the company moves forward and buckles up to meet new challenges.

EA eases the process of collecting, accessing, and understanding the data that helps the governance process. Organizations are represented through data inventories created by enterprise architects, based on semantic models. Essential facts and figures are extracted from company resources and used to map business strategies, processes, and IT infrastructure.

Tying business data with a data dictionary can be automated to create the basis for tracking business data lineage. That way, the architects are enabled to analyze the impact of a potential change that might happen in near future, bearing in mind new industry trends. Streamlining digital transformation efforts prepares an organization for market changes and helps leaders plan accordingly.

New regulations, such as the **General Data Protection Regulation (GDPR)** and other data privacy laws, have accelerated companies' compliance processes. The documentation of GDPR and the impacts on their applications can be streamlined. Letting authorities know that personal data is being processed with all regulations under consideration is essential. GDPR practices have made compliance easier and simpler. With this workflow, **data privacy officers** (**DPOs**) can easily document GDPR processing activities by reusing applications created by enterprise architects. Detailed information about business processes and applications is at their disposal to review and analyze, including diagrams, flowcharts, and other detailed properties.

Enterprise architects leading digital transformation

Some may believe enterprise architects are out of touch with the realities on the ground, where day-to-day work gets done. They believe enterprise architects live in a bubble, where they plan on ideal situations and scenarios that are hard to implement in reality. They might even claim that enterprise architects find it difficult to demonstrate the business value that results from EA because they don't know enough about core business operations.

However, in agile environments that are common among most businesses in today's modern digital age, enterprise architects are the business partners who drive and facilitate digital business transformation. They anticipate and predict market innovations and customer behavior changes and plan for the future accordingly. By working closely with agile teams, they contribute significantly to digital transformation initiatives to put the company on the right path:

- Enterprise architects not only make strategic recommendations for the most effective business outcomes, but they continue to assess business opportunities throughout the quarter or a set period. They are the ones who keep in touch with emerging technologies and the latest business trends to evaluate the potential long-term impact. Constant changes in the market and relevant industries have an impact on IT systems, and sometimes, this results in the building of an entirely new ecosystem. These changes are anticipated by the enterprise architects. Their role as business partners exhibits and represents the value that is rooted in the collaborative efforts of people, modern processes, appropriate applications, and productive infrastructure.

- Each company, whether it's on purpose or not, is in a race toward ultimate success. Making valuable investments and spending time, effort, and energy to adapt to and adopt emerging technologies is the best way to stay in the game and compete with other companies.

- According to a Forrester report, 86% of respondents from leading companies believed that technology is the most important factor in driving business strategy. Today, enterprise architects help companies understand and analyze the impact of emerging and strategic technologies. They help determine the value that digital business platforms can deliver in the modern enterprise. They have their eyes out in the market and are in a better position to anticipate new trends and opportunities.

- Enterprise architects are well-equipped to recognize and communicate market trends to decision-makers. They are likely to recommend the adoption of new technologies that are potentially valuable, especially those that are comparatively new or those that could prove to be disruptive in the marketplace. Based on these suggestions, IT leaders begin to brainstorm, analyze, and determine the impact that such technologies could have on the business and figure out whether they will move their company ahead of their competitors or not.

- It's important to note that an emergent EA design can present a number of challenges, as the development teams are often unaware of broader business goals, technical resources, and business standards. However, agile teams are empowered and well equipped to design the architecture they need for a streamlined technology workflow based on the 11th principle of the Agile Manifesto: "*The best architectures, requirements, and designs emerge from self-organizing teams.*"

- In the past, enterprise architects have been accused of designing "architecture for the sake of architecture." They were considered detrimental to business growth. The reality is the opposite, and the business world has taken note and recognized their value. Enterprise architects are an organization's most influential leaders, with the ability to foresee the future and make recommendations based on it. They are responsible for growth initiatives and implementations. They leverage company assets and resources to explore new business opportunities by paying close attention to market trends. The value they bring to their organization is what sets the pace for business success:

Who is an enterprise architect?	• Software architect who oversees the complete system architecture, business processes, and IT infrastructure • Plays a major role in reducing complexity associated with digital transformations and establishing rules and processes around technology usage
What is the role of an EA in digital transformation?	• Execute digital programs, such as cloud computing and online business models, and simplify and modernize a company's IT system • Role is to reduce complexity to a minimal level so that the company can capitalize on digital technologies, develop product-development methodologies, and respond to customers' needs more quickly
What steps can corporations take to empower EAs?	• Assign more responsilbity to EAs and encourage implementation of their policies and guidelines • EA team to routinely provide business units with technology costs of any important decisions taken by them • EA to gain a direct line of communication to decision makers

Figure 2.3 – The enterprise architect's role in digital transformation

Taking the first step is almost always the hardest part in any field of life, whether that step is to establish a brand-new business, enroll in an online course, or build a new house. The beginning is the toughest phase. The same is true with EA.

Steps for getting it right the first time – core foundation

Companies that are new to EA can find it both complicated and overwhelming. Some might not be able to comprehend the impact that transformation will have on business outcomes.

Setting up the right foundation for the overall success of EA can also be a challenging task. And what happens once the initial planning phase is over? What is the next phase? Setting up the right strategy, making a plan, and then sticking to it will ensure the best outcomes.

Here is a step-by-step process to see how all of this works, starting with communication.

Get every stakeholder's input on matters that may or may not have an impact on the transformation. Establishing a clear understanding of the real purpose and motives behind EA is one of the most essential steps in the whole process. If the team is not aligned on the importance and value of EA for business productivity, the process might not offer the most effective results. Collecting the data of all the company resources that the teams utilize for their day-to-day business affairs can help evaluate the impact.

Once the strategic steps are nearly done on paper, sharing them across functional areas to ensure everyone is on the same page is absolutely essential. That way, every stakeholder can communicate their concerns, identify any loopholes, and address issues that can be fixed before the process begins. It makes sense to begin with practical matters and get started with the actions to bring about the actual transformation.

Here are essential steps for building the right core foundation for the first time to ensure a successful EA:

- **Evaluate any current foundation driving execution**

  Often, companies stick to outdated methods of articulating business strategies and then aligning IT. These processes have worked great in the past, but today, with so many innovations and digital advancements, companies might discover that IT is a bottleneck rather than a strategic asset. Generally, any new initiative in a company takes around 2 years to operationalize. Employees need time and space to get used to a new system to establish a strong understanding of the updated way of running operations. To implement a new system to support a strategic initiative, teams can give it at least a couple of years before evaluating the potential outcome. The problem with this infrastructure is that while the company spends time getting used to it, there can be many new advancements in the industry.

  Top IT and business management buy-in is ideal for an efficient management EA initiative. The business functions and processes must be described using relevant artifacts and should be in line with the scope. In other words, business and IT must be on the same page to define the scope of the EA. To ensure the maximum productivity of EA, the content needs to have certain characteristics that are well in sync with modern industry trends.

- **Evaluate the operating model**

Every initiative needs a blueprint to define the direction that a particular project is going to take. For the team to follow guidelines and align to a plan, there must be proper documentation to put them on track. When it comes to the digital business world, this guideline is called an *operating model*. It is known to be the first layer in the foundation for execution in EA. This comprehensive model defines the business process of standardization and explains the need for an integration that enhances the value for a particular set of customers or other target audiences.

Put simply, the operating model is a stepping stone of the business strategy as it indicates how the process takes its course, the ultimate goal, and the value that will be created, delivered, and captured by the business units at the end of it. Enterprise architects are capable of analyzing the business processes, system linkages, and data to support every aspect of the business model. There are certain elements in the business model that play a significant role in determining the operating model, including customer segments, key activities, resources, and partners.

All of these elements come together to provide a map that helps identify the current potential and capabilities of an organization. This mapping is conducted over a course of time where stakeholders sit together and evaluate the process. Data and characteristics from the business model are provided to facilitate the mapping matrix. This mapping process and criteria work well to evaluate the enterprise's particular business model and innovation parameters.

- **Define processes and goals for the EA**

Put simply, the primary objective of EA is to create a roadmap or blueprint to put the organization on the right track for a transformation process. A set of valuable information and company data that must be included are IT assets and business processes. Without the background knowledge of the company's resources, determining a future can be pretty tough.

Enterprise architects are well trained to analyze data from the past and design a strategic plan to exploit the current capabilities of an organization and bring change. Other common goals include promoting team alignment and standardization. The best way to do that is to ensure each and every stakeholder is aligned and the communication between and across the teams is smooth. Ensuring a unified environment across teams and organizations is crucial to this process.

As part of the EA process, an organization's structure, roles, and responsibilities are outlined. EA models offer an overview of an organization's structure and provide a long-term perspective. Business processes, including information systems and technologies, are described. New technologies and processes are also adopted.

The enterprise architect is a guiding agent to help an organization plan its goals and work toward achieving them over time. The use of available resources and technology to fulfill these aims is also directed in the guidelines. The following is a list of the general goals of any EA:

- **Effectiveness**

    Setting realistic yet highly motivating goals is what EA is all about. The core foundation establishes a workflow for essential and accurate processes by overseeing each and every aspect of the operations. Often, the blueprint and roadmaps define the guiding principles on how to achieve the ultimate goal and produce the deliverables set out by the business.

- **Efficiency**

    A company has a certain set of resources that are exploited in the most productive way to keep the business operation going. The enterprise architect offers a plan and determines the ability to reuse these resources. By eliminating redundancies, they ensure the best contribution of each employee's resourcefulness set out in the identified EA framework. Business process modeling and workflow mapping can produce greater collaboration.

- **Agility**

    Multiple procedures being carried out to achieve a single goal can be a devastating approach. But the enterprise architect specializes in combining legacy technology with modern ones and facilitates the adoption process. In addition, their business model assesses any technology risks with the constant monitoring of metrics and analytics. This explains the need to identify when and how to evolve IT in alignment with business goals.

- **Continuity**

    Consistency is the way to ensure great outcomes. Especially when it comes to big corporate organizations, every plan, strategy, or initiative is an ongoing process that takes years to turn into a fruitful decision. Maintaining mission-critical business operations is crucial for businesses because the risk of teams breaking down or management losing interest in an initiative is quite common. The enterprise architect helps ensure continuity through the standardization of business and IT processes.

Moreover, to meet the business and IT needs of the organization, the EA development process integrates different viewpoints within an organization.

EA management process

Enterprise architecture management (EAM) enables and drives business value using EA. It defines the direction that an organization needs to take for smooth and seamless implementation, strategy building that ensures optimal outcomes, and governance to plan and set the right roadmap for the company's vision, goals, guidelines, policies, and principles.

The EAM process has multiple roles within an EA:

- It defines the right path for activities related to EA. All of the stakeholders within an organization must take the direction set by EAM.

- It works as a bridge between business strategy and EA when it comes to communication, collaboration, and maintaining the connection.

- It leverages the core values of EA for the process of business transformation.

Furthermore, communications, monitoring, control, and other activities that take place on a recurring basis are managed under the EAM process to ensure the development and deployment of EA support and the delivery business value.

EA governance process

All the information related to the ongoing processes is required to be shared and evaluated across the board. This is where the EA governance process plays a vital role. Through this process, teams identify, manage, audit, and disseminate all of the information needed to manage the EA. Apart from managing and controlling, there are hundreds of processes going on within an organization that must be monitored, such as architecture principles, policies, decisions, recommendations, deliverables, contracts, and agreements. The EA governance process ensures that they are being executed correctly at the appropriate times.

Project engagement process

The relationship between EA and the delivery of projects holds special importance in the EA process, as it provides direction to anticipate business changes. Additionally, new market trends that might emerge based on customer behavior within the next 3- to 5-year period are predicted.

The EA model is the primary source of information that sets the foundation for individual delivery projects. By the end of delivery projects, the solution architecture that has been crafted is linked back to the current EA.

EA compliance process

Compliance with rules, laws, and regulations is assessed against the EA assessment criteria, standards, qualities, service-level agreements, and architecture requirements. This complex yet crucial process is conducted in multiple stages and the tasks that are performed are detailed next.

Strategizing on priority

In today's constantly evolving digital world, businesses must stay ahead of innovation to keep their place in the race. EA leaders play a vital role in helping organizations catch up with the latest trends. They cannot rely on legacy architectural practices, as they are not relevant today. EA leaders apply their critical capabilities to define a new vision for EA for the companies and how it would be beneficial.

Enterprise architects should focus their time and resources on prioritized elements within the architecture model. Usually, these priorities are based on both the scenarios and practices that are opted for globally. EA offers relevant business value based on current trends related to each business priority:

Key Business Priority	Enterprise Architecture Value
Business transformation	Assert business goals, redesign business models, assess impacts, design and communicate future, prioritize and plan changes, and accelerate requirements.
Strategic planning	Provide a business and enterprise framework for objectively prioritizing investments within and across portfolios based on strategic alignment and rationalization.
Customer experience	Provide root-cause analysis for experience results, inform experience decision making (e.g., priorities, available capabilities), assess impacts bidirectionally (i.e., experience and business/technology environment), and translate experience into action.
Agile execution	Provide big-picture direction and common language, focus execution teams on the right enterprise priorities, and accelerate requirements.
Resource optimization	Provide a business and enterprise lens for optimizing resources (e.g., processes, system applications) for cost/simplification reasons and assist efforts of related disciplines (e.g., business process management and operational excellence).
Regulatory compliance and changes	Provide a business and enterprise framework for assessing, addressing, and communicating regulatory impacts and risks; demonstrate compliance with end-to-end traceability from policy to business and IT assets.
Emerging technologies	Assert business goals, redesign business models, identify key applications for emerging technology, assess impacts, design and communicate future, prioritize and plan changes, and accelerate requirements.
Cross-organization coordination	Provide a business and enterprise framework for assessing, designing, planning, and executing mergers, acquisitions, joint ventures, joint initiatives, and startups.

Figure 2.4 – Key business priorities and EA value

IT engagement model architecture and implementation

The defining principles of an EA model include the mission, goals, objectives, responsibilities, and resources within an organization. Taking everyone along on the journey of transformation is one way to ensure fruitful outcomes.

Creating and sharing engagement models across the board helps all stakeholders understand the scope and ultimate EA objectives. A communication plan, followed by funding details and innovative ideas, is documented in the charter.

Here are a variety of components of engagement models:

- EA ensures collaboration among various teams in an organization. It's essential to be in touch with the ground realities of business processes. That is why each model comes with an engagement purpose. It defines the reasons for interaction between EA teams and other groups.

- Participants include all stakeholders that are a part of the process, including the EA team and the groups they interact with, to achieve the identified goals.

- Artifacts are extracted from the data based on analytics, and then evaluated or modified by this engagement type to be used as future reference.

- Communication approaches ensure that all participants are on the same page in terms of successes, failures, capabilities, and opportunities. It ensures that this type of engagement is the most effective.

- The timing of an engagement defines the amount of time a certain task will take. It evaluates the total duration of the process related to the engagement purpose.

For a better understanding of these engagement purposes, here are four common categories of EA engagements:

- Engagements solely focused on creating support for EA along with strategy building, portfolio management, and governance.

- Engagements focused on evaluating, recognizing, collecting, and drafting artifacts. These elements are responsible for defining the current situation of EA and how it will look in the future.

- Engagements focused on making an impact on the current workflow to support the EA's intermediate and future states.

- Engagements that focus on influencing future outcomes and decisions that relate to the EA's intermediate and future states.

Developing a consistent mindset, strategies, and actions to understand engagement purposes can have additional purposes and approaches, but the major ones have been discussed already.

Testing the core foundation for business agility

Some of the reasons EA is an important element in the enablement of enterprise architecture are outlined next.

Agile teams are focused on value creation

EA allows organizations to reuse their valuable assets across delivery teams. When companies work on innovative projects, it is crucial to maintain the flow of ongoing processes. Therefore, when agile teams have high-quality assets available to reuse, they are able to focus on creating a new valuable solution.

Common guidance enables greater consistency

Roadmaps and blueprints set by enterprise architects are capable of ensuring great outcomes. When teams follow these guidelines, their work results in greater quality. EA facilitates learning about new assets, getting accustomed to new processes, and gaining an understanding of how things operate in a new business environment infrastructure. Moving between teams is convenient and effective because it's easier for team members to catch up on their progress and share their skills and learnings with other team members.

Agile architecture enables disaggregation

The ability to allocate tasks to the teams with the most relevant and appropriate skill sets is a great talent on its own. When a business solution is based on highly cohesive components, spreading work among smaller teams gets easier. That way, the delivery time is reduced by reducing the risk of organizational complexity.

EA scales the agile methodology

When carried out efficiently across an organization, agile strategies can offer extraordinary outcomes. Companies can experience a smooth workflow paired with a seamless transformation process.

A disciplined, agile approach to EA enables organizations to scale agile strategies across the enterprise. Effective leadership and a defined set of principles play a major role in setting a solid foundation.

Leadership principles and how they relate to enterprise architects

An organization's culture, ultimate goals, mantra for innovation, team interactions, and what keeps team members focused and motivated all come together to define a company's discipline. In order to ensure that EA has maximum impact on an organization's infrastructure, the team must exercise strong organizational discipline to build and leverage a solid foundation for EA success.

Committing and removing barriers

Stakeholders must embrace the discipline of being a valuable asset to the team and a contributor to the operating model. When it comes to the implementation of standard processes, data, and technology, these stakeholders play a vital role.

Not only do employees need to abide by the organization's regulations, but management must embrace them, too. Rigor in these areas helps pursue strategic opportunities that leverage a company's foundation by focusing on the opportunities that can make a measurable difference and are a great fit for the business. To build an effective foundation for execution, businesses shouldn't base their strategies on customer demands and competitor initiatives. Instead, they should take a leading approach and come up with a strategy that is all about identifying opportunities to leverage existing capabilities.

A company needs a driving force to be able to execute the plans it has set for itself. An enterprise architect is at the forefront when it comes to a company's ability to execute its strategies. Although the roadmap is designed by EA, the need for the attention and dedication of senior management still holds great importance. With multiple board members and decision-makers, having everyone on the same page while taking important steps can be difficult.

When an enterprise architect takes action based solely on what they think is right, it can lead to more harm than good. Therefore, senior management must keep an open mind, let go of ego, and be involved in the articulation of the EA. By taking responsibility for converting an architecture into a foundation for sustainable execution, management can make a big difference by reinforcing governance.

Emphasizing strategic planning

If you're looking to align your agile resources and get them well in sync with your company guidelines, organizational strategy is a great way to move forward. Often, enterprise architects get stuck with day-to-day matters instead of focusing on strategic planning. To avoid such distractions, communicating all aspects of the process with teams across the board is a powerful approach. Better outcomes can be ensured by working closely with business and IT, drafting roadmaps and target dates, and visualizing the end results.

Being the commander and leading the way

A team performs better when they have a leader who leads by example. An organization needs skilled employees, but the leader is the one who encourages that team to put forward their best work. The commander provides details about the core direction and strategy to their staff with the understanding that things can change.

They offer space for the team to settle down and get used to new developments while maintaining their managing intent. The journey matters, but what most people will remember is the end result. That's what the goal should be: to deliver on the architect's intent.

Displaying the value of business architecture

Which is better: telling people how someone solved a problem or showing them the journey they took to solve it? Practical examples – sharing the journey – tends to be more effective. Company leaders must lead by example because actions speak louder than words.

Often, organizations spend most of their time trying to sell the virtues and benefits of business architecture. But too often, in the process, they fail to implement these qualities in their business architecture. Once an EA team gets past introducing business architecture within the organization, the best and the only way to sell it is by fully implementing the plan.

Summary

Market trends and technology are constantly changing, and organizations that don't evolve with them struggle to stay relevant. Paying close attention to the customer's behavior and understanding how they approach innovation and technology can offer a lot of insight into upcoming trends. Enterprise architects are the specialists who look into these elements and come up with innovative strategies. They anticipate and predict the changes that might happen in the market based on a variety of factors, and they help organizations to better equip themselves to deal with them.

In the process of this analysis, data evaluation, and strategic operational planning, enterprise architects often come across many challenges. Sometimes, management is not as involved as they could or should be, teams are not well structured, or tasks are not appropriately allocated. In the wake of these challenges, communication and collaboration among different groups can fail.

Redefining and designing the whole organizational structure can be a monumental task, but applying the right strategy and talent to approach each step can help facilitate the process. Some companies might not get it right the first time, which is not unusual. Teams and individuals need space and time to get in sync with one another and to get used to the transformation process. The role of leadership plays an important in EA. Nothing helps more than having a manager who motivates team members and sets the right example through their actions.

The next chapter is about the **Amazon Web Services (AWS)** cloud. We will explore and shed light on this transformational technology and the guiding rules to ensure positive outcomes when applying it. With EA, cloud capabilities provide the freedom to explore and take risks with technological advancements. Additionally, we'll address the principles that support the process.

3
Applying Enterprise Architecture to the AWS Cloud

An **enterprise architecture** (**EA**) sets the foundation for a streamlined workflow. So, basically, when we talk about a team of technicians, developers, database, and network engineers, they all use the same framework for their day-to-day organizational operations. Creating a consistent and defined standard for business planning, design, and implementation of the workload in the cloud is facilitated by EA. To explore this further, we will discuss the following topics in this chapter:

* Introduction to EA in **Amazon Web Services** (**AWS**)
* AWS EA tenets and EA domains
* AWS services that support EA activities
* Working backward with AWS
* Governance, auditability, and change management

Enterprise architecture in AWS

A centralized workflow establishes a way for building a workload, determining a roadmap for current and future operations and the path that should be taken to reach the ultimate goals set by the stakeholders.

Once an EA is agreed upon by every individual involved in the process, the same operational methods are followed across the board. It sure comes with multiple benefits, including better clarity in the workload, prevention of competitive interests within your organization, and better compliance. The primary objective of every business, apart from a valuable financial outcome, is to provide services that fulfill customers' needs. For an organization to execute its customer-centric strategy, EA guides its business, information, process, and technology decisions.

Business architecture domain

Every company has a set of guidelines and standard regulations that are followed across the board. These define a blueprint for each business growth initiative and implementation. To fulfill the roles of these innovations, the business architecture domain describes the functional capabilities that a company holds to achieve the ultimate goal. The *What* and *Who* of a business growth strategy is addressed in a way that contributes to establishing what is the organization's vision and the objectives behind any new development. Apart from that, the teams, groups, or capable individuals who will be assigned to execute the defined services are also covered.

Application architecture domain

The role of each and every application that a company's operations rely on is determined in this step. Interactions and relationships between the applications and the core business processes within the organization are established here. In simple words, the *How* of a business strategy is determined by figuring out how the previously defined business services were implemented.

Data architecture domain

Data is the most important asset of any business in the world and defines the past, present, and potential future of services. This step describes the data assets of an organization and the way it is being exploited to improve business and customer satisfaction. The analysis ultimately results in an evolved business process.

Technology architecture domain

No company can have smooth and seamless operations without modern technological assets. Especially in today's advanced digital universe, describing the software and hardware that's required by an organization for business and application services is absolutely essential.

Cloud initiatives and traceability across the IT landscape

Thriving businesses love nothing more than the ability to respond faster to customer needs and modern business requirements, and for that, the perfect resort is EA, which provides agility and ensures resilience among development teams. Moreover, with the cloud, the enterprise has all the freedom to take risks when it comes to new technological advancements. However, without full control over operations in a company, things may not be as productive and convenient. Better compliance, security, and workload management can be ensured by having the right control.

Job descriptions and defined roles are a major part of the traditional **information technology** (**IT**) operating model. The stakeholders of these models are developers, engineers, and server administrators. Such models allow organizations to consume the cloud as an **end-to-end** (**E2E**) team that's working in an aligned infrastructure. An IT organization adopting a cloud-first strategy means that all actors use a similar framework for their decision-making process and managing the system.

Mixing up two different methods by adopting an EA model while operations still run through traditional silos can have a devastating impact. Without a standardized adoption, a company is likely to end up with no centralized management and compliance. A team that is working toward the same goal should take the same road toward the finish line. When the methods or approaches of an initiative are not aligned, competition within an organization cannot be avoided. There would be a lot of confusion among the IT department regarding critical matters such as workload being deployed, security vulnerabilities, integrations, crucial metrics, and so on. Without centralized management, companies can never be sure about their security standards as there is no control or audit trail.

Creating a combination of scalable cloud applications and services reduces delays or issues that computers or network devices may encounter in infrastructure provisioning and device management. When we talk about AWS, we mean the market leaders of services to define **infrastructure as a service** (**IaaS**) and **platform as a service** (**PaaS**) in cloud environments. Setting the goals for an architecture regarding the outcome is the first step before implementing the EA in any of the AWS services.

Before you incorporate architecture in the cloud, make sure that all the required assets are at your disposal and that the team is well aware of them. Cloud solutions set the guidelines for organizations regarding crucial elements, including profit maximization, the principles of work continuity, agility, scalability, flexibility, and network or data security.

Properly embedding EA domains in a cloud architecture can avoid many issues by building a strategy and fulfilling business expectations. Having architects focus their energy on collaboration to make the most out of the business strategy can prove to be extremely beneficial.

EA facilitates the standards for business planning and implementation of the workload in the cloud. Moreover, it enables businesses to improve their customer services for greater outcomes using a blend of scalable cloud applications.

AWS EA tenets and EA domains

The quality and consistency of decision-making play a major role in the overall process and outcome of an initiative. To ensure the best possible infrastructure, certain AWS EA principles need to be considered. They are a set of guidelines to be followed as they describe the big picture of the enterprise, specifically the technological capabilities and their impact on the institution. The principles are well in sync with the business mission and goals, and each one of them has a unique definition and implementation process.

All information about the organization's ultimate goal, set of agendas, and mission is defined by enterprise principles to ensure harmony among processes in a company. Within a **business unit (BU)** or **organizational unit (OU)**, IT, **human resources (HR)**, domestic operations, or overseas operations are important elements of any enterprise principle. Principles that are used to inform architecture development need to be well aligned with the architecture capability (stable building blocks that define what an organization does) defined by the organization itself.

Establishing a sustainable architecture practice within an organization can be achieved by adhering to the same approach that is used to establish any other capability—such as a **business process management (BPM)** capability—within an organization.

These principles ensure a level of collaboration and consensus across the enterprise that leads to better decision-making. Architecture principles set the foundation for an effective process by governing the architecture process, its maintenance, implications, and impacts. They often restate other enterprise guidance in a way that effectively guides architecture development. Deployment of all IT resources and assets across the enterprise are also monitored and defined by the architecture principles as they form a basis for making future IT decisions. Nonetheless, all aspects of the architecture principles are tightly knit with the business objectives driving forces behind it.

Components of architecture principles

Each architecture principle should have associated rationale and implications statements. When deployed appropriately, they can effortlessly promote understanding and acceptance of the principles themselves collectively. The process ultimately helps in explaining and justifying the reasons behind adopting certain principles, and should include the following aspects:

- **Name**: Should be easy to remember and should represent the essence of the rule. No specifications are necessary for this section, such as a specific technology platform. Ambiguous words such as *support*, *open*, and *consider* can create a bit of confusion. Always remember to avoid unnecessary adjectives and adverbs.

- **Statement**: Should clearly communicate the fundamental rule by eliminating any ambiguity. Principle statements for managing information are similar for most organizations.

- **Rationale**: Should highlight the business benefits of adhering to the principle, using corporate vocabulary. Point to the similarity between technology principles and the principles governing business operations. Mention the relationship with other principles and intentions regarding a balanced interpretation. Describe use-case scenarios of following guidelines set by these principles.

- **Implications**: Should highlight business and IT requirements for carrying out the principle regarding resources, costs, and activities. Clearly state the impact on the business and the consequences of adopting a principle. Answer questions such as *How does this affect me?*. Mention that some outcomes are speculative and potential, rather than fully analyzed.

Developing architecture principles

Key stakeholders within a system come together for the development of architecture principles. The principles are put together by enterprise architects and are implemented after the approval of the Architecture Board. One of the most important requisites includes clear traceability that leads to a comprehensive articulation to guide the decision-making process. The principles ensure that the architecture and implementation of the target architecture are well aligned with business strategies and objectives. Here are the elements that influence architecture principles:

- The enterprise mission of the company justifies their planning at each step toward a certain goal of enterprise.

- An enterprise's **strengths, weaknesses, opportunities, and threats** (**SWOT**) influence the principles to a great extent. Moreover, current initiatives define a roadmap for future business strategies.

- External elements that define market trends such as **time-to-market** (**TTM**) imperatives, customer behavior, and so on, along with existing and potential legislation.

- The existing assets and infrastructure of an organization have a huge impact on architecture principles, such as information resources including systems documentation, equipment inventories, network configuration diagrams, policies, and procedures.

- The latest technological and business trends—for example, predictions about economic, political, and market factors that influence the overall enterprise setup.

Qualities of principles

It takes varied factors to determine whether a principle is good, great, or simply a waste of effort. A poor set of principles becomes redundant quite quickly and results in a lack of credibility. A combination of fancy words gathered on a piece of paper does not define a principle's value or whether the decision-makers agree on it or not. Values that are rooted deep in a company's foundation and followed unconsciously across the board are something we can safely call a good set of principles. They are defined in a language that is understandable by each stakeholder and is not complicated or unnecessarily lengthy. Principles that can be endorsed by the management provide a firm foundation for making architecture and planning decisions. They build policies around future strategies, procedures, and standards to support the resolution of contradictory situations. We have listed five criteria to help distinguish between a set of good and bad principles. According to this list, a good principle has the following attributes:

- **Understandable**: Something that is too complicated to grasp can never make a deep and long-lasting impact. However, the underlying tenets that are easily understandable by individuals throughout the organization have made it to our list of good principles. Its purpose should be clear and unambiguous so that the risk of internal or external violations can be minimized.

- **Robust**: Principles should enable decision-makers to make valuable decisions about architecture followed by the implementation of policies. Each principle should be sufficiently definitive on its own and precise enough to support the ongoing decision-making process in unconventional situations.

- **Complete**: A attribute of principles that not only governs the management of company information about the business but also covers every situation perceived regarding technology and other advancements.

- **Consistent**: The kind of principle that is relevant to the overall process of business strategy and offers a balance in interpretations. Adhering to one principle shouldn't violate the spirit of another. A consistent, scalable, and flexible interpretation of every word in the document is essential.

- **Stable**: Businesses are constantly evolving as per customer behavior, and principles should be enduring enough to accommodate changes. There should be scope for adding, removing, or altering principles based on these changes.

Applying architecture principles

The way an enterprise uses and deploys IT resources and assets within an organization is decided by stakeholders leveraging the architecture principles. They are used every step of the way to ensure a productively smooth process followed by maximum outcomes, as explained in more detail here:

- Architecture principles guide the creation of a roadmap and facilitate the process whereby the enterprise makes conscious decisions about EA.

- Architecture principles work as a guiding force that exerts an influence on the selection of products and solutions followed by establishing relevant evaluation criteria.

- Architecture principles are, in a nutshell, drivers for defining requirements related to the business and technology of the architecture.

- Architecture principles aid the process of evaluating existing implementations. This process helps in compliance with the defined architectures. Using analysis reports, valuable insights are utilized for transition activities to define and implement architecture goals.

- The architecture principles' implication statement provides valuable inputs for future transition initiatives and planning activities. Moreover, it sets the foundation for primary tasks, resources, and potential costs to the enterprise.

- When it comes to architecture governance activities, architecture principles provide support for architecture compliance assessments. Also, they enable the system to initiate a dispensation request within the local operating procedure. This is accomplished by assessing the health of a system/application/solution to determine its conformance to a target reference architecture's standards and guidelines, including detecting patterns and technology anomalies.

While applying architecture principles, choosing the right one as per the situation can be a difficult and complex job. The wrong pick can often lead to devastating outcomes. In order to avoid any confusion or finger-pointing in the future, the rationale for such decisions should always be documented. Companies or departments might not feel the need for continuous documentation at that particular point. However, it should be a common practice to bring everything on record by having it in written form. A principle often seems self-evident, but the guidance in a principle could be complicated and have multiple aspects to it. While being multidimensional, principles should be obvious as they help ensure decisions that lead to the desired outcome.

Those who violate principles might take things lightly, and letting such matters go can set a wrong precedence. A declaration of principles may not contain specific penalties, but it can actually cause operational problems and affect the ability of the organization to fulfill its mission in the long run.

An example set of architecture principles

Higher management reaching a mutual agreement on a number of principles can be a tough task as too many principles can reduce the flexibility of the architecture, and too few will not have the right level of impact. Some organizations document principles for each level within a department; others, however, prefer to define only high-level principles.

Take the following diagram as a reference for both the typical content of a set of architecture principles and the recommended format for defining them:

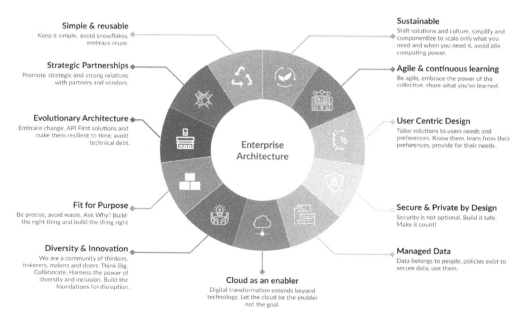

Figure 3.1 – Architecture principles and format for defining them

Next, we move on to business principles with their rationale and limitations. Each principle is unique and defines a particular situation under which the users derive their own meanings and face certain constraints.

Business principles

Principle 1 – Primacy of principles

Statement: All organizations within the enterprise must adhere to the following principles of information management.

Rationale: In order to ensure that the information provided to the decision-makers is consistent and measurable, all organizations must align their infrastructures and abide by the principles.

Implications:

- This principle helps avoid exclusions, favoritism, and inconsistency. Otherwise, it is capable of undermining the management of information.

- Information management initiatives are incapable of implication without being examined for compliance with principles.

- Change the framework of the initiative to resolve conflict with a principle.

Principle 2 – Maximize benefits to the enterprise

Statement: Maximum benefits to the enterprise are ensured by information management decisions as a whole.

Rationale: Maximum **return on investment** (**ROI**) requires information management decisions to stick to enterprise-wide strategies. *Service above self* is what this principle is all about. Any decision or step that is taken with a broad-minded approach while keeping in mind the enterprise-wide perspective turns out to be more effective than ones that are made from any particular organizational perspective. No individual or a group will detach from the benefit of the whole enterprise.

Implications:

- Bigger goals require bigger risks and drastic decisions, therefore enterprise-wide massive benefits require changes in planning strategy. This step needs decision-makers to go beyond IT to bring about this change.

- Letting go of the organization's preferences might be required, or bringing them down in the priority list could be needed for the greater benefit of the entire enterprise.

- The entire enterprise should be on board to decide on the application development priorities for the entire enterprise, and application components should be shared across the board.

- An enterprise plan must always set the foundation for conducting information management initiatives. Meanwhile, individual organizations pursue initiatives that are in accordance with blueprints established by the enterprise.

- With the changing need of redefining principles based on special circumstances, priorities must be adjusted. For that purpose, a comprehensive enterprise representation forum should reach a decision.

Principle 3 – Information management is everybody's business

Statement: Information management decisions that are made for accomplishing business goals must be backed by all organizations in the enterprise.

Rationale: All organizations in the enterprise must be fully involved in all aspects of the information environment. That is the only way to ensure that information management is aligned with the business. All information users play the role of key stakeholders in the implementation of technology that ultimately addresses a business need. Business experts from across the enterprise and technical staff come together as a team to take responsibility for developing and sustaining the information environment that defines the goals and objectives of IT.

Implications:

- Working toward a common goal as a team. Each stakeholder must take responsibility for developing the information environment.

- Sufficient and sustainable resources required to implement this principle need to be provided consistently.

Principle 4 – Business continuity

Statement: Enterprise operations are maintained despite any system interruptions.

Rationale: Imagine a day at your workplace without desktops, laptops, the internet, or a communication platform such as Slack. How unproductive would that day be? This is all because we are greatly dependent on system operations. With them being more pervasive, enterprises must consider the reliability of such systems throughout their design and use to ensure the uninterrupted flow of information. Certain tools are essential for conducting day-to-day operations, thus business premises throughout the enterprise should be equipped with capable ones to continue business functions regardless of external events. Extra steps need to be taken to avoid any kind of disruption in case of hardware failure, natural disasters, and data corruption. An alternative information delivery mechanism must always be in place.

Implications:

- Natural disasters or system failures are a part of the process, hence a reliable alternative must be put in place in advance and managed.

- Periodic reviews, vulnerability testing, and designing of mission-critical services should ensure uninterrupted business function through alternative capabilities.

- When the system is being put in place by enterprise architects, matters such as recoverability, redundancy, and maintainability should be addressed at that time.

- The impact of applications must be assessed for the enterprise mission. This helps in coming up with a recovery plan.

Principle 5 – Common business applications

Statement: Business processes and applications that are used across the enterprise for the execution of a process are better than having duplicative applications that are only provided to a particular organization.

Rationale: Duplicative resources mean increased cost and proliferate conflicting data.

Implications:

- Organizations dependent on applications that only serve a particular organization instead of the whole enterprise must replace these with ones that are adaptable enterprise-wide. Establishment and adherence to a policy requiring this are crucial.

- Similar/duplicative capabilities cannot be developed by organizations that are dedicated to them. Expenditure of scarce resources can be decreased by having a joint-application approach that will be more effective and cost-efficient.

- Enterprise decision-making supported by data and information will be standardized to a much greater extent.

- Organizational capabilities producing different data will be replaced by enterprise-wide capabilities.

Principle 6 – Service orientation

Statement: The design of services that mirror real-world business activities creates an architecture along with business processes.

Rationale: There are no boundaries when it comes to the flow of information, and the service orientation delivers enterprise agility.

Implications:

- Business descriptions are utilized by service representation to provide context such as business goal, process, policy, service interface, and so on, and services are implemented using service orchestration

- Unique requirements are placed on the infrastructure, and open standards are used for implementations to realize location transparency

- Implementations are often constrained or enabled by context and must be described within that context

- Strong governance of service representation and implementation is required

Principle 7 – Compliance with the law

Statement: Enterprise information management processes stick to all relevant policies and regulations.

Rationale: Adhering to laws, policies, and regulations in the enterprise policy will not preclude business process improvements leading to changes in regulations.

Implications:

- The enterprise complies with laws, regulations, and policies regarding the collection and management of data

- Education and access to the rules are ensured by the enterprise

- Updated laws and regulations may drive changes in processes or applications

Principle 8 – Protection of intellectual property

Statement: Protection of an enterprise's **intellectual property (IP)** is absolutely essential. It must be reflected in IT architecture, implementation, and governance processes.

Rationale: A major part of an enterprise's IP is hosted in the IT domain.

Implications:

- Actual protection of IP assets is implemented in the IT domain. Trust in non-IT processes can be managed by IT processes as well, such as email, mandatory notes, and so on.

- A security policy for the governance of human and IT actors is required to improve the protection of IP. This eliminates compromises and reduces liabilities.

Data principles

Principle 9 – Data is an asset

Statement: Data is of great value to the enterprise and is managed accordingly.

Rationale: Real and measurable value of data can never be underestimated as it facilitates the decision-making process. Data is carefully managed just like all other company assets to set the foundation of a business strategy. The enterprise is well aware of where the data is, whether a team can rely upon its accuracy, and whether it can be extracted when needed.

Implications:

- Three principles combine together to form this: data is an asset, shared, and accessible.

- Ensure that all organizations within the enterprise understand the relationship between the value of data, sharing, and accessibility.

- Teams must be authorized to manage data for which they are accountable.

- Adopt the approach of *data stewardship* and let go of *data ownership*.

- Don't let obsolete or inconsistent data pass to enterprise personnel as this can adversely affect decisions across the enterprise.

- A data steward who manages data ensures data quality as well.

- Develop procedures to prevent, identify, and correct errors in the information. Fix processes that produce flawed information.

- An enterprise-wide forum should decide on changes in the process suggested by the steward.

- Data stewards accountable for who is responsible for properly managing data are assigned at the enterprise level.

Principle 10 – Data is shared

Statement: Data that is essential for executing duties is accessible to the organization, hence this is shared across enterprise functions and organizations.

Rationale: To improve the quality and efficiency of enterprise decision-making, it is essential to maintain timely, accurate data in one application and then share it, rather than maintaining duplicate data in multiple applications. There is a wealth of stored data in the enterprise, but it is organized in hundreds of stovepipe databases. The ability to share these islands of data across the enterprise will determine how fast it can collect, create, transfer, and assimilate data.

When data is shared, we will be able to make better decisions as there are fewer sources of more accurately managed data to rely on. Data that is transferred via the network will be more efficient because data entities are reused without having to enter data again.

Implications:

- Three principles combine together to form this: data is an asset, shared, and accessible.

- Ensure that all organizations within the enterprise understand the relationship between value, sharing, and accessibility to data.

- Abide by a common set of policies, procedures, and standards governing data management to ensure easy access short- and long-term.

- Invest in software that is capable of migrating legacy system data into a shared data environment.

- Develop standard models and other metadata to create a repository system to make it accessible after efficiently storing it.

- Adopt and enforce data access guidelines for new application developers when legacy systems are replaced. Ensure that data in new applications remains accessible and continues to be used by new applications.

- Adopt common methods and tools to create, maintain, and access data shared across the enterprise.

- Data sharing requires a significant cultural change.

- In no circumstances will the principle of data sharing compromise confidential information.

- All users will rely on data to execute their respective tasks. Ensure that the most accurate data is being relied upon for decision-making.

Principle 11 – Data is accessible

Statement: Data is accessible for users to perform their functions.

Rationale: Providing users with access to information enables them to make quick and effective decisions and to respond to requests for information and service in a timely manner. Using information must be considered from an enterprise perspective to allow wide access by a variety of users.

Implications:

- Three principles combine together to form this: data is an asset, shared, and accessible.

- Ensure that all organizations within the enterprise understand the relationship between value, sharing, and accessibility to data.

- Provide ease of accessibility with which users obtain information.

- The information must be accessible and displayed in a way that can accommodate a wide range of enterprise users.

- Understanding the data is essential. Individuals should not misinterpret information.

- Access to data does not mean the user has access rights to modify or disclose the data.

Principle 12 – Data trustee

Statement: A trustee is responsible for the quality of each data element.

Rationale: When data is entered multiple times, its integrity may be compromised, so the data trustee will be solely responsible for eliminating redundant effort and data resources. It is one of the advantages of an architected environment to be able to share data within the enterprise. It becomes increasingly important that the single authority making decisions is the data trustee.

> **Important note**
>
> In contrast to a steward, a trustee is responsible for data accuracy and currency, whereas a steward may also be responsible for standardization and definition.

Implications:

- With a real trusteeship, data ownership issues are resolved, allowing all users to have access to the data. Therefore, a cultural shift from data *ownership* to data *trusteeship* may be necessary.

- The data trustee is accountable for meeting quality requirements for the data.

- The trustee should have the ability to provide user confidence in the data based on data sources.

- Identify the true source of the data so that the data authority can be assigned the responsibility of a trustee. However, classified sources will be revealed.

- Once information is captured electronically, it should be validated as close to the source as possible. To ensure the integrity of the data, **quality control** (**QC**) measures must be implemented.

- Sharing data across organizations makes trustees accountable for the accuracy and currency of their data elements. Therefore, trustees must recognize the importance of their trusteeship role.

Principle 13 – Common vocabulary and data definitions

Statement: The definitions of data are consistent across the enterprise, and users have easy access to the definitions.

Rationale: To facilitate data sharing across headquarters, the data that will be used in developing applications must be defined in a common way. This will enhance communication and facilitate effective dialogue. The systems must also be interfaced, and data exchanged.

Implications:

- We are led to believe that this issue is adequately addressed due to the existence of people with *data administration* job titles. This task requires a significant amount of additional energy and resources and improving the information environment relies heavily on it. A large community addresses the issue of data element definition, which is separate but sufficiently related, like a common vocabulary.

- The enterprise must establish an initial common vocabulary for the business.

- The definition effort will be reconciled with the corporate *glossary* when a new data definition is required.

- Multiple parochial meanings of data must give way to enterprise-wide definitions to avoid ambiguity.

- Need for coordinated data standardization initiatives.

- Responsibilities must be assigned for functional data administration.

Principle 14 – Data security

Statement: Data protection against unauthorized use includes, but is not limited to, the protection of pre-decisional, sensitive, source selection-sensitive, and proprietary information. In addition, the typical features of national security classification apply.

Rationale: The necessity to restrict access to secret, proprietary, and sensitive information must be weighed against the open sharing of information and the release of information via suitable legislation.

To minimize undue conjecture, misunderstanding, and improper usage, **work-in-progress (WIP)** material must be preserved. Existing regulations demand that national security and data privacy be protected while allowing free and open access.

Implications:

- Gathering information in any form will make a huge objective requiring a survey and de-characterization methodology to keep up with fitting control.

- This review and declassification are handled by appropriate policy and procedures. Regular reviews of the information are important as access to information is based on a need-to-know policy.

- Separate systems to contain different classifications should be revamped.

- See if the current system or solution is too expensive to manage unclassified data on a classified system. Combine the two by placing unclassified data on the classified system, where it must remain.

- Identify security needs to provide access to open information in a secure way.

- Restrict access to *view only* or *never see* for security purposes.

- Decide on the labeling of data for access to pre-decisional, decisional, classified, sensitive, or proprietary information.

- Design security into data elements from the beginning.

- Safeguard systems, data, and technologies against inadvertent or unauthorized alteration, sabotage, disaster, or disclosure.

- Manage duration of protection for pre-decisional information using new policies in consideration of content freshness.

Application principles

Principle 15 – Technology independence

Statement: Applications are autonomous of explicit innovation decisions. This way, they can work on multiple innovation stages.

Rationale: Technological independence allows applications to be developed, upgraded, and operated in the most cost-effective and timely way. However, the innovation that is dependent on external factors such as vendors becomes the driver rather than the user requirements themselves.

Every IT-related decision makes us dependent on that technology. This principle ensures that application software is not dependent on specific hardware and operating systems software.

Implications:

- Standards supporting portability are essential.

- Most applications for **commercial off-the-shelf (COTS)** and **government off-the-shelf (GOTS)** applications are technology- and platform-dependent.

- Subsystem interfaces to enable legacy applications need to be developed. They interoperate with applications and operating environments within the EA.

- Use middleware to decouple applications from specific software solutions.

- Java and future Java-like protocols could be opted for as they give a high degree of priority to platform independence.

Principle 16 – Ease of use

Statement: Applications are easy to use, along with a transparent underlying technology so that users can concentrate on tasks at hand.

Rationale: Ease of use is a positive incentive for user adoption. The more a user has to understand the underlying technology, the less productive they are. Rather than developing independent systems to do the same task outside of an enterprise's integrated information environment, the integrated information environment encourages users to work within it.

Using a system should be as straightforward as driving a different car since most of the knowledge required to operate it will be similar to that required to operate other systems. Training will be kept to a minimum, and improper use of the system is extremely unlikely.

Implications:

- It will be necessary for all applications to have the same *look and feel* and support ergonomic requirements; hence, a common look-and-feel standard must be created, along with usability test criteria that can be applied to all applications

- An interface should not be constrained by narrow assumptions about the location, language, system training, or physical capabilities of the user

- A variety of factors affect the ease of use of an application, including linguistics, physical attributes of the user (visual acuity, ability to use a keyboard and mouse), and skill in technology use

- Technology principles

Principle 17 – Requirements-based change

Statement: Changes to applications and technology are only made in response to business needs.

Rationale: Through this principle, the information environment will change in response to the business's needs, rather than the business adapting to IT changes.

By changing technology, business needs may change and, therefore, unintended effects on business will be minimized.

Implications:

- An EA will be used to examine proposed changes prior to implementation.

- Technical improvement and system development will not be funded without a documented business need.

- We will develop and implement change management processes conforming to this principle. This principle may clash with the principle of responsive change. We must ensure that response to legitimate business needs is not hindered by requirements documentation.

- Business needs should be kept in focus, not technical needs—managing change in a responsive manner also falls under this category.

Principle 18 – Responsive change management

Statement: It is imperative that changes to the enterprise information environment are made in a timely manner.

Rationale: The enterprise information environment must be able to accommodate the needs of people in order for them to be expected to work within it.

Implications:

- There must be ways to manage and implement change without creating delays.

- A user who feels the need for change needs to speak with a *business expert* who can enlighten them and help implement it. Adopting this principle may require additional resources.

- In order to implement changes, the architectures should be kept up to date.

- This will result in a conflict with other practices such as the maximization of enterprise-wide benefits and applications.

Principle 19 – Control technical diversity

Statement: Maintaining expertise in and connectivity between multiple processing environments is not trivial due to technological diversity.

Rationale: In order to support alternative technologies for computing environments, there is a real, non-trivial cost of infrastructure. There are further infrastructure costs associated with maintaining multiple processor architectures connected together. Keeping the number of supported components to a minimum simplifies maintenance and reduces costs.

Standard packaging will simplify implementation; deployment impacts will be predictable; valuations and returns will be predictable; testing will be redefined. Technical administration is controlled better when limited resources focus on a shared set of technologies.

Implications:

- This principle directly ties policies and procedures that govern the acquisition of technology.
- Technology choices are highly affected by available ones within the blueprint.
- Technology that evolves with modern requirements will have to be developed and put in place.
- The technology blueprint will be modified based on improvements in operational efficiency.

Principle 20 – Interoperability

Statement: Data, applications, and technology should be interoperable using defined standards.

Rationale: By providing consistency, standards make it easier to manage systems, increase user satisfaction, and protect existing IT investments, maximizing their return while reducing costs. Interoperability helps ensure support from multiple vendors for their products and facilitates supply chain integration.

Implications:

- The use of industry standards and interoperability standards will be followed unless there is a compelling business reason to implement a non-standard solution
- A process for defining standards, reviewing and revising them periodically, and granting exceptions must be in place
- Current IT resources must be identified and documented

All the principles provide a stepping stone to set the right foundation for an effective workflow. Moreover, the need for AWS services that ensure efficient EA activities remains crucial.

AWS services that support EA activities

Organizations are often packed with talent, software, hardware, and so on, but knowing which ones to utilize for a particular project or task is necessary. Out of an extensive AWS catalog, companies find the most effective ones to support activities in the corporate architectures, such as AWS Organizations, **Identity and Access Management (IAM)**, CloudTrail, Service Catalog, CloudWatch, and so on.

There are certain stakeholders of AWS services that support EA activities defining *who*, *why*, *what*, *where*, and *how* aspects of the infrastructure, as illustrated in the following diagram:

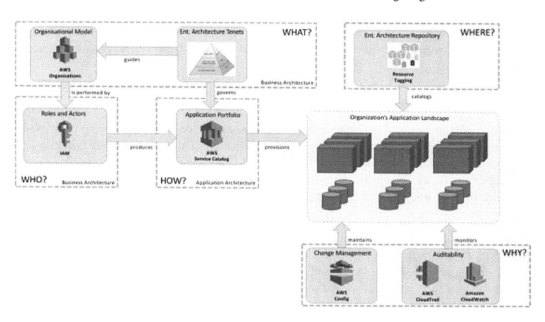

Figure 3.2 – Different aspects of an infrastructure that supports EA activities

Within infrastructure, the business architecture domain defines actors, software, and other tools, compliance with governance bodies, change management, and an EA repository.

Roles and actors

Actors include an organization, a person, or the system executing business activities. Being well aware of each and every aspect of the business and understanding the role of each actor can enable you to create definitive listings. Organizations evolve with time and that is how they stay relevant. In order to facilitate the smooth transitional process, the relationship between each actor and their role needs to be well defined. Any enterprise can model actors and roles in two stages. Usually, organizations have a corporate directory with all the information in it. Other than that, some companies reinforce these elements with AWS IAM solutions.

Application portfolio

Any software plays a significant role in attaining a company's objective, whether they are in-house or external, long-term, or short-term. Application portfolio management is detailed information about which applications a company uses. It is an essential part of the application architecture domain in EA. Through this biodata of applications and other software, the company sets the standard for the utilization of applications. AWS can help streamline the management of commonly deployed applications while providing consistent governance and meeting compliance requirements. Audits and compliance with regulations are efficient and hassle-free when AWS provides a single location where organizations can centrally manage these applications. Keep in mind this only applies to AWS-related services, and organizations may have other environments, architecture, or services within the enterprise. Offering a particular version to users, configuring the services, and controlling access can all be easily managed with the AWS cloud.

Governance and auditability

Compliance with internal and external services to your organization is crucial to ensure that every operation is streamlined as per the requirements and regulations. This is where CloudTrail helps by giving your organization transparency across its entire AWS landscape. The event history of all activities provided by CloudTrail simplifies security analysis, resource change tracking, and troubleshooting. Ultimately, the process of governance, compliance, and operational auditing is made much easier and error-free.

CloudWatch, the monitoring service for AWS cloud resources, helps collect and track metrics, monitor log files, and automatically react to changes in your AWS resources. Events based on the application behavior are triggered by this service as well. CloudTrail and CloudWatch make a powerful duo as they have a huge impact on audit functions and architecture governance.

Change management

The transition process going on within an organization or a system is managed effectively by EA. The primary objective of this monitoring is to ensure that organizational operations continue to be productive and deliver as per the business strategy. To automate this activity, AWS Config is leveraged as it lets you assess, audit, and evaluate the configurations of your AWS resources. The process of reviewing changes is made easier, which leads to an effective evaluation of compliance against the configurations specified in your internal guidelines.

EA repository

What is the ultimate goal that an organization is working toward? Which resources are being exploited to achieve that goal? What kinds of IT assets does a company have when it comes to internal and external operations? Well, all this information can be found in an EA repository. It reflects the organization's technology, data, applications, and business artifacts and the relationships between these components. A while ago, companies used to spend millions of dollars on off-the-shelf products to meet their repository need. However, with cloud services, things have changed to a great extent, and AWS tagging and resource groups are now letting companies organize their AWS landscape by applying tags at different levels of granularity.

They offer labeling, collecting, and organizing resources and components within the services. Another major benefit that comes with AWS services is that managing applications' businesses and technical components of the target landscape globally are made possible. Together, AWS Config, tagging, and Resource Groups make it easier to detect a rogue server or shadow application in a target production landscape.

Customer obsession is one of Amazon's customer-centric guiding principles. The company's approach begins with focusing on the customer and then builds products to delight that customer. AWS helps figure out customer needs to come up with innovation and improvements.

Working backward with AWS

Working backward is a fundamental part of the AWS innovation process. AWS begins by determining what the customer needs and wants, and then makes improvements based on their requirements.

The product team at Amazon thinks through all of the reasons why a certain product is developed and why anyone would be interested in it. A compelling news release is then drafted to announce the product and convince the target customer to opt for it. This announcement should take readers into an imaginary world where their lives would be incomplete without this product. That's the only way to be impactful.

Amazon services do not just represent a software structure but also an organizational structure. By working backward, a better offering can be created for your customers. Small teams are allocated to a certain product to work together for maximum productivity with a strong ownership model as if it were a start-up on its own. Individual and undivided attention is paid to aspects such as who the customers are and what they are looking for. Working backward is a process we employ to ensure service meets the needs of a customer by starting with the customer and working backward until you have the minimum set of technology requirements to reach your goals.

The working backward product definition process sets the basis for what is going to be built. It typically has four steps, as outlined here:

1. Writing a press release that describes everything about the product: why it's important for you, what it does, what changes it will bring to your life, and why it exists. What are the features and benefits of this product and which problem in your life does it suggest a solution for? A press release is expected to be straightforward and crisp. A press release determines how people outside of the organization will see the product.

2. Writing **frequently asked questions** (**FAQs**) that include queries people may have in their minds regarding the product after reading the press release. Add questions that define what the product is good for. Put yourself in the shoes of someone who is thinking about using the product or is already using it, and consider all the questions you would have as a customer.

3. Defining the mighty customer experience. Jot down the customer experience based on different points of view a customer might have about the product. For products with a **user interface** (**UI**), build mock-ups of each screen that the customer uses. For web services, write use cases describing ways people could use the product. In a nutshell, tell stories of how the product solved issues that the customer had.

4. Writing the user manual. Guideline step-by-step instructions about how the customer will use the product. Answer the *How to* and then tell the customer everything they need to know to use the product. If the product is to have different types of users, write a different manual for each type.

By the end of this exercise, the team will be much clearer about what they are planning to build. The set of information in these documents will be readily available to smoothen the process. At this point, the whole team will have a shared vision of the product you are going to build.

AWS keeps modifying the framework based on customer feedback. A while ago, they updated the framework based on the findings from thousands of reviews carried out by AWS solution architects. Customers who needed more guidance on operating the cloud were provided sufficient assistance by adding a sixth pillar to the framework: capturing best practices for sustainability.

Here's a list of the full set of pillars:

*   **Security**: Protection of assets through risk assessments and mitigation strategies while maintaining delivery of business value.

*   **Reliability**: The system should be able to recover from service failures. In situations such as these, it should dynamically acquire computing resources to continue meeting demands and mitigate disruptions.

*   **Performance efficiency**: Use resources in an efficient way to meet system requirements. Technologies must evolve with changing needs.

- **Cost optimization**: The ability to make cost-effective choices without opting for suboptimal resources.

- **Operational excellence**: Monitoring systems that deliver business value and constantly improve processes and procedures.

- **Sustainability**: Identifying ways to reduce energy consumption and improve the efficiency of your workloads by evaluating their design, architecture, and implementation.

The AWS Well-Architected Framework determines a set of best practices for the preceding pillars and offers a set of questions to help understand where you stand. AWS created a series of whitepapers in response to customers' requests on being more prescriptive on how to architect on the cloud, in the context of each pillar.

Governance, auditability, and change management

The governance, auditability, and change management of an organization's architecture are key factors in effective IT/business integration, tracking the outcome, and management of workflow, which is why they have increasingly become a board role.

Governance

The purpose of this section is to shed light on IT and architecture governance so that business responsibilities for the activities and artifacts of architecture can be explained.

Architecture governance characteristics

EA and other architectures are managed via architecture governance at an enterprise-wide level. It includes the following characteristics:

- To ensure the effective introduction, implementation, and evolution of architectures across the organization, a system of controls must be implemented for overall architectural components and activities

- Developing and implementing a system to ensure compliance with internal and external standards and regulations

- The establishment of processes that allow the preceding processes to be managed effectively within agreed parameters

- Establishing practices to ensure accountability both inside and outside the organization, in line with clearly identified stakeholders

Levels of governance within the enterprise

Architectural governance usually operates as part of a hierarchy of governance structures, which—particularly in large enterprises—may include multiple domains such as corporate governance, technology governance, IT governance, and architecture governance, with distinct disciplines and processes. Within the overall enterprise, each of these domains of governance may exist at various geographic levels—global, regional, and local.

Nature of governance

Strategic planning is less about strict adherence to rules and more about providing guidance, as well as ensuring a fair and equitable distribution of resources to ensure the sustainability of a company's goals. In essence, governance refers to ensuring that business is conducted properly.

Here, we enumerate the basic principles of corporate governance as identified by the **Organisation for Economic Cooperation and Development (OECD)**:

- A discussion of shareholders' rights, roles, and equitable treatment
- A discussion of disclosure and transparency and board responsibilities
- Ensures strategic guidance of the organization
- Ensures efficient monitoring of board management
- Ensures accountability of the board for the company
- Board reviews and guides the corporate strategy
- Board monitors management performance aligned with the business objectives

In corporate governance, separate rights and responsibilities are assigned to the board, managers, shareholders, and other stakeholders, along with rules and procedures for making decisions on corporate affairs. Furthermore, it provides a framework by which company objectives are set, as well as a way to monitor progress toward those objectives.

EA governance capabilities and its elements consist of multiple factors that need to be addressed for smooth operations. Their benefits are highlighted in the following screenshot as well:

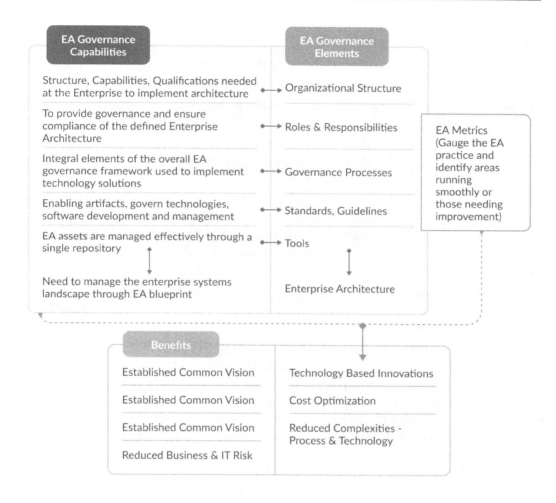

Figure 3.3 – EA governance capabilities and elements

Characteristics of governance

The following characteristics highlight the value and necessity of governance. Organizations should adopt this approach while dealing with all involved parties:

- **Discipline**: All stakeholders must adhere to procedures, processes, and authority structures put in place by the organization.

- **Transparency**: All decisions that may or may not affect IT/business will be made available for inspection by an authorized organization.

- **Independence**: Potential conflicts of interest may occur, hence a decision-making process and other mechanisms will be established.

- **Accountability**: Governance boards are responsible for actions or making decisions, hence are authorized and accountable for their actions.

- **Responsibility**: Each stakeholder or investor must abide by laws and responsibilities toward the organization.

- **Fairness**: Unbiased decisions, processes, and implementation will be ensured. They will not be allowed to create unfair advantages for any one particular party.

Technology governance

As technology permeates every aspect of an organization, technology governance is a critical capability, requirement, and resource for it. The use of technology for the purpose of research, development, and production of its goods and services is carried out and monitored during this stage. Its scope is broader than just IT governance activities.

Many organizations have a balance that favors intangibles over tangibles that require management, according to recent studies. Considering that virtually all these intangibles are informational and digital assets, it is readily apparent that businesses are relying more on IT and IT governance. It is therefore becoming increasingly important for IT governance to be as effective as possible.

Moreover, they indicate that businesses are increasingly dependent not just on information but on the processes, systems, and structures by which it is created, delivered, and consumed. Many industries are moving to add value through intangibles, so risk management must be considered key to understanding and navigating new challenges, threats, and opportunities. Increasingly, businesses rely on IT not only to run smoothly and profitably, but also to build their reputation, brand, and—ultimately—their values.

IT governance

IT governance institutionalizes best practices for planning, acquiring, implementing, and monitoring IT performance to ensure the enterprise's IT assets support its business objectives. In order to link IT resources and information to corporate goals and strategies, IT governance provides a framework and structure.

Over the last few years, IT governance has become an essential component of an enterprise's governance. Business functions and processes are increasingly dependent on IT, and to gain a competitive advantage, businesses must manage the complex technology that is scattered throughout the organization in order to respond quickly and safely to needs. As a result of increasing reports of information system disasters and electronic fraud, regulatory environments around the world are increasingly demanding tighter enterprise control of information.

Now, the management of IT-related risks is widely recognized as an important pillar of enterprise governance. In conclusion, top management must endorse an IT governance strategy and establish an appropriate organization for implementing it, clarifying who is ultimately responsible for their enterprise-wide integration and who owns the enterprise's IT resources.

AWS architecture governance

AWS enables customers to provision and operate their environment for business agility and governance control. AWS Management and Governance services, along with **cloud centers of excellence (CCoEs)**, provide resources to builders that reduce vulnerabilities and maintain compliance across the organization by defining preventive and detective controls.

Cloud governance is a combination of processes, people, and technology that drives cloud adoption and improves an organization's agility without compromising security. The concept of *safety* is important as cloud governance encompasses more than just cyber security.

With decentralized governance, safety standards and costs can be controlled. This also ensures much better responsiveness and agility. In order to deploy the appropriate resources and define best practices, it's important to develop a critical mass of AWS experience, establish operational processes, and build a CCoE. This gives the following benefits as well:

- **Scale**: Highly dynamic cloud resources are managed at a massive scale through AWS Management and Governance services.

- **Simplicity**: A single AWS control plane reduces complexity for customers as they can manage and govern their resources on AWS and on-premises.

- **Third-party solutions**: Management and governance system extensions are a huge part of AWS. It offers a broad partner ecosystem for customers.

- **Cost savings**: AWS Management and Governance services let customers assess their resource utilization and identify efficient and less costly ways of working.

Auditability

Having well-defined and functioning EA principles and processes in place is what this section determines: an infrastructure that meets current business needs and prepares for future requirements. These requirements are aligned with the overall enterprise approach. Here's a list of some of the audit's specific roles to assess:

- Transparent planning and decision-making related to EA are ensured through sufficient governance.

- There is adequate alignment between the IT and business-effective EA via development and implementation processes.

- Performance measurement and monitoring should be done by EA to ensure maximum outcomes and achieve key benefits.

As documented by the **Center for Internet Security (CIS)** Cloud Platform Foundations Benchmarks, the **General Data Protection Regulation (GDPR)**, and the **Payment Card Industry Data Security Standard (PCI DSS)**, AWS Audit Manager's prebuilt frameworks help translate evidence from cloud services into auditor-friendly reports.

AWS Audit Manager simplifies assessing risk and compliance with regulations and industry standards by automating continuous audits of your AWS usage. In addition to automating evidence collection, Audit Manager allows you to scale audit capability on-demand as your business grows and reduces the *all-hands-on-deck* manual effort often associated with audits. It is simple to evaluate if your policies, procedures, and activities—referred to as controls—are effective with an audit manager. As an audit approaches, AWS Audit Manager can help you manage stakeholder reviews of your controls and build audit-ready reports with a great deal less manual effort.

The AWS Management Console allows you to start using Audit Manager immediately. You can tailor a framework and its controls to meet your company's specific needs. Audit Manager collects and organizes relevant evidence—such as snapshots of resource configuration, user activity, and results from compliance checks—based on the framework you select. Therefore, to begin your assessment, simply select a prebuilt framework, and evidence will be collected and analyzed automatically.

The AWS CloudTrail service, enabled by default, helps you enable governance, compliance, and operational and risk auditing of your AWS account. All activities are recorded in a CloudTrail event. You can view recent events in the CloudTrail console by going to **Event history**.

Change management

This section aims to establish an architecture change management process for the new EA baseline that is achieved with the completion of the preceding activities. The process typically provides guidelines for the continual monitoring of new developments in technology and changes in the business environment. Furthermore, it also initiates a new architecture evolution cycle.

Change management approach

A change management process is designed to ensure that architecture changes are managed in a cohesive and architectural manner. They also ensure that the implemented EA is dynamic—that is, capable of growing rapidly in response to changes in business and technology environments.

The change management process determines the circumstances in which the EA is allowed to change after implementation, the process by which that will happen, and when the development cycle will initiate again for a new architecture. Within an enterprise, the architecture change management and the architecture governance processes are closely related.

The governance body establishes criteria to judge whether a change request warrants just an architecture update or whether it warrants starting a new cycle of the **Architecture Development Method (ADM)**. To avoid any unpleasant outcome, the governance body must continue with changes that are directly related to business value. It is difficult to prescribe guidelines for establishing these criteria because companies perceive risk differently. However, with the ADM, the criteria become clear for specific needs as the maturity of the governance body improves.

Drivers for change

Multiple technology-related drivers set the foundation for architecture change. Top of the list is new technology reports, asset management cost reductions, technology withdrawal, and standards initiatives. These requests are managed through an enterprise's change management and architecture governance processes. Moreover, these architecture changes are facilitated and motivated by certain business drivers, as outlined here:

- Business-as-usual developments
- Business exceptions
- Business innovations
- Business technology innovations
- Strategic change

These requests often result in a total redesign and development of the EA, in many cases.

The change management process

Project management methods are an example of management techniques and methodologies that are used for managing change. Change management processes in other fields such as systems development or project management can be adapted for use in architecture by enterprises that already have one in place.

Identifying how changes will be managed, which processes will be followed, and which methodologies will be used is a critical step in change management. In addition to a filtering function, the process must determine which phases of the architecture development process are impacted by requirements. If only migration is affected by changes, the architecture development phase will not be concerned with these changes.

This section outlines an approach to change management focused on supporting a dynamic EA that may be considered for use in the absence of a similar process today.

The change management process approach is based on architectural changes classified into one of the following categories:

1. A simplification change is handled via change management techniques.

2. An incremental change is capable of being handled via change management techniques as well. Partial re-architecting might be required, depending on the nature of the change.

3. The re-architecting change puts the whole architecture through the architecture development cycle all over again.

These three choices can also be described as simplification, incremental change, and re-architecting. A simplification change is often motivated by a desire to reduce investment, an incremental change by a desire to maximize existing investment, and a re-architecting change by the need to increase investment to find new opportunities to exploit.

The following activities are undertaken to determine whether a change is simplification, incremental, or re-architecting:

1. Registration of all events that may impact the architecture

2. Resource allocation and management for architecture tasks

3. The process responsible for architecture resources assessing what should be done

The key is to always remember that all changes should add value to the business. Change management should be based on minimizing business risk while increasing productivity and minimizing wasteful effort or cost. In addition to providing predictable, testable outcomes to changes, it should also eliminate the need for submitting changes to scale infrastructure to meet business demands, as well as automatically recovering from failures and rolling back failed changes. Ultimately, automation can deliver more business value, which is what change is about, by reducing change-related risks and increasing business agility.

Cloud automation, integration, and deployment tools make it possible for the business to make small, frequent changes that reduce risk and increase business value. Processes need to be adapted to reflect what is actually being changed, such as increased change and decreased risk. On a concluding note, considering the risk of not implementing a change or experiencing delays is always better than avoiding it all the way. Not to forget, the primary aim of managing change is to streamline business risk.

AWS Change Manager simplifies the way you can request, approve, implement, and report on operational changes to your application configuration and infrastructure on AWS and on-premises.

Summary

Organizations that are obsessed with customer needs and stay one step ahead of the rest to catch up with the latest industry trends know the key to enterprise success. A consistent and comprehensive strategy for business planning, design, and implementation of the workload in the cloud, facilitated by EA, is the right way to move forward. Every company has a set of guidelines and regulations that each stakeholder adheres to. Moreover, technological advancements with time are crucial for keeping the company moving toward growth and innovation.

Cloud helps EA with all the freedom to take risks when it comes to new technological advancements as it offers better compliance, security, and workload management. One of the most successful business techniques of strategizing the next move based on a hypothetical unpleasant situation proves quite productive.

Certain principles used to inform architecture development need to be well aligned with the architecture capability defined by the organization itself. These principles are defined based on their characteristics, implications, and rationale for different circumstances, as discussed in this chapter.

The next chapter focuses on the new digital environment that requires more adaptive conceptualizations of EA in order to achieve the desired impact. Digital transformation has implications for EA, as we explore.

Part 2 –
Enterprise Architecture
Frameworks

Moving forward, understanding the most popular frameworks for EA is what we're hoping to achieve in this section. You should buckle up to take a deep dive into AWS frameworks for architects, **The Open Group Architecture Framework (TOGAF)** in real application scenarios, and the readiness assessment process.

Redefining and designing a whole organizational structure can be a nerve-wracking task, but a high skillset and the right strategy to approach each step can help facilitate the process. By looking more into the objectives of EA and the benefits that are proven to be effective within the industry, you will learn to enable digital transformation with collaboration across an enterprise.

Most professionals find it challenging to prescribe the frameworks for enterprises to ensure that EA can kick off and move in the right direction. To facilitate that, AWS offers prescriptive guidance frameworks, including Migration Readiness Assessment, Cloud Adoption Framework, and Well-Architected Review, and aligns them with frameworks such as TOGAF.

By understanding the current state of a business's cloud journey and the outcomes of its business targets, you will identify its business objectives for its migration to the cloud.

At the end of this part, the book explains the process of approaching each phase of the TOGAF Architecture Development Method during AWS cloud transformation. The purpose here is to explore the non-functional architectural aspects of the cloud.

Nonetheless, this part concludes with the most simple yet critical management lesson – the leadership role plays an important part in EA. Nothing helps more than having a boss who is a motivating factor and sets the right example through their actions.

This part of the book comprises the following chapters:

- *Chapter 4, Available Frameworks for an Enterprise Architecture*
- *Chapter 5, AWS Prescriptive Guidance Frameworks*
- *Chapter 6, TOGAF Framework in Action with AWS*

4

Available Frameworks for an Enterprise Architecture

In this chapter, we will explore common frameworks and use cases, and identify common potential risks and benefits of particular **enterprise architecture** (EA) approaches. We also will cover several types of risks and how to assess risk when implementing an EA.

Finally, we will consider tools available to assist in the EA journey and share examples of tools and services that can ease the migration of an existing system to an EA-ready system.

In this chapter, we will cover the following topics:

- Use cases for EA and objectives
- **EA frameworks** (**EAFs**) and methodologies
- Technology and risk management
- EA collaboration and reporting
- EA and digital transformation

Use cases for Enterprise Architecture with objectives

In the right hands, enterprise architects can assist their companies in navigating the digital transformation that could have substantial benefits for their organizations in the long run. This would enable their companies to ensure compliance with regulations. As an example, consider the **General Data Protection Regulation** (**GDPR**) of the **European Union** (**EU**).

A number of new rules have been imposed on the management of end users' personal data by this regulation. A company that fails to comply with GDPR will be fined up to 20 million euros or 4% of its global annual turnover for the prior fiscal year. In order to demonstrate GDPR compliance, enterprise architects need to ensure that all relevant data is collected and presented in a clear and concise manner.

Business architects have the ability to add value in three specific areas: enabling growth, ensuring compliance, and reducing complexity. Organizations must continually innovate to stay competitive. It is common for organizations to struggle with implementing key **information technology (IT)** trends—such as microservices, the **Internet of Things (IoT)**, and cloud migration—that carry the potential to increase their market share. In addition to accelerating **time to market (TTM)**, creating new revenue streams, reducing hardware costs, and reducing costly complexity, these trends can be extremely valuable to companies. In the future, enterprise architects will be in a position to support their companies' digital transformations, which—if done correctly—could result in reduced costs and greater profits.

The uninhibited growth of IT in the past few years has resulted in duplicated systems that bring along with them multiple drawbacks and overlapping capabilities. These systems generate inconsistent data that is overly complex. Enter enterprise architects. Their role is to tackle these problems head-on by providing a roadmap to manage and reduce complexity, which contributes directly to reducing costs.

As a top-level architect, an **enterprise architect** is responsible for EA design. Consequently, they have a broad scope of responsibilities. In EA, IT assets and business processes are mapped along with a set of guiding principles that help drive a continuous discussion about business strategy and how it can be expressed through IT.

A **solutions architect** is one level higher than an application architect, who is a specialist in a specific application. A solutions architect focuses on the solution, while an enterprise architect focuses on the organization as a whole. An **application architect** focuses on one function. These roles don't interact with clients often, so they do not require much business experience. With experience, many solutions architects go on to become enterprise architects.

An effective EA that has strong foundations and is well aligned with the business objectives and technical strategy can offer great benefits to an organization. Some of the more specific objectives of an EA are listed here:

- **Business operations**:

  - Reduced cost of business operations

  - More agile organization and workflows

  - Shared business capabilities that can be accessed across the organization

  - Lower change management costs

  - Higher business productivity to ensure greater efficiency

- **Digital transformation and IT operations**:

  - Extended reach of the enterprise through enhanced digital capabilities

  - A harmonized environment is ensured by combining all enterprise components

  - Reduced expenses of software development, support, and maintenance

  - Higher portability ratio of applications

  - Convenient system and network management with an improved interoperability

  - Better communication regarding critical enterprise issues

  - Easy to upgrade system components

- **Better IT investments**:

  - Elimination of complex elements in the business and IT

  - Higher **return on investment (ROI)** for current business and IT networks

  - Easier outsourcing of business and IT solutions

  - New and lower-risk investments, accountability, and more effective outcomes

- **Faster, simpler, and cheaper procurement**:

  - Accessible information governing procurement in a coherent plan to simplify the process of making buying decisions

  - A faster procurement process to boost overall speed and flexibility while maintaining architectural coherence

  - Capability for multi-vendor open systems

  - Enhanced ability to secure more economic, IT, and business capabilities

The value of a system is more easily recognized where the need for it is higher. The same is the case with EA; it works most productively for large corporations that are struggling to simplify their highly complex IT environments. The business model that lacks varied capabilities produces a critical need for effective EA.

Nine most common EA use cases

Here are the nine most common use cases where an EA is the recommended solution for addressing challenges and leveraging opportunities.

Post-merger management

Multiple businesses can merge or come together to combine their services, in different circumstances. Smaller companies are acquired by bigger companies, financially struggling companies join up with more successful organizations, and successful best-of-breed companies are acquired by companies seeking to add capabilities to their product portfolios. These events are called **mergers and acquisitions (M&A)**.

The post-merger phase can be complex, and it is crucial for all parties involved to work together, as this integration phase is no easy feat. All information about company policies, assets, capabilities, and more must be shared and understood. Applications, servers, business capabilities, employees, processes, and other artifacts must be carefully considered for what they provide pre- and post-merger.

On average, 70-90% of acquisitions fail. To ensure a smooth, seamless, and successful journey through the process, effective strategies for accelerating growth and scaling operations are essential.

Although many factors contribute to M&A not succeeding, one is that businesses pause operations to focus on integration. In the integration phase of a successful M&A initiative, EA enables key stakeholders, such as **chief financial officers (CFOs)** and **chief operating officers (COOs)**, to make faster and more credible decisions.

M&A fail and consume unintended resources when the companies involved fail to successfully integrate or anticipate needed synergies. These challenges are huge from a technology standpoint. When multiple companies are concerned, the unification and transformation of technologies must occur without disrupting business as usual.

During a merger or acquisition, it is essential to ensure that the initial state of both IT landscapes is documented. This is where EA proves to be especially helpful in answering essential structural questions, such as the following:

- What infrastructure is in place for maintaining records at each company?
- How is company data stored and retrieved when required?
- Where does the company store its supporting documents?

Enterprise architects propose best-fit solutions from concrete data after considering these questions and finding answers.

Application rationalization

Businesses are often focused on driving economic growth rather than aligning the IT landscape. Consequently, different applications are put in place at different points in time, based on needs or requests communicated from different departments.

Business leaders may not realize that having a sprawling IT ecosystem full of overlapping applications, varying life cycles, and redundant technologies often encounter multiple integration issues and inefficiencies that may affect the company's operations at the enterprise level. In addition to increasing IT spending by hundreds of millions of dollars, a complex, rigid IT ecosystem also directly decreases the **quality of service (QoS)** and customer satisfaction.

EA provides an opportunity to review applications in use across the business, recognize and address integration failures, eliminate redundant applications, and streamline processes for reviewing and selecting applications in the future.

Integration architecture

Integration architecture (IA) is critical for valuable applications. Some applications are built from scratch, while others run on their preconfigured settings, and some others use a combination of the two.

Integration is a challenge, as the most valuable applications are those that work together to create seamless solutions, and every business has different needs. Retail and e-commerce applications need to integrate with inventory systems, **human resources (HR)** applications need to sync with calendars, marketing applications need to work with **customer relationship management (CRM)** programs, and so on.

Integration is defined by the complexities and dependencies of multiple applications running on multiple platforms in different locations, which makes the term *simple integration* a contradiction. Statistics suggest that 70% of all integration projects are unsuccessful. Technical difficulties or problems with the software are rarely responsible for these failures. The problems are caused by management problems, constantly changing software, ambiguous standards, and a lack of clarity in accountability.

EA provides a foundation and roadmap for integrations across an organization. It also defines resources and processes necessary to ensure that integration capabilities are considered, managed, and executed successfully.

Technology risk management

Risk management requires establishing a strategic view of an organization to understand possible challenges. Doing this requires an informed view of current products, processes, applications, and infrastructure, as well as an understanding of the risk and security aspects of each. Without knowing what the primary risks are, C-level teams cannot fulfill their management responsibilities. The ability to understand these relationships is essential in assessing the effects of business decisions.

Business analysts can use these tools to analyze enterprise risks associated with—for example— developing new products and initiatives, outsourcing business processes or IT systems, or assimilation of another organization after a merger. This will allow them to balance the enterprise's risk propensity against potential consequences.

Furthermore, executives and operational management are rightly concerned about the spread of risks across the organization. Risks from one part of the organization can affect other parts of the organization. Consider the example of a system failure, break-in, power outage, fraud, or another mishap. How would these events affect critical business processes, services, clients, partners, and markets? By creating insights into these relationships and dependencies through EA, you are able to prevent or mitigate disasters in the future.

Technology is essential to the success of organizations in all industries. Any technology carries some inherent cyber risks, which can be found in innumerable forms. The most common, yet preventable, situations resulting in data breaches are caused by IT outages, legacy applications, and their supporting infrastructures. Based on IBM's *Cost of a Data Breach Report 2021* (`https://www.ibm.com/security/data-breach`), the average cost of a security breach is $4.24 million **United States dollars** (**USD**) globally. The average cost of a breach in the US is much higher, at $9.05 million per incident. An attack on an organization's cybersecurity system can have a significant impact on its financial standing, customer retention, and brand reputation.

There are probably over a million different types of technology products offered by the 20 largest technology vendors alone. Their components change every day, and the need to monitor new versions as life cycle information changes is an important element of IT management. Outdated components need to be upgraded based on these changes.

There are many risks associated with maintaining obsolete technology, including the following:

- The technology doesn't support the business
- Higher complexity
- Security vulnerabilities
- Compliance issues
- Lack of skill and support from vendors
- Lower IT flexibility

Technology products undergo about 2,500 information changes daily. Keeping track of all of it would be impossible to do manually.

Data compliance

Compliance with data privacy laws and regulations is how organizations show they follow formal standards and procedures for ensuring sensitive data is protected from loss, theft, corruption, and misuse. Organizing, managing, and storing data requires compliance with regulations that organizations must follow to avoid financial, legal, and other penalties that could be levied against the business and/or individuals who lead it.

Various industries, governments, states, countries, and even continents have varying regulations regarding data compliance. The three elements an organization must focus on when it comes to data compliance relate to data, actions, and penalties. Regulations identify the type of data that should be protected and actions that must be taken to protect that data. If an organization doesn't comply with these actions, regulations outline the consequences.

The cost of compliance is steep, but the penalties for non-compliance are even higher. Under GDPR, for example, any organization processing the personal information of EU citizens must comply with GDPR regardless of where their business is located. As with many regulatory mandates, GDPR offers many advantages, such as requirements for data standardization that will benefit organizations and their transactions with other businesses. For most organizations, data compliance has affected their approach to data management.

Standards governance

EAs and other architectures are managed and controlled by architecture governance at an enterprise level. Architecture governance normally operates within a hierarchy of governance structures and not in isolation. It works in the larger enterprise, such as corporate governance, technology governance, IT governance, and architecture governance, and can include all of the distinct architectural domains with their own disciplines and processes.

The enterprise may have multiple levels of governance—global, regional, and local—over its life cycle. Large corporations can benefit from standardized IT: they can reduce training time, cut maintenance and support costs, have better bargaining power with vendors, and improve communication.

It is common to combine standardization with centralization, a process by which an IT department gains more control over hardware and software purchases, because every new piece of software equipment added to the IT arsenal will require installation, maintenance, personnel training, repairs, patches, upgrades, and so on. Standardization can be disadvantageous, as technologies change very rapidly, and processes need to be updated when technology changes. Businesses also use alternative concepts, such as radical agility, to prevent stifling innovation across the enterprise.

Monoliths to microservices

Many businesses are being forced to rethink their architecture as digitalization accelerates rapidly. Customers expect companies to make their products available on as many digital channels as possible to meet their constantly increasing expectations. Multinational corporations have grown to become monoliths over time, as they develop very complex structures that make it difficult to perform swift or timely changes.

It is not sufficient to apply scale to individual elements of an architecture; the entire application must be prepared for scale. Introducing microservices architecture into software development can reduce application throughput times. Since microservices can be built and deployed independently, not only do they enhance productivity and flexibility, but they also increase the resiliency of applications. Teams can build microservices from the ground up or decompose legacy monolithic applications into microservices. They enable cloud-native development, whether they're deployed on-premises or in the cloud.

A reputation for complexity surrounds microservices. Furthermore, not every monolith is well suited for being converted to a set of microservices. In order to determine when and where microservices are useful, enterprise architects play a crucial role. Furthermore, they lay the groundwork for a cultural shift that is required for microservices to succeed.

When it comes to legacy issues and missing information, companies that have adopted microservices still face the same challenges as those that haven't adopted them. As a result of microservices, monoliths can be broken down, enabling rapid changes, short release times, and team autonomy. Software releases created with microservices are deployed up to five times faster than those created without them.

Cloud transformation

The process of moving data, applications, networks, and infrastructure to a cloud environment is known as cloud transformation. Moreover, the cloud in all its forms—including on-demand environments, smart development, and **artificial intelligence** (**AI**)—is a technology to be harnessed. The cloud may seem like the perfect solution if legacy technology, processes, and infrastructure are preventing an organization from achieving a desired competitive advantage. There are many big consulting firms that can help teams design their **cloud transformation strategy**. Although many steps and guides are provided to help teams make the transition, in the end, it's really all about moving applications to the virtual world.

Defining and analyzing changes executed toward the achievement of organizational goals forms the basis of EA, so organizations applying an EA approach are likely aligned with their goals.

With the availability of cloud computing, new service-driven business models have been developed that drive product and service value. A number of benefits are associated with cloud computing, such as cost savings, efficiency improvements, shorter development cycle times, and faster TTM. In addition to improving asset utilization, reducing operational expenses, and redefining the relationship between IT staff and management, moving to the cloud can help companies dramatically cut costs.

As business and IT strategies are increasingly influenced by the cloud, a roadmap from legacy to cloud needs to be implemented by enterprise architects. Achieving cloud transformation success is challenging due to complex business environments and rapidly changing infrastructure. A successful transition to the cloud requires a number of organizational, operational, and technical modifications. Several factors influence cloud adoption along the way, including budget limitations, the need for exponential scale, and increasing complexity in corporate policies and regulations.

IoT architecture

Digital transformation is driving an increase in the need for enterprise architects to manage the growing complexity of IT. Consumers find IoT-powered smart devices useful or convenient for their lives. For example, a fuel monitor that dispatches a fuel truck when a propane tank meter registers below a certain percentage can save time that would have been spent monitoring the meter manually and calling the fuel company to schedule a refill. Similarly, enterprise architects should consider how IoT can benefit their organizations.

EA can integrate IoT in three generic ways, as outlined here:

- In the first case, you can choose to rely on the services provided by the device manufacturer. Exporting and importing files are the two main methods of transferring data between existing corporate systems, while custom **application programming interface (API)** connections can be used to transfer data automatically.

- In a second option, an IoT value chain can be built by implementing separate services for data storage, data communication, data analytics, and data integration. While this approach can be quite a challenge, many IoT applications will be handled more successfully using this method.

- A third option would be to connect IoT devices directly to enterprise management systems, such as **Systems Applications Product (SAP)**, or build an in-house intermediate application to achieve this goal.

With IoT, companies can launch products faster, get big data insights in real time, create new services and business models, and reduce costs. However, security and privacy risks, a lack of standard oversight, and the integration of IoT devices all pose significant challenges.

EAFs and methodologies

EAFs provide guidelines for creating and using EAs that describe a model of a system's architecture. Tools and approaches are provided to facilitate enterprise architects' work to optimize different architecture domains across the enterprise. They integrate disparate, fragmented manual and automated processes into an environment that is responsive to change and supported by the implementation of business strategies.

EAFs determine how organizations can most effectively achieve their current and future business goals. While EAFs have evolved over the last five decades, there are a few that have been developed and improved over time and are still in use today.

The Open Group Architecture Framework

The initial development of **The Open Group Architecture Framework** (**TOGAF**) took place in 1995. Newer editions or models offered improved iterations and theories, as was usual at the time in the field of EA. TOGAF was heavily influenced by the US **Department of Defense's** (**DoD's**) own EAF, called the **Technical Architecture Framework for Information Management** (**TAFIM**).

TAFIM was abandoned by the US DoD within a few years of TOGAF's introduction. Today, over 20 years later, it continues to be a worldwide success. Organizing IT efforts cross-departmentally, and aligning IT initiatives with business goals is a part of TOGAF, as are other common IT management frameworks.

Before an EA project begins, TOGAF helps businesses define and organize requirements, keeping the project moving efficiently and with few errors. This framework aims to help enterprises organize and address all critical business and strategic needs through four objectives, as outlined here:

- Use a common language among users, from key stakeholders to team members. As a result, everyone will understand the framework, content, and goals in the same way, and communication barriers can be addressed or removed.

- Achieve EA freedom by avoiding proprietary solutions—a combination of tools, processes, and unique capabilities businesses develop or acquire to gain a competitive edge. TOGAF is free, as long as it is being used internally and not for commercial purposes.

- Save time and money by utilizing resources more efficiently.

- ROI must be measurable.

A common EA subset consists of four domains, as outlined here, and the TOGAF standard is designed to support all of them:

- Organization, governance, and key business processes are defined by the business architecture.

- In an organization's data architecture, data assets and data management resources are described logically and physically.

- Application architectures describe how applications are going to be deployed, their actions, and their interactions with the core business processes of an organization.

- Technology architecture is a set of logical requirements for deploying business, data, and application services. It includes IT infrastructure, middleware, networks, communications, processing, standards, and so on.

TOGAF provides a proven and repeatable **Architecture Development Method** (**ADM**). Architects establish an architecture framework, develop architecture content, transition architectures, and guide their realization. These activities are executed within an iterative cycle of continuous architecture definition and realization, which enables organizations to transform their businesses in a controlled manner while meeting business goals and opportunities.

An ADM includes the following phases:

- During the preliminary phase, activities such as customization of TOGAF and the definition of architecture principles are considered in the preparation and initiation of the architecture capability creation:

    A. Architecture vision is the first phase of the architecture development cycle. In this phase, organizations identify key stakeholders, detail the architecture vision, and explain how to obtain approval to move forward with architecture development.

    B. The business architecture is developed to support the agreed-upon architecture vision.

    C. Information systems architectures are created to describe how these architectures will support the architecture vision.

    D. Technology architecture is designed to support the architecture vision.

    E. Opportunities and solutions are identified for initial implementation, and delivery vehicles are identified.

    F. A detailed implementation and migration plan is finalized.

    G. Implementation governance sets up the execution plan and accountability structure for the project.

    H. Procedures for managing changes to the new architecture are established.

- The final phase is also a continuous and ongoing activity, to examine how requirements are managed throughout the architecture development life cycle.

An architect implementing an ADM will generate a number of outputs as a result of their work, including **process flow diagrams** (**PFDs**), architectural requirements, project plans, and project compliance assessments. An ADM provides a framework for the definition, structure, and presentation of major work products organized according to TOGAF architecture.

The following three categories describe the type of architectural work product within the context of use by an architecture content framework:

- **Deliverables** are work products that are contractually specified and, in turn, reviewed, agreed upon, and approved by the stakeholders. A project's deliverables consist of documents that are archived at project completion or moved into an architecture repository as a reference model, a standard, or a snapshot of the architecture landscape at a specific time.

- **Artifacts** are architectural products that describe a certain aspect of architecture. In general, artifacts fall into three categories: *catalogs* (lists of things), *matrices* (showing relationships between things), and *diagrams* (pictures of things). A use-case diagram, a business interaction matrix, and a requirements catalog serve as examples. The architecture repository will store the artifacts of an architectural deliverable.

- In an enterprise capability, a **building block** represents a part of the enterprise capability that may be reused in combination with other parts to construct architectures and solutions. The level of detail of building blocks can depend on the stage of the architecture development process. Early in the process, building blocks can simply consist of names or outlines. In the future, a building block can be decomposed into multiple supporting building blocks, along with detailed specifications.

Architectures and solutions can be considered building blocks, as detailed here:

- As per **architecture building blocks** (**ABBs**), an enterprise may require a customer services capability, which can be supported by many **solution building blocks** (**SBBs**), such as processes, data, and application software.

- In SBBs, there are components that implement the required capability; for example, a network is an artifact that can be described with complementary artifacts and then used to implement enterprise solutions.

An architect implementing an ADM will generate a number of deliverables, maintaining them in an architecture repository. The ADM provides a framework for the definition, structure, and presentation of major work products in the architecture.

No two organizations are the same, so it is important to be able to customize the approach to meet each organization's specific needs. The Enterprise Continuum allows enterprise architects to map a tailored approach.

Enterprise Continuum

As part of the TOGAF standard, there is the concept of the Enterprise Continuum, which sets the broader context for an architect and explains how generic solutions can be adapted and tailored to meet the unique requirements of each organization.

The Enterprise Continuum is part of the architecture repository, a method of classifying architecture and solution artifacts as they change from generic foundation architectures into organization-specific architectures. The Enterprise Continuum includes the concepts of Architecture Continuum and Solutions Continuum.

Making work products available to individuals and teams across an organization is a critical aspect of EA and ensures consistency across an EA team.

Architecture repository

By using an architecture repository, the TOGAF standard supports the Enterprise Continuum by storing different types of architectural output, created by the ADM, at different abstraction levels. In this way, stakeholders and practitioners at different levels can communicate and collaborate. In developing an organization-specific architecture, architects are encouraged to leverage all other relevant architectural resources and assets available in the Enterprise Continuum and architecture repository.

A TOGAF architecture delivery model is an organization's process life cycle based on a governance framework that operates on multiple levels within an organization and produces outputs that reside in an architecture repository. Enterprise Continuum models provide a useful context for analyzing architectural models. They depict building blocks, their relationships, and the constraints and requirements associated with the development cycle.

Here are the major elements of an architecture repository:

- The architecture metamodel is a set of tools designed to tailor an architecture framework and content for use within specific organizations.

- Governance of the architecture repository is supported by the architecture capability through parameters, structures, and processes.

- The architecture landscape represents assets deployed across the enterprise at various levels of abstraction to satisfy the architecture objectives of the enterprise.

- New architectures must comply with the **Standards Information Base** (**SIB**). They may include industry standards, selected products and services from suppliers, or service sharing already in place within the organization.

- To support the creation of new EAs, the reference library provides guidelines, templates, patterns, and other forms of reference material.

- An enterprise governance log records governance activity across the organization.

- The repository of architecture requirements provides the architecture board with a view of all authorized architecture requirements.

- The solutions landscape represents architecturally the SBBs that have been planned or deployed by an enterprise to support the architecture landscape.

The architecture repository builds the capability for the organization to implement, support, and repeat new EAs at scale.

Establishing and maintaining an EA capability

For architectural activities to be effective within an organization, it is imperative to establish organizational structures, roles, responsibilities, skills, and processes that promote architecture as a business capability.

When an EA process is operating at maturity, business capabilities and operations are tracked, and the resource pool and professional development are aligned with roles and responsibilities required under the architecture.

One of the most effective frameworks that are widely used in EA is the **Zachman Framework**, which is used for identifying and tracking critical elements of an organization's people and processes that support EA.

Zachman Framework for EA

John Zachman introduced his framework for information systems architecture in 1987. The Zachman Framework applies the understanding that the same complex item can be described for different purposes in different ways, using different kinds of descriptions.

An architectural artifact is organized using the Zachman Framework—a design document, specification, or model addressing both the target audience of the artifact (for example, business owners and system builders), as well as the specific issue being addressed (for example, data and functionality).

The Zachman Framework is based on a **two-dimensional** (**2D**) model used for arranging artifacts in the architecture industry. In building architecture, the **first dimension refers to the players involved**. Construction of physical buildings—for instance—may involve several players or stakeholders, including the owner who pays the bills, the contractor who manages the design, and a zoning board that ensures building codes are followed.

Different architectures are prepared for each player by the architect and comprehensive information is demanded by all players, but what constitutes completeness varies for each player. In addition to the building's functionality and aesthetics, the owner is interested in a detailed description.

Construction materials and the construction processes are of particular interest to the builder. There is no concern over where the wall studs are placed, or which nails or shingles are used. Certain practices are observed—for example, one practice might be to build a house with bedroom windows aligned with the sun in the morning, regardless of where the sun rises in the morning.

In terms of a specific artifact organization, the second defining aspect is the descriptive focus of that artifact: the *what*, *where*, *when*, *who*, and *why* of the project. The second dimension exists independently of the first dimension. Neither the builder nor the owner should be unaware of *what*, but what the owner knows may differ from what the builder knows. Who asks the question will determine the answer.

The Zachman Framework suggests that the same complex item can be described for different purposes differently, using different descriptions. Any complex object, such as manufactured goods, can be completely described using Zachman's 36 categories, made up of six columns and six rows and taking the form of a 2D matrix.

Included in the Zachman Framework are these perspectives of the system:

- **Planner's View** (**Scope Contexts**): Describes the organization's purpose and strategy and provides a basis for the other views

- **Owner's View** (**Business Concepts**): A view of the organization that shows where automation can be applied

- **Designer's View** (**System Logic**): This view describes how the system will meet the information needs of the organization

- **Implementer's View (Technology Physics)**: How production constraints will be met as part of the implementation of this system

- **Sub-Constructor's View (Component Assembles)**: This view shows details specific to an implementation of a specific system element

- **User's View (Operations Classes)**: This view enables the user to observe the system's operation

Another EAF emerged in response to US legislation designed to improve the way the federal government acquires, uses, and disposes of IT.

Federal Enterprise Architecture Framework

In response to the *Clinger-Cohen Act of 1996*, **chief information officers (CIOs)** established the **Federal Enterprise Architecture Framework (FEAF)** in 1999. The FEAF allows federal agencies and other government agencies to share processes and information.

An architecture can be categorized according to FEAF categories of business, data, applications, and technology architectures, as explained in more detail here:

- Business architecture defines what is done, who did it, how it was done, and when and why it was done

- Data architecture determines the information used by the agency to do business

- Application architecture is a collection of all IT resources, such as computers and software that process the data according to business rules

- Technology architecture comprises the technology that facilitates the previously mentioned phases

Federal EA (FEA) is the method or the architectural result of implementing that methodology for a specific enterprise. In terms of how it can apply to companies in the private sector, FEA is viewed from a methodology perspective.

Although there is a lot more to FEA than its reference models, five of them can be referred to as part of FEA, one representing each activity area—business, service, components, technical, and data.

The FEA process

The FEA process focuses on developing a segment architecture for an overall enterprise subset, as follows:

- Analyze the segment's architecture to determine a simple but concise vision that relates to the segment's organizational structure

- Establish an architecture target for the segment, define goals, develop design alternatives, and set the EA for the segment that includes business, data, services, and technology architectures

- Justify the investment and determine the ROI
- Establish milestones and performance measures for assessing the success of the project, including a plan and task list

FEA integrates strategic, business, and technology management as part of organization design and performance improvement.

Yet another EAF was developed by Gartner, a firm that provides analysis, research, and strategy services for organizations.

Gartner's EAF

As organizations plan for the future, Gartner's EAF is designed to influence and support their decisions. It focuses on a constant state of adaptation. This model is used to assess the enterprise's present state, identify appropriate investments in technology and procedures to achieve the desired future state, manage the enterprise during the transition, and plan investments for the future.

This framework brings together three constituents: business owners, information specialists, and technology implementers. Success depends on how well an organization can unify these three groups behind a shared vision that drives business value. The key to success is to drive profitability, not check off items on a process matrix. According to Gartner, EA must focus on where an organization is going rather than on where it is now.

An organization has the opportunity to clearly articulate the nature, scope, and impact of the EA changes being made by creating an EA vision. A business, technical, information, and solutions architecture for an enterprise can be considered as soon as the organization establishes this common vision for the future.

Those changes must be prioritized according to the business value they will bring. EA involves creating the best possible template or platform to maximize the use of IT systems. There is no inherent antagonistic relationship between the four frameworks analyzed here. Every one of them serves a different purpose and has unique pros and cons.

Benefits of each EAF

Through the Zachman Framework, classification and organization are addressed. The TOGAF model is the best to employ if the process is the problem. FEAF is a good framework for analyzing the most highly complex and interconnected enterprises. The Gartner EAF is the most effective way to start if vision is the main problem. To evaluate these frameworks based on how they address an organization's unique needs and circumstances, it is essential to possess a thorough understanding of the organization.

TOGAF is marketed as an EA methodology and framework, and it is distinct from the Zachman Framework in that it provides implementation guidelines for creating artifacts. It places a greater emphasis on methodology and process. The TOGAF Certification Program has gained traction among enterprise architects, most of whom strive to become TOGAF-accredited.

TOGAF has two important components for defining a common language: the content framework describes the set of key artifacts produced for supporting architecture, while the **Technical Reference Model (TRM)** provides a model and taxonomy for generic platform services.

Technology and risk management

A risk management program's goal is to identify preventive and control measures to mitigate risks associated with specific activities and valuable assets. Many risk management efforts are narrowly focused, functionally driven, and disjointed. Therefore, each risk activity uses its own language, metric, and customs, leading to a fragmented view of risks. There is an inability to anticipate, control, or manage interdependent risks when there are no connections between risks and no holistic view of risk. Aiming to address the interoperability and standardization challenges in risk management, this book proposes a coordinated approach involving risk management, governance, and EA. It helps map and trace identified risks back to enterprise artifacts modeled within the EA, supporting an organization's strategic priorities. While we are at it, let us shed some light on two levels of risks that need to be addressed, as follows:

- **Initial level of risk**: Prior to determining and implementing mitigating actions, categorize the risks
- **Residual level of risk**: Identifying and categorizing risks after mitigation

Risk management steps

There are several key steps involved in risk management, which we can cover now.

Risk classification

Any EA activity involves risk, and the ADM does as well. Risk classification is useful from a management perspective so that mitigation can be executed as quickly as possible. Among the ways that risks are classified is with respect to the impact on the organization, meaning that certain levels of governance are required for risks with particular impacts. In addition to time (schedule), cost (budget), and scope risks, others might include those related to client relationships, contracts, technology, scope, complexity, and environment (corporate).

The management of risks can also be delegated by identifying domains of the architecture. While classifying risks as business, information, applications, and technology is useful, corporate EA directorates should consider adopting or extending organizationally specific ways of expressing risk, rather than modifying them. At the end of the day, EA risks are corporate risks and should be classified and appropriately managed in a similar manner, or even more so.

Risk identification

There will be a great deal of risk involved with maturity and transformation readiness assessments. Determine a strategy to address the risks during the transformation, then identify the risks.

For specific factors associated with architecture delivery, **Capability Maturity Models (CMMs)** may be used to first identify baseline and target states and then identify actions needed to achieve the target state. If the target state is not achieved, risks can be discovered. It is important to complete risk documentation as part of a risk management plan, for which templates are available in certain project management methodologies, such as the **Project Management Book of Knowledge (PMBOK)** and **Projects IN Controlled Environments 2 (PRINCE2)**, as well as with some government methodologies.

It is usually incorporated into these methodologies to execute contingency planning, track and evaluate levels of risk, react to changing risk levels, and document, report, and communicate risks to stakeholders.

Initial risk assessment

In order to identify risks, it is necessary to classify them according to their frequency and effect based on scales used within the organization. Putting together an initial risk assessment combines effect and frequency.

Measurement of effect and frequency does not come with any hard-and-fast rules. However, guidelines are based upon existing risk management best practices. The effect could be assessed using the following example criteria:

- **Catastrophic** infers financial losses that are critical enough to cause the organization to fail.

- **Critical** determines a loss of productivity and no ROI in the IT systems. It affects more than one **line of business (LOB)**.

- **Marginal** indicates a small financial loss in the LOB and a lower ROI in the IT department.

- **Negligible** infers a relatively minor impact on the ability of an organization to deliver services or products.

The frequency can be indicated as *Frequent, Likely, Occasional, Seldom, or Unlikely*. In general, a potential plan for assessing corporate impact can include these categories of risk:

- **Extremely High Risk (E)**: The transformation is likely to fail and with severe consequences

- **High Risk (H)**: Significant parts of the transformation effort are likely to fail and result in the failure to achieve some goals

- **Moderate Risk (M)**: Failure of some transformation efforts will jeopardize the success of some goals

- **Low Risk (L)**: Some goals will not be achieved in their entirety

Organizations can assess the impact of these risks using a common structure for corporate risk impact assessment, as illustrated here:

Corporate Risk Impact Assessment					
Effect	**Frequency**				
	Frequent	**Likely**	**Occasional**	**Seldom**	**Unlikely**
Catastrophic	E	E	H	H	M
Critical	E	H	H	M	L
Marginal	H	M	M	L	L
Negligible	M	L	L	L	L

© The Open Group

Figure 4.1 – When assessing risk, organizations can use this assessment
chart as they consider and rank risk related to their EAs

There are many approaches for risk mitigation and assessment that organizations can use, including residual, monitoring, and governance risk.

Risk mitigation and residual risk assessment

A risk mitigation strategy includes identifying, planning, and taking action to reduce risk to a manageable level. It could be as simple as monitoring, accepting, or assuming the risk, or it could be as complex as a **business continuity plan** (BCP) requiring complete redundancy (with all the associated cost, scope, and time implications).

The risk assessment must be done systematically and pragmatically due to its implications. As high-impact risks are mitigated in order of frequency, each risk has to be addressed separately.

Conduct residual risk assessment

After the mitigation effort has been identified for each risk, re-evaluate its effects and frequency, as well as recalculate the impacts to determine whether the mitigation has made a significant difference. Resource-intensive mitigation efforts are often necessary, and a large expenditure for little or no residual risk should be questioned. Residual risk refers to risk left over after the initial risk has been mitigated.

Risk monitoring and governance

IT governance frameworks—and, possibly, corporate governance—may approve residual risks, as well as business acceptance of residual risks. In order to ensure that the enterprise is addressing residual risk rather than initial risk, the execution of mitigating actions must be carefully monitored after acceptance of the residual risks.

In *Phase G*, also known as implementation governance, where risk monitoring takes place, risk identification and mitigation assessment worksheets are maintained as governance artifacts. By implementing governance, you will be able to identify critical risks that haven't been mitigated. You may need to repeat an ADM cycle for these issues.

One of the final considerations when implementing EA is how to understand, implement, and manage collaboration and reporting to track the effects of change.

Business owners should assess their susceptibility; that way, data breaches and IT outages caused by vulnerabilities can be prevented by taking precautions against them. Some of the most promising technologies have emerged in the past few years, including cloud computing, AI, IoT, and blockchain.

If it is unclear how EA works, stakeholders will not support it. In the absence of stakeholder participation, EA programs often end up in a massive failure. As a result, management may question the value of EA artifacts because they are not being used in projects. Before starting EA programs, all stakeholders must be educated and made aware of EA's value.

The *ivory tower* enterprise architect approach suggests that your chances of getting buy-in from most stakeholders are highly unlikely. Rather than imposing content on an organization, an enterprise architect leads the EA process. The architecture board represents the key stakeholders in the architecture and governs its implementation.

A chief architect who is an ineffective leader may understand EA well, but with a lack of management skills, even a good organizational structure and staffing levels cannot overcome critical issues. As a result, there is a lack of progress or a confusing architectural design. Ideally, the role of a lead architect should be filled by an individual with strong soft skills—such as enthusiasm, communication, and passion—in addition to being well respected and strategically minded.

Not establishing effective governance early on will have a devastating impact later on. All information related to architecture management, contracts, and implementation must be identified, managed, audited, and disseminated through governance processes. In the absence of governance processes, people are at risk of developing their own working styles, and no monitoring and audit tools to guide architectural design will be available. Enterprise architects should resist the temptation to set governance processes after more architecture content is available and instead, should develop governance and content at the same time.

Communication problems might not seem like a big issue but can lead to some serious misunderstandings within an enterprise. A program's success often depends on good and continuous communication of its value and progress.

In some organizations, EA focuses mainly on technology, which has a much narrower scope than technical architecture. Business, information, and solutions architectures are all included in EA. It is possible for non-technical people to make technical decisions, while enterprise architects become too reactive and tactical when technology and business goals do not align.

Do the baseline *current-state* architecture first. Program goals will determine whether or not this is a risk. When an EA is being used to merge companies or for the creation of a new enterprise vision and strategic goals, this baseline architecture should not be used. Prescriptive guidance is provided in EA, but it is absent from current-state architecture. As a consequence, EA value will not be delivered on time and good future-state architecture will not be created.

EA collaboration and reporting

Through EA tools, organizations can determine both the need for and the impact of change. Integrated modeling captures the relationships and interactions between partners, operating models, capabilities, individuals, processes, information, applications, and technologies within and between an ecosystem. Those systems serve as central repositories for capturing data and metadata about the artifacts an enterprise cares about and the processes associated with them.

These artifacts are represented by models that define relationships between them, as well as help to describe and shape the future of the enterprise. EA tools help IT and the company as a whole make better investment decisions. In combination with operational performance data, models can improve business outcomes and help build and operate digital platforms more effectively.

Many organizations take the approach of engaging the assistance of EA service experts. One such organization is **International Brands Limited (IBL)** Group, a world-class conglomerate that manages a diverse portfolio of companies across consumer retail, healthcare, pharmaceuticals, distribution, and e-commerce. Brands on IBL Group's client list include Johnson & Johnson, Red Bull, Mars, and Kellogg's.

IBL was on a mission-critical SAP data migration journey. IBL leadership wanted to make the business more agile, achieve cost efficiencies, and improve stakeholder management. Downtimes were causing delays in delivery and loss of revenue. At risk were relationships with their customers and supply chain partners.

The team enlisted the assistance of NorthBay Solutions, an **Amazon Web Services (AWS)** Premier Partner, to guide its team through the data migration. The consulting team analyzed requirements, created a detailed roadmap, and developed a plan to migrate groups of servers in waves.

The work with NorthBay Solutions allowed IBL to realize a 30% improvement in performance, without any increase in **total cost of ownership (TCO)** after migrating to AWS.

What are the features of EA software?

Timelines allow users to plan, strategize, and execute long-term projects. They also make it easier for users to identify various phases and keep track of their progress. A roadmap displays strategies—along with the various relevant resources, departments, and assets—visually. In addition, they can assist with tracking progress and monitoring standards as projects are implemented.

In addition to analytics, users will also be provided with tools to analyze productivity, resource usage, and standards compliance. Planning for the future and strategizing for the task and project in question can be improved with this information. Furthermore, collaboration is the act of collaborating on tasks and projects within a platform. Next comes asset management, which refers to a tool for managing all of an organization's assets and resources.

Budget hierarchies describe how elements of a budget structure are linked. A reporting structure can be defined and managed by administrators, along with access rights for each report. Also, the developing models of business systems are based on standards.

Managing the workspace, supporting colleagues, enabling collaboration, and building confidence within your most complex projects is the approach for Sparx Systems. In addition to TOGAF and Zachman, the platform supports several industry standards for the design and implementation of IT software and business systems. As an added benefit, Sparx Systems' Enterprise Architect tool is cloud-based and allows global collaboration, model simulation, and complete traceability from requirements to deployment.

Sparx Systems makes its Enterprise Architect solution available in four different editions that are tailored to different scenarios. Organizations, groups, and individuals use the software to model and manage complex information. Visually connecting structures and behaviors allows organizations to build a coherent, verifiable model of what is or what will be.

Specifically, the Sparx solution has tools built into Enterprise Architect that can help teams manage complexity, as follows:

- Diagrams to represent business and strategic concepts
- Reusable model patterns and domain-specific profiles
- Tracking and version management
- Secure access based on roles to allow the right people to participate

Organizations can formally capture and track requirements from design to build to deployment and identify whether proposed changes have an impact on initial requirements, using an impact analysis to build the right system. The built-in requirements management features in Sparx Enterprise Architect can be used to define a requirement model, track system requirements, report requirements, and analyze proposed changes.

As a result of Sparx Enterprise Architect's highly crafted patterns and reusable model structures, it will expedite your development work and help you achieve accurate and stunning models that leverage a strong and proven foundation. You can reduce noise by focusing on one modeling challenge at a time. Push other technologies and tools into the background as you concentrate on business analysis, strategy, or software design.

EA and digital transformation

Businesses have always benefited from strategic planning. However, with the urgency of digital transformation and the complexity of these initiatives, such planning has become even more critical. This complex technology is connected with the business context through EA to drive desirable business outcomes.

Different organizations have varied meanings of digital transformation that include technology trends such as the shift to cloud services, the adoption of AI and **machine learning** (**ML**), advanced analytics and big data infrastructure, the emergence of IoT, the rise of **robotic process automation** (**RPA**), and more.

In business and organizations, digital transformation is defined as the ability to effectively leverage the challenges and opportunities of mixed digital technologies in a strategic and prioritized manner in response to current and future shifts in society. Organizations can react faster to market changes by transforming; this allows them to be as flexible and dynamic as possible. Financial services are an example of one industry where it has become a competitive necessity.

The cloud offers businesses the ability to deploy **software-as-a-service** (**SaaS**), RPA, and AI at a rapid pace. Because many projects need to move at a much faster pace, digital transformation changes everything for enterprise architects and **enterprise project management offices** (**EPMOs**). As with the print press and the internet, this digital revolution can be compared to the invention of the printing press. All enterprises are questioning business models, technology has gained importance in the process, and enterprises are faced with new challenges on almost every next move in this era of collaboration.

What does digital transformation mean for enterprises?

Everyone is affected by the digital revolution, hence companies must find new ways to collaborate to succeed in these times. Digital transformation happens at its own pace, and it cannot be viewed as a one-size-fits-all process. Enterprises maintain their own unique IT legacy systems and processes, and they are subject to different external regulatory requirements and market pressures. Successful enterprises treat the transformation as an ongoing process because industry maturity affects the path to digital excellence. A variety of strategies and paces are used in this process in order to address business needs.

For enterprises of all sizes, technology is gaining importance as business models are being questioned. Despite the move from the periphery to the center of enterprises, knowledge is still dispersed. Because of a lack of transparency, local decisions are made disregarding the implications of those decisions for the organization as a whole. Digital transformation is more likely to fail when it is centrally managed, which makes it crucial for enterprises to make distributed knowledge available across the board.

Successfully implementing digital transformation with EA

As a general rule, digital transformation is extremely complex, individual, and very expensive. The first step to implementing frameworks—which often fail—is to understand and then improve your business data, as well as your IT infrastructure. Your EA can be determined and filled with sufficient data once you have completed this step.

To better understand the application that matters most for a business and the evolving trend regarding this application, we must know to address the basics, finding the right people in the business who can give the right definition of an application and the business individually as well as together. Then, use their answers on IT as a beginning point and find a simple model to create transparency on this view.

Managing application portfolios in such a situation is extremely helpful. You will be able to develop a first-shot classification of user groups and business capabilities after having gathered first sight into how IT applications are viewed from the business side. Combining a high-level assessment of the business criticality report and the functional and technical fit of the business with the application can prove effective. It becomes an invaluable tool for the business and IT to spot improvement opportunities quickly.

Dealing with operational issues

As soon as you begin working on a strategic project, an operational question distracts you. EAs know all too well the challenges of staying current with the latest operating systems, responding to urgent requests for business support from unknown groups, and cutting costs by eliminating redundancies. Identify these issues proactively to avoid distractions before they become a problem. You are distracted because you don't know which applications are affected by an operating system or major database update. When you know which major technology is used by your top business applications—omit any details—you can take proactively calculated decisions.

Business support requests usually come from out of nowhere; however, having compiled your application portfolio landscape, you will be in the driver's seat. Specifically, try to get an assessment of which user groups and capabilities your business deems most vital, and focus on the problems surrounding those groups. The application portfolio landscape contains all the information you need and use to deal with traditional requests for cost-cutting. All you need to do is pinpoint low-hanging fruit before your competitors do. As soon as you have penned down the key applications, the most pressing improvements, and taken care of any operational concerns, it is time to get serious about data and how it drives your business. Typically, this is accomplished at two different levels of granularity. The key data objects that drive the business are of primary importance at the business level. Nothing more can be said than that the needs of your stakeholders should be your top priority. Concentrate on their value to your company, and they will form the coalition you desperately need.

Following the creation of the first business value, EAs are able to look further into the future because of the level of trust between peers and management. Providing the enterprise with ways to implement target architectures is their responsibility. Nonetheless, they need to keep in mind that focusing on creating business value and high-quality data is imperative to avoid fallacy.

At the end of this chapter, we conclude that despite the fact that EA has often been put forward to help businesses innovate and transform, it has traditionally been focused on standardizing processes and integrating technology rather than continuously adapting to change. The new digital environment requires more adaptive conceptualizations of EA in order to achieve the desired impact. Digital transformation has implications for EA, as we explored. Existing approaches to EA address integration and coherence within an organization, but they often fall short when it comes to the complexities associated with digital ecosystems. In a digital environment, we postulate that adaptive capabilities are needed that transcend the concept of dynamic capabilities.

Summary

The role of enterprise architects is to take on these problems head-on by providing a roadmap to manage and reduce complexity, which contributes directly to reducing costs. Enterprise architects ensure that IT is aligned with business goals and standards.

Within an EA, the primary objective is to ensure a reduced cost of business operation, an agile organization and workflow, shared business capabilities and access across the organization, and more. In the light of these goals, enterprise architects fit best in multiple use cases such as mergers, integrations, risk assessment, management, and so on. The EA also includes governing principles that discuss how business strategy can be realized through IT implementation.

In the absence of stakeholder participation, EA programs often end up being a massive failure. EA often focuses only on technology, which has a much narrower scope than technical architecture. Business, information, and solutions architectures are all included in EA.

Lastly, digital transformation is defined as the ability to effectively leverage the challenges and opportunities of mixed digital technologies. Business organizations handle this in a strategic and prioritized manner in response to current and future shifts in society.

Successful enterprises treat digital transformation as an ongoing process because industry maturity affects the path to digital excellence. Conclusively, the new digital environment requires more adaptive conceptualizations of EA in order to achieve the desired impact. Digital transformation has implications for EA.

In the next chapter, we will cover prescriptive guidance from AWS on migration to the cloud. We will cover how to identify business objectives for cloud migration, a review framework, readiness assessment phases, and adoption and delivery frameworks.

5
AWS Prescriptive Guidance Frameworks

Several departments and major business processes are impacted, including the **information technology (IT)** framework, in the process of transitioning to the cloud. Planning ahead is crucial for a successful migration but translating business goals into a migration plan takes time.

An overview of the steps involved in planning and implementing your cloud vision is discussed in detail in this chapter.

We will cover the following topics in this chapter:

- Understanding the current state of the cloud journey and target business outcomes
- Identifying business objectives for your migration to the cloud
- **Amazon Web Services (AWS)** Well-Architected Framework review
- AWS **migration readiness assessment (MRA)** phases
- **AWS Cloud Adoption Framework (AWS CAF)**
- **AWS Engagement Delivery Framework (AWS EDF)**

Understanding the current state of the cloud journey and target business outcomes

No matter where you are on the cloud journey, whether you're just getting started or you're at the halfway point, it isn't over. The organization is required to constantly review its strategy, no matter where it is in its cloud journey, to ensure that it is getting the most out of the services it aims to offer. Since technology and services are always changing, businesses need to use them to continually improve their operations. Changing the path of the journey is key to staying competitive, growing the business, and ultimately succeeding. In order to ensure that organizations are on the right path and have improved their business acumen, cloud adoption strategies need to be created or reviewed.

Those who have already taken the plunge should review best practices related to security, availability, automation, and cost management to make sure their investment is getting the best return. The next step is to outline a solution and fill in the details after the journey has been outlined and a roadmap has been drawn up.

It is not necessary to rush into the cloud, nor is it necessarily a *cloud-native* solution that is the right fit for your business. Here are some key considerations and steps to defining a cloud strategy that will deliver value to your business:

- **Articulate your vision**

  Ensure that your cloud strategy takes into account the business objectives of your organization when documenting your vision for the enterprise's future use of the cloud. Considering a long-term view of your objectives and the associated benefits of cloud computing, such as moving from proprietary solutions to **software-as-a-service** (**SaaS**) solutions, will help in decision-making within the business and gain buy-in from key stakeholders.

- **Present a strategy and roadmap**

  After the vision has been bought into by the company, steps are taken to get it molded into a cloud strategy. A comprehensive roadmap is laid out that guides both short- and long-term undertakings.

- **Understand your asset landscape**

  When determining your strategy and assessing benefits, it will be helpful to have a comprehensive view of the infrastructure and software assets in your business. Maintaining and replacing assets cost money, and their expected useful lives should also be considered, as well as qualitative aspects, such as the degree of customization and the complexity of the migration process.

- **Look to improve the operating model**

  Organizations should consider reshaping their processes when they move to the cloud. Regardless of whether the process is in the cloud or not, even with better technology, it can still be flawed; technology alone won't make it better. It is best to involve a wide range of stakeholders in the process to identify improvements that can be accomplished in the cloud. Thus, lifting-and-shifting systems can be avoided, skipping the need to change them again later on.

  An important factor to consider will be the balance between retaining in-house solutions and custom functionality and a cloud-native approach. Additionally, consider streamlined processes for the back office, such as system integration and **business continuity** (**BC**) plans, as well as those processes used by employees and customers.

- **Vendor selection**

  Establishing a cloud roadmap begins with choosing the right vendors. It is imperative that you conduct due diligence on your vendors in order to be sure they provide the best possible solutions, support, and cost model. Verify that the future state meets your risk appetite by considering both the resilience of the vendor and the criticality of the processes being migrated. In light of increasing cloud adoption, regulators could recommend that certain companies develop a multi-cloud strategy in light of the systemic risk of cloud failure.

- **Resource management**

  Cloud computing requires specialized skills—for example, project management, cloud architecture, **user experience (UX)**, data architecture, and expertise in software development. New roles include cloud security professionals and network specialists after go-live. To meet resource requirements, care should be taken to balance the onboarding of new staff and third-party support with the redeployment of headcount from retired systems.

- **Benefit and cost analysis**

  Cloud computing features many benefits, among them scalability, flexibility, reduced complexity, and cost smoothing. SaaS deployments to complete outsourcing of platforms and infrastructure will result in different benefits. It is likely that the business will experience some short-term disruption, regardless of the circumstances. To present a complete business case, it will be important to understand both the short- and long-term impacts, including data transformation and migration requirements. As you consider savings and projected costs, keep in mind the challenges inherent to modeling, particularly if current IT costs are not sufficiently granular.

- **Security in the cloud**

  A cloud-based solution may increase the attack surface or points of entry of the organization and expand its digital perimeter. When implementing network, data, and cybersecurity controls within a cloud environment, it is essential to think about how they will be deployed, both before and after the migration. It will be necessary to consider both regulatory requirements and third-party privacy concerns when storing or processing data overseas, especially as it relates to data held or processed abroad. Successful, secure cloud deployment also requires mature processes for data governance and data leakage control.

- **Cloud governance**

  To ensure that cloud applications, data, security, and controls receive adequate accountability and ownership, the IT governance model will need to be amended. It is important to mitigate the risk of shadow IT activity and ensure that the cloud environment is properly controlled, such as licensing management and capacity monitoring.

- **Operationalizing**

  New ways of working need to be embedded immediately through training and awareness exercises. In cases where cultural changes are needed, such as implementing agile project management practices, they cannot be underestimated. Within the new environment, ongoing audits and regulatory requirements—including cross-border data sharing—should be considered. The final step would be to review and update policies and procedures pertaining to core business areas such as backup and **disaster recovery** (**DR**), change management, service delivery, and vendor relationship management.

Multiple business departments and critical business processes will be altered as a result of the change. Hence, an enterprise cloud journey entails more than just technical changes.

Stages of a cloud journey

A migration plan that incorporates business objectives is time-consuming, but advanced planning is essential to a successful migration. An overview of how to plan and deliver your cloud vision will be covered in this section.

Step 1 – Making the business case

It is an important business decision to embark on a cloud journey. Before adopting a cloud infrastructure, businesses should evaluate its business implications. Cloud computing differs from traditional IT setups, and decision-makers should be aware of this. Assessing the implications of benefits, risks, compliance, security, and data control for the company as a whole and its IT activities—in particular—is essential. Identify which systems and applications should be migrated first, and what the expected costs and **total cost of ownership** (**TCO**) of the cloud deployment are.

Step 2 – Identifying the right applications

The design of every application varies, so cloud environments might not be suitable for every application. In the event that the application is cloud-friendly, you can simply *lift* and *shift* it over to the cloud. Lift-and-shift migration is by far the easiest migration to make since there is no code modification required, but there may be times when the application only needs a few tweaks before being migrated to the cloud. When the whole application needs to be rewritten, that is the worst-case scenario.

Assessing your architecture and its complexity is the best and most cost-effective way to ensure efficiency. Decide whether you can completely migrate to the cloud or whether it's better to shift only a few applications to the cloud while keeping the others on-premises.

Step 3 – Selecting a cloud service provider

The next step is to choose a cloud environment after you have analyzed and inventoried your environment. Each **cloud service provider** (**CSP**) has its own architecture and its own set of characteristics, licensing, and support capabilities. When assessing a cloud provider, you should ask the following questions:

- *Are your workloads compatible with the cloud's architecture?*

  In order to reduce code changes and overhead, you might prefer a cloud environment requiring fewer modifications to applications.

- *How does the provider implement cloud services?*

  There are public and private cloud offerings from most cloud vendors. You should check whether the vendor provides capabilities for complex cloud environments if you plan to implement a multi-cloud or hybrid cloud architecture.

- *Would it be possible to use your own existing licenses on the cloud?*

  Managing licenses can be complicated and costly. Check whether your existing license is compatible with the software and, if not, determine ahead of time which license you need and what its costs are.

- *In terms of support, what is needed before, during, and after migration?*

  There are cloud providers that provide tools and little support, while others offer assistance from start to finish.

In addition to security, compliance, and **service-level agreements** (**SLAs**), there are many more aspects of cloud migration to consider, but you should begin by considering the preceding questions.

Step 4 – Initial adoption

In order to move to the cloud, most companies adopt SaaS first. Platforms such as **customer relationship management** (**CRM**), office productivity tools (Office 365 and Google Workspace), accounting, **human resources** (**HR**), and collaborative tools such as Slack, Asana, or Trello are among the less critical applications. Software solutions that are critical to a company's success—such as warehousing, production, and **enterprise resource planning** (**ERP**)—are normally tightly integrated with core operations. You can move an entire infrastructure to the cloud by implementing **platform-as-a-service** (**PaaS**) solutions. A transition to a cloud-based solution will often require pilots and **proofs of concept** (**POCs**), an approach known as *repurchasing*.

In the initial stages, **infrastructure as a service** (**IaaS**) can be used for non-critical applications, test and development environments, batch processing, and data archiving. Develop a cloud governance strategy as your organization adopts cloud solutions. Develop business processes that cover both on-premises and cloud environments, create access policies, and implement monitoring and security tools.

Step 5 – Full migration

Your cloud migration should now be complete with all the necessary information. However, it is important to keep in mind that much of the execution process is actually testing, and performing a pilot is an excellent way to accomplish this. Applications that require ongoing operation cannot sustain a long period of downtime, especially mission-critical ones. To verify this, it is always better to test your plan, and then move forward with it. Put a recovery strategy in place, in case of an issue.

Step 6 – Post-migration

Your migration is complete, but your journey has not been completed. We can now begin comparing performance before and after migration. Be sure that you are aligning cloud performance with SLAs from your provider and your own performance goals. You should be vigilant for issues that come up in the new cloud environment, detect unexpected changes, and fine-tune applications and infrastructure accordingly.

Cloud migration challenges

You will probably face some challenges during your cloud migration project, and here are some tips for overcoming them:

- **Interoperability**

  Adapting existing applications to interact with cloud environments may require refactoring or complete rewrites. A decision should be made whether to move the dependency of the application to the cloud as-is or transition to a cloud-based counterpart.

- **Availability**

  It may be necessary to temporarily shut down business systems during the migration process. Unexpected downtime may also occur during migrations. Establish a DR plan that is compatible with the cloud, to ensure business operations are not interrupted and customers are not inconvenienced.

- **Data security and integrity**

  As well as the risk of data loss or corruption, migrations to the cloud can also open the door to hackers. During the migration process and in the target cloud environment, determine the risks and compliance issues you may face, and adjust your security strategy accordingly.

- **Cloud expertise**

  Traditionally, your IT department might not have the experience to handle cloud environments. Data center expertise and experience managing physical servers do not directly translate to the cloud. Cloud experts should be recruited or contracted to provide solutions to these issues, such as training teams and providing sandboxes for experimentation.

Challenges at every step of the way during your cloud migration project are inevitable; however, what matters the most is how you overcome them and emerge stronger than before. When you're well prepared for the migration with great resources and strategies, the outcome is extremely beneficial. We will look deeper into this in the next section.

Three possible outcomes of cloud readiness

Effective strategic planning, as well as modern tools and techniques, is absolutely essential for cloud migration to be a success. When executed properly, here are some positive outcomes that you will experience:

- The path of what we call the *stages of adoption* is generally followed by organizations considering large-scale migration to AWS. It is important to assess your organization's readiness at each stage and to determine which parts of the environment are sufficiently mature to move to the next stage.

  The project phase (or POC phase), for example, includes organizations planning their first workload to move to the cloud. During this phase, no foundational constructs or unified AWS accounts are required. However, tagging must be properly performed before a larger migration initiative can be planned. In the absence of this, migrations may be delayed due to issues with the foundation.

- Another major outcome of a readiness assessment is identifying strengths and weaknesses. Based on strengths, the organization determines which teams and practices are ready for wide adoption. To ensure successful cloud migration, these areas do not require additional work. Weaknesses are areas that need to be addressed so that cloud migrations can be enabled. The earlier gaps are addressed, the easier the migration process will be, and the less likely the chances of project delays.

- In order to grow the areas of strength in your organization and close gaps, you need to put an action plan in place. For projects to be successful, owners should be assigned, and deadlines should be set. To advance your cloud initiative, we recommend engaging your internal process improvement and organizational change teams. The teams usually have tools for analyzing current capabilities, communicating, and planning buy-in, which is helpful.

Accessing the organization's readiness, identifying strengths and weaknesses, and bridging the gaps between teams play a major role in a successful cloud migration process. Moving forward, the aims and goals for the migration will be discussed.

Identifying business objectives for your migration to the cloud

Cloud migration strategies can only be devised once you understand why you are moving to the cloud. Here are some of the most common reasons companies move to the cloud:

- To avoid maintenance costs of data centers
- To have enhanced scalability
- To improve resilience with higher capabilities
- To enhance remote collaboration among teams

To ensure that all team members understand the purpose of the business, it is also important to gain agreement on the business objectives. Identifying what to move to the cloud will be much easier once you understand the business rationale behind switching. A migration journey involves lots of decisions, including planning a migration strategy, choosing a CSP selecting a deployment model, and so forth. The only way to make the right decisions along the way is to have well-defined and realistic goals.

A readiness assessment consists of four tasks. Let's have a look at each of them.

Readiness assessment meeting

An assessment of readiness begins with scheduling the meeting and inviting the required attendees, such as the following:

- The **chief executive officer (CEO)**
- The chief architect
- The **chief information officer (CIO)**
- The **managing director (MD)**
- The **business unit (BU)** owners
- IT finance
- The security leader
- The network leader
- The application development leader
- Infrastructure leader
- The operations leader
- The application owners

These entities are some of the biggest stakeholders in an organization who contribute toward the long-term success and efficiency of teams across the board.

Conducting stakeholder interviews

An hour or 2-hour-long interview with the executive team is followed by interviews with key stakeholders or personas. A kick-off meeting is a crucial part of the assessment process since it starts the entire process, and this is what you should aim to do:

- In the kick-off meeting, determine a set of core applications that will be assessed over the next 2 weeks in relation to the organization's business priorities. Make sure the applications are aligned with these priorities.

- To create alignment and executive commitment to resource allocation, host a 2-day workshop where key business and technology leaders are aligned with respect to priorities.

This workshop will determine the most important results that can be delivered through a modernization initiative. In order to achieve the defined outcomes, determine current capabilities, architectures, and skills. Establish a cloud management team, cloud business office, and cloud platform engineering team as key participants in the operation model.

The workshop should be led by a modernization program manager and data specialists, infrastructure specialists, and modernization architects. Stakeholders decide upon success factors, a methodology, and typical outcomes at the end of the vision workshop. As a result, the organization will have a full understanding of its focus and commitment during the next phase.

Gathering information using resources

Gather information by using an application modernization questionnaire, analyze the gathered information, document observations, and determine the next stages through the following steps:

1. Identify applications that will be replatformed, refactored, and replaced, and create a journey guide so that everyone can understand the ecosystem. Make a prioritized list of workloads that should be modernized, and then create a modernization blueprint for those workloads.

2. Make sure you meet the requirements, so before you create a blueprint, complete all prerequisites. Verifying the drivers of application modernization includes testing their effectiveness, performance, integration, and serviceability, and determining their application adoption path.

3. Perform accurate asset alignment. To support prioritized workloads, identify which proposed and existing assets are needed.

4. Iterations and releases need to be defined. The allocation of time for modernization iterations needs to be determined. Before you change production processes, decide which releases to perform.

5. Make sure your organization is ready for modernization by identifying appropriate actions for each area. For the first few applications you're planning to modernize, you should ensure a seamless migration experience. Don't provide an action plan for all applications during this first pass. By adopting an iterative approach, you will achieve agility and speed while maintaining quality and security.

6. Set deadlines and identify owners. At least one owner and due date should be provided for each action.

Once the application to be replatformed and replaced is identified and processed based on prioritized workload, only then is the appropriate action taken.

Conducting a debrief meeting

Develop a roadmap based on the findings and risk factors identified in the debrief meeting, outlining business plans and paths for each application. Some factors you might analyze are noted here:

- Sorting, ranking, and sequencing applications

- Models of interim and target operations

- Requirements relating to technology and regulation

- The migration of large amounts of data

- Conversion of a variety of data types

Observations and activities that result from this help set the right tone for achieving those outcomes. In the debrief, stakeholders should be aligned and agree on the next steps, during which certain topics will be explored in depth, followed by implementation and momentum-building.

In the process of assessing applications for readiness, we produce the following:

- A summary of observations and next steps in an out-brief deck

- A meeting set for reviewing outputs and identifying the next steps

- Estimating and proposing use cases including **statements of work** (**SOWs**) and **minimum viable products** (**MVPs**)

Having successfully completed a vision workshop, the extended modernization team should launch an inception engagement lasting for 1 week, which would include the following:

- Aligning stakeholder groups

- Determining high-level technological solutions to achieve business objectives

- Establishing a roadmap detailing milestones and phases of MVP development

- Utilizing AWS Control Tower automation to create your first cloud foundation using landing zone templates

A joint execution team will be expected to communicate the vision and set expectations with senior business and technology leaders in your organization. Nevertheless, most of the workshops will be aimed at the modernization working teams, where owners of applications, technical leads, business owners, and architects should be included.

With AWS, your business development team will have access to technology modernization and **end-to-end** (**E2E**) support for application architecture, design, development, mobile capabilities, testing, and collaboration solutions. With the right people and the right setup, you can help modernize your legacy applications by combining proven processes, intelligent automation, data and patterns, and open standards.

AWS Well-Architected Framework review

Cloud computing platforms such as AWS and others offer many benefits. You can have access to powerful IT infrastructure for an affordable price without investing in on-site hardware. Thus, you can scale your IT operations and infrastructure to match your business performance, and reduce them as required during a slow period.

Your business will save time and money with cloud computing, which will free up more resources for other initiatives within your organization. With our Well-Architected Framework, you can fully take advantage of the cloud computing power of AWS. An AWS Well-Architected Framework review can help you figure out whether you're following the framework correctly and looks at your cloud architecture in a systematic manner. The AWS Well-Architected Framework report assesses whether you're following it and where you might improve.

The AWS Well-Architected Framework provides recommendations that help optimize how your organization develops, maintains, and upgrades applications on AWS. When building systems on AWS, you can learn about the pros and cons of each decision you make. Here are some additional advantages:

- Improving AWS workloads over time by applying AWS design principles

- To ensure performance and cost optimization, it is crucial to plan for future workloads that are as secure and reliable as possible, as well as ensuring they are as efficient as possible

- Being able to make informed decisions about your architecture in a cloud-native way, as well as knowing how your design decisions affect your products or services

- You can also use AWS-sponsored funding programs to enhance your AWS workload by leveraging usage credits for each submitted and approved workload

AWS' Well-Architected Framework incorporates six core elements—operational excellence, security, reliability, performance efficiency, cost optimization, and sustainability, described in more detail here:

- **Operational excellence**

  Supporting the development and running workloads in a high-performance manner, gaining insight into their operations. Improvement of processes and procedures to assure business value is also delivered.

- **Security**

  Cloud technologies can be used to improve your overall security posture by protecting your data, systems, and assets with cloud technologies.

- **Reliability**

  Workload reliability involves the ability for workloads to perform their intended functions correctly and consistently when they're supposed to. Workloads must be capable of being operated and tested throughout their entire lifetime. An in-depth guide to implementing AWS workloads that are reliable is provided here.

- **Performance efficiency**

  As demands and technologies change, efficiency refers to the ability to utilize computing resources efficiently.

- **Cost optimization**

  The ability to run systems at the lowest possible price while delivering maximum value to the business.

- **Sustainability**

  The ability to reduce energy consumption and increase efficiency over time to continuously improve sustainability impact. We maximize the benefits of provisioned resources while minimizing the total resources needed across all components of a workload.

Six core elements incorporated by AWS' Well-Architected Framework are presented in the following diagram:

Figure 5.1 – Factors that contribute to the AWS Well-Architected Framework

The architecture team should be capable of creating architectures and following best practices. A virtual community of AWS principal engineers can review designs and help new teams understand AWS best practices. This will help new teams acquire these capabilities or existing teams raise their bar. Best practices are made visible and accessible by the principal engineering community. Lunchtime presentations are one way they do this; for example, by discussing real-life examples of best practices. During the talks, new team members will be able to view recordings of the talks.

Our experience running internet-scale systems on AWS has led to the development of best practices. The best practice is usually determined by data, but **subject-matter experts** (**SMEs**)—such as principal engineers—are also crucial. Principal engineers ensure that teams follow best practices as new ones emerge through their community work. Our internal review processes will incorporate these best practices in time, as well as mechanisms to ensure compliance. We have codified our principal engineering thinking in our Well-Architected Framework, which serves as a customer-facing implementation of our internal review process. Field roles, such as solutions architect and internal engineering teams, have been integrated into it. By using the Well-Architected Framework, you can utilize these learnings on a scalable level.

A well-architected enterprise architecture based on the needs of customers can emerge by using the method of a principal engineering community with distributed ownership. **Chief technology officers** (**CTOs**) and other technology leaders should conduct Well-Architected reviews across their entire portfolios to better understand the risks. Using this approach, you can identify themes across teams that your organization can address through training, lunchtime discussions, or other mechanisms that allow your principal engineers to share their thoughts with other teams on specific topics.

General design principles

There are five general cloud design principles identified by the Well-Architected Framework. Let's look into them one by one, as follows:

- **Stop guessing your capacity needs**

  You might end up spending nearly all your time on idle resources or dealing with the performance implications of low capacity if you make a poor capacity choice when deploying a workload. These issues can be solved with cloud computing. Your capacity can be adjusted up or down automatically, based on your needs.

- **Test systems at the production scale**

  The cloud enables you to quickly set up production-scale test environments, test successfully, and then decommission resources on-demand. The cost of a virtual test environment is fractional to the cost of testing on-premises since you only pay when the test environment is running.

- **Automation for easier architectural experimentation**

  You can automate your workloads to save money and avoid manual effort, thus creating and replicating them at a low cost. Monitoring your automation will allow you to audit any changes that have been made and, if necessary, revert to previous parameters.

- **Allow for evolutionary architectures**

  Architecture decisions are typically implemented as static, one-time events in a traditional environment during the life cycle of a system, with a few major versions. The initial decisions made by the business and its context may inhibit a system's ability to meet changing business requirements as the business evolves. A cloud-based solution with automated and on-demand testing minimizes the risk of design changes affecting the end product. Businesses can use this as a standard way of incorporating innovations into their systems over time.

- **Drive architectures using data**

  Your architectural choices can be tracked in the cloud to determine how your workload reacts to your architectural choices. Using this information, you can improve your workload based on facts. You can use the code in your cloud infrastructure to make informed architectural decisions, improving it over time.

Cloud design principles identified by the Well-Architected Framework play a major role in enhancing architectural decision-making over time.

Improving through game days

Regularly schedule production simulations to check your architecture and processes. As a result, you will be able to identify areas for improvement and gain experience dealing with events within an organization.

Reviewing architectures should be done consistently, without blaming anyone, and encouraging digging deep. There should be no audit in this process; it should only be a conversation. It is intended to identify critical issues and areas for improvement when reviewing an architecture. The review will lead to a set of actions aimed at improving customer experiences.

Taking responsibility for the architecture of the team is everyone's job. Instead of holding a formal review meeting, team members who design architecture should continually review their design with the Well-Architected Framework. When your team utilizes a continuous approach, the architecture can be updated as the functionality is implemented, and improved as new features are added.

In AWS, well-architected systems and services follow AWS's internal review process. **Root cause analysis (RCA)** focuses on design principles that influence the architectural approach; it also includes questions to ensure that people don't overlook areas that often feature in RCA. We look at RCA whenever there is a significant issue with an internal system or service, or when a customer contacts us, to see whether we can improve the review process. In the product life cycle, reviews should be conducted at key milestones, early on in the design phase so that one-way doors can be avoided, and before the initial launch of the service. Adding new features and implementing new technologies will continue to increase your workload after going into production. As a workload grows, its structure will change. For its architectural characteristics to not degrade as they evolve, it is imperative that you follow good hygiene practices. If you make significant architecture changes, a Well-Architected review should be part of the process.

It is important to ensure that all the right people are engaged in the conversation if you are going to use the review as a one-time snapshot or independent measurement. Review times are often the first opportunity for a team to really grasp what they've done. It is helpful to have informal conversations about another team's architecture to glean answers to most questions when reviewing the workload of another team. If an ambiguity or perceived risk remains, you can follow up with one or two meetings to gain clarity or dig deeper into the issue. Having reviewed the issues, you should have a list of priorities based on the business context. The impact of those issues on your team's day-to-day work will also need to be considered. You could solve recurring problems earlier, freeing up time you could use to create business value. Your review will be updated as you address issues and see how the architecture improves.

After a review has been conducted, you will understand its value, but you may first encounter resistance from a new team. To resolve some objections, you can educate the team on why a review is beneficial. Moving forward, we will look at different scenarios that might have an impact on the review at a later stage, as follows:

We are too busy! (Generally said just before a big launch)

Here's how to respond:

- The launch of a big product will go smoothly if you prepare it beforehand. Through a review, you can find out whether any problems were overlooked.

- It is most important to conduct reviews early in the life cycle of your product so that risks can be identified and mitigation plans can be developed.

There is no time to act on the results! (This is frequently said before a major event such as the Super Bowl.)

Here's how to respond:

- The events mentioned previously cannot be changed. Would you like to experience these risks without knowing how they relate to your architecture? You still need playbooks to handle them if they arise, even if you do not address all of them.

We don't want others getting insight into how we implemented our solution!

Here's how to react to this:

- It is evident that none of the questions in the Well-Architected Framework reveal any commercial or technical proprietary information if you point the team at them.

Your organization might identify thematic issues as a result of multiple reviews with different teams. If you examine a group of teams, you may find that they have issues in a particular pillar or topic.

The following diagram presents a cycle of review within an AWS cloud infrastructure:

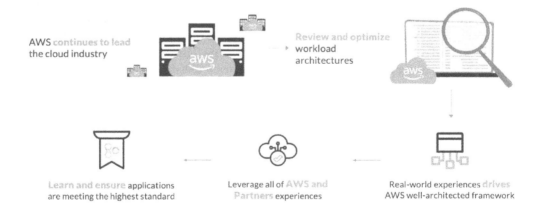

Figure 5.2 – AWS review cycle

As part of your comprehensive review, you will need to identify any mechanisms, training, or principal engineering talks that might assist you in addressing these thematic issues.

AWS MRA phases

Rather than merely describing your workload, an MRA should document what you need to migrate to AWS. It will assist you in anticipating risks, costs, and necessary processes, as well as potential migration paths. AWS migration readiness is enhanced when you perform an MRA, preparing you for every situation and preventing problems from arising.

By working with an MRA, your company can make well-informed, data-driven migration decisions and address any questions you may have. In a comprehensive MRA, you should ask the following questions:

- Do I have a good case for migrating to AWS? Find out whether AWS might not be the right solution for your needs before investing time, money, and effort in a migration.

- If I move my workload to AWS, which re-architecture will I need? The re-architecture of applications that aren't easily portable should be planned and budgeted for.

- In this case, would a *lift-and-shift* migration be useful? Consider taking a different approach to AWS if your applications require extensive redesign.

- What would be the cost of migrating to AWS? You may need help first estimating migration costs since AWS only offers pricing for computing resources and data storage and transfer.

- How would an AWS migration assist your business? The benefits of AWS vary greatly depending on the computing needs of your firm, so you may be able to find benefits specific to your firm. By knowing these details, you will be better prepared to migrate.

- After a successful migration, how much will this workload cost? You'll need to take into account several factors to get an accurate cost estimate. However, to budget properly, these factors must be taken into account.

To make informed decisions about cloud migration, MRAs are vital. In addition, answering these questions requires a complex process involving a variety of figures.

Participants from different parts of the organization will participate in an interactive workshop led by an experienced architect or consultant. They will gather key information about AWS's Cloud Adoption Framework to indicate cloud readiness. You'll receive a full debrief along with recommendations following the workshop. You can conduct this assessment on its own or integrate it with other workshops and migration services.

AWS CAF

To deliver a comprehensive digital transformation, you will need the AWS CAF. By leveraging this, you will be able to identify and prioritize transformation opportunities, assess and improve your cloud readiness, and iteratively evolve your roadmaps throughout the transformation process. Let's focus on digital transformation and emphasize the use of data and analytics. As part of the framework, six perspectives are identified (**Business**, **People**, **Governance**, **Platform**, **Security**, and **Operations**), accounting for 47 discrete capabilities.

A successful digital transformation requires alignment across four key domains: **Technology**, **Process**, **Organization**, and **Product**. AWS recommends four iterative and incremental cloud transformation phases based on the capabilities and transformation domains, as follows:

- **Envision**: Display how the cloud will benefit your business. In this phase, you will participate in an interactive workshop led by a facilitator to identify transformation opportunities.

- **Align**: Identification of capability gaps across foundational capabilities. This phase also takes the form of a facilitator-led workshop and results in an action plan.

- **Launch**: Demonstrate incremental business value through pilot projects in production.

- **Scale**: Extend pilot programs to the desired level of scale to achieve business benefits.

As digital technologies proliferate, changes are occurring faster, and competition is increasing in many sectors. As it becomes increasingly difficult to sustain competitive advantages, companies are increasingly forced to reinvent themselves every few years. Additionally, citizens' expectations and behaviors are driving government agencies to improve the provision of digital services. Using digital technologies in a digital business world helps companies adapt to market changes, delight customers, and accelerate their business outcomes.

AWS is used by millions of customers, including start-ups, enterprises, and governments, digitalizing and optimizing business processes, migrating and modernizing legacy workloads, and reinventing operating models. Their business outcomes are improved—including lower costs, reduced risks, and improved operational efficiency—as a result of cloud-powered transformation. Their agility improves, and they create new revenue streams as well as improve employee morale and customer satisfaction. It takes a set of foundational organizational capabilities for you to effectively leverage the cloud for digital transformation (your cloud readiness). As shown in the following diagram, with the AWS CAF, thousands of organizations around the world are accelerating their cloud transformation journeys by identifying these capabilities and providing prescriptive guidance. Here, you can see the elements that contribute to product transformation within an organization:

Transformation Domains

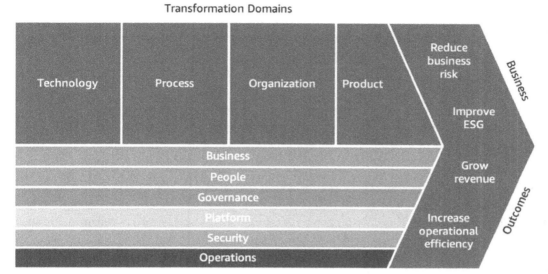

Foundational Capabilities

Figure 5.3 – Contributing factors for product transformation within an organization

In the preceding diagram, there is a value chain that consists of technologies, processes, and organizations that enable product transformation. Reducing risk, improving **environmental, social and governance (ESG)** performance, and increasing revenue and operational efficiency are a few of the business outcomes.

Cloud transformation value chain

Using the cloud for migration and modernization of legacy infrastructure, applications, and data and analytics platforms is central to technological transformation, as detailed here:

- According to cloud value benchmarking, moving from on-premises to AWS reduces the cost per user by 27%, increases the number of **virtual machines (VMs)** managed per administrator by 58%, and decreases downtime by 57% and security events by 34%.

- Business operations can be digitized, automated, and optimized through process transformation. Analytical platforms are a powerful tool for extracting actionable insights from data. **Machine learning (ML)** can be used to improve operational efficiency in a range of areas, including customer service, employee productivity, fraud detection, and forecasting. In this way, you can improve customer and employee satisfaction while improving operational efficiency and operating costs.

- An organization's transformation focuses on reinventing its operating model—how it orchestrates efforts to provide value to customers and align with its strategic goals. Utilizing agile methods to rapidly iterate and evolve while organizing your teams around products and value streams will help you become more responsive and customer-centric.

- Business model transformation entails reimagining your product/service offering and revenue model through new value propositions. You may be able to take advantage of this to reach new customer segments. Using AWS reduces **time-to-market** (**TTM**) by 37%, increases code deployment frequency by 32%, and reduces time to deploy new code by 38%, according to the *Cloud Value Benchmarking* report.

Capabilities facilitate the utilization of resources (people, technology, and any other tangible or intangible assets) by an organization to accomplish a specific goal. Using AWS CAF capabilities, you can improve your ability to leverage the cloud effectively to drive digital transformation. The **Cloud Native Computing Foundation** (**CNCF**) groups its capabilities into six categories—**Business**, **People**, **Governance**, **Platform**, **Security**, and **Operations**.

Your cloud transformation journey is composed of a set of capabilities owned or managed by different functionally related stakeholders, as discussed next.

AWS CAF perspectives and foundational capabilities

Your cloud investments will be more successful if you keep your business goals in mind. CEOs, **chief financial officers** (**CFOs**), **chief operating officers** (**COOs**), CIOs, and CTOs comprise this group. Here are some approaches to take:

- Bringing a people perspective to the cloud journey accelerates our strategy to help organizations move more rapidly to the continuous growth of a learning culture. CIOs, COOs, CTOs, directors of the cloud, and senior leaders across functions and departments are usual stakeholders.

- A governance perspective helps you maximize benefits and minimize risks associated with your cloud initiatives. **Chief transformation officers** (also known as **CTOs**, along with chief technology officers), CIOs, CTOs, CFOs, **chief data officers** (**CDOs**), and **chief risk officers** (**CROs**) are typical stakeholders.

- Building an enterprise-grade, scalable, hybrid cloud platform, modernizing existing workloads, and implementing cloud-native solutions are only a few benefits of a platform perspective. Typical stakeholders are CTOs, engineers, and technology leaders.

- Your cloud workloads and data are more secure when you take a security perspective. Stakeholders in security management include **chief information security officers** (**CISOs**), **chief compliance officers** (**CCOs**), internal auditing specialists, and security engineers and architects.

- By understanding operations, you can ensure your cloud services are delivered to a level that meets business requirements. A number of stakeholders participate in this process, such as IT service managers, infrastructure and operation leaders, and site reliability engineers.

Once AWS CAF perspectives and foundational capabilities are identified, we move forward to diving deep into the journey of cloud transformation.

Cloud transformation journey

Cloud-based business outcomes are demonstrated in the **Envision** phase. The process identifies and prioritizes transformation opportunities in line with your strategic business objectives across the four transformation domains. Here's what you can do to obtain maximum value from this process:

- The ability to demonstrate value as you progress through your transformation journey will be enhanced by relating key stakeholders and measurable business outcomes to your transformation initiatives.

- *Phase A* of the alignment process examines gaps across AWS CAF perspectives, identifies dependencies across organizations, and surfaces stakeholder concerns and challenges. Developing cloud readiness strategies, ensuring stakeholder alignment, and facilitating organizational change management will help you become more cloud-ready.

- During the launch phase, pilot initiatives are delivered in production, and incremental business value is demonstrated. In order to influence future directions, pilots need to be highly impactful. Learning from pilots will help you adjust your approach before scaling to full production.

- As part of the scale phase, your cloud investments should be scalable, and your business value will be sustained as needed.

Some foundational capabilities may not need to be addressed at once. Your cloud transformation journey will require you to develop foundational capabilities and improve your cloud readiness.

AWS EDF

Migrations to the cloud are prepared and implemented using agile methodologies. The process involves the following:

- To be able to respond to change, consider structuring your work as epics and stories

- Prioritizing the backlog and producing it

- Making a progress report

- Ensuring that business needs are efficiently and effectively tied to technology initiatives through a migration roadmap

Agile development involves starting small, iterating, evaluating, managing, and scaling huge stories. Discussed next are the steps involved in making the process seamless.

Preparation

Here are the steps involved in the migration preparation:

1. Form two scrum teams with two pizzas each that are made up of internal resources defined in the readiness and planning phase. Teams should be divided into functional and technical roles. In addition to enabling migrations, these teams prepare the business to do enterprise-scale migrations:

   A. *2-Pizza Team 1* structure and resources—business case development, program governance, people skills, and **center of excellence** (**CoE**)

   B. *2-Pizza Team 2* structure and resources—application discovery, application migration, landing zone, security, and operations integration

2. The migration readiness assessment results will be reviewed in a planning meeting with both scrum teams.

3. *AWS Wave 1* will deal with 10 to 30 on-premises applications that should be migrated to AWS.

4. Plan and prioritize all workstreams from existing migration patterns based on *pre-baked* epics.

5. The migration of applications will be divided into eight 2-week sprints.

6. Create a migration plan that includes resources, a backlog, risks and mitigations, and roles and responsibilities, such as **Responsible, Accountable, Consulted, Informed** (**RACI**).

Considering these pointers, you can identify which resources are responsible for managing risk that occurs during the project.

Implementation

The following steps are involved in the migration implementation:

1. Create sprint schedules and targets with both teams for each sprint.

2. The epics should be reviewed, broken down into stories with acceptance criteria, and organized into sprints *1* through *8*.

3. Each 2-pizza team needs to meet daily for cadence.

4. Faster feedback and uninterrupted workflow are two important outcomes of this meeting. By creating daily scrums, the scrum leader communicates progress, resolves blockers, and reports on deliverables.

5. Build an implementation oversight meeting plan for communications and reporting. Ensure teams are working well and are delivering value using agile metrics.

6. Focus on managing sprints with the following primary objectives:

    A. The ability to understand, enable, and mobilize a workforce is key to learning by doing.

    B. Build to full migration capacity by starting small and achieving early success.

7. Build a list of outputs, best practices, and lessons learned that can be used in migrations at scale.

8. Using *Wave 1* as a guide, create blueprints for agile migrations. Lay the groundwork for the planning and readiness phases.

Gaining experience and confidence as you work through these initial *Wave 1* migrations is beneficial. As part of this process, you will select which migration patterns and tools work best for your organization. Testing operational and security processes is also included in the process. A list of application groupings based on common patterns is created to recognize patterns within the portfolio (for example, common architectures and technology stacks). The result is a standardized migration process for groups of applications.

Value-adding outcomes

When you apply this agile model to operating at scale, you can accelerate your progress toward business outcomes. The agile approach results in the following value-adding business outcomes:

1. The *7 Rs* of migration should be applied to application selection.

2. Planning movement waves with migration tools—develop priority lists of move groups with migration tools.

3. Testing and deploying various components of your landing zone will validate its functionality.

4. **Development operations** (**DevOps**)—Foster the continuous development of new features, fixes, and updates with the DevOps model.

5. Automate the migration process using vendor tools.

6. Use the *AWS Prescriptive Guidance* catalog to find migration patterns.

7. The goal is to design target state architectures for the migration of servers, data, and applications.

8. Resources will be trained on AWS services and will gain hands-on experience migrating.

9. Running an AWS operation runbook enables you to verify the operating model.

10. Migration management—handle migration scopes, schedules, resource plans, issues, and risks.

By accelerating the process of improvement toward migration, these elements prove to be extremely effective and beneficial.

Summary

To stay competitive, grow a business, and succeed, you must change your path of travel. Cloud adoption strategies need to be created or reviewed to make sure that organizations are on the right path and are improving their business acumen. When defining your vision for how your organization will utilize the cloud in the future, ensure that your cloud strategy takes into account the business objectives of your company. Whether it's for short-term or long-term initiatives, a comprehensive roadmap should be outlined, followed by a migration plan that incorporates business objectives, which is time-consuming.

After understanding why you are migrating to the cloud, you can formulate a cloud migration strategy. Cloud computing is commonly used to avoid data center maintenance costs, enhance scalability, improve resilience, and enhance remote collaboration among teams. As a customer of AWS, your business development team has access to technology modernization as well as E2E support for application architecture, design, development, mobile capabilities, testing, and collaboration solutions. AWS's Well-Architected Framework can help you optimize how you build, maintain, and upgrade applications on AWS.

Your organization could address themes across teams through training sessions, lunchtime discussions, or other mechanisms that facilitate communication among principal engineers on specific topics. AWS CAF will enable you to identify and prioritize transformation opportunities, assess and improve your cloud readiness, and iteratively enhance your roadmap as you transform your organization.

The next chapter is about understanding **The Open Group Architecture Framework** (**TOGAF**) architecture domains and exploring cloud ecosystems in the context of AWS. We will also review reference architecture and models to learn more about each phase of a TOGAF **Architecture Development Method** (**ADM**) in an AWS cloud transformation.

6

TOGAF Framework in Action with AWS

In contrast to traditional waterfall processes, architecture can be developed in an iterative manner. Evidently, Agile-Scrum methodologies have proven to be successful because they emphasize iteration. In this process, documentation and proper planning do not have to be neglected. In fact, they should be encouraged.

In this chapter, we will cover the following topics:

- TOGAF – **Architecture Development Method (ADM)** phases and approaches
- Cloud architecture development method
- Cloud ecosystem reference models
- Enterprise architecture principles of the cloud ecosystem

TOGAF – ADM phases and approaches

Our goal is to develop an Information Systems architecture that functions efficiently and effectively. But remember, this is not to create endless and unnecessary artifacts. Generally, agile projects involve iteration during the requirements phase. Projects rarely have clearly defined and understood business requirements, without needing to elicit and clarify them beforehand.

Listed in the following table are the ADM phases. Each phase covers a specific role and describes the essential aspects:

Preliminary Phase	Creating an architecture capability requires preparation and initiation activities, such as customizing TOGAF, selecting tools, and defining architecture principles.
Requirements Management	Business requirements should be incorporated within every step of the TOGAF project. An ADM phase handles, deals with, and prioritizes requirements based on their identification, storage, and input and output.
Phase A: Architecture Vision	TOGAF projects should have a clear scope, requirements, and expectations. Establish an architecture vision and identify stakeholders. Establish a Statement of Architecture Work and validate the business context. Gain approvals for any changes.
Phase B: Business Architecture Phase C: Information Systems Architectures Phase D: Technology Architecture	The following four domains are to be developed: 1. Business 2. Information Systems – application 3. Information Systems – data 4. Technology Build the baseline and target architectures for each case and assess the gaps.
Phase E: Opportunities and Solutions	Identify the building blocks identified previously, and determine the vehicles that will deliver them. Identify the transition architectures required if an incremental approach is needed.
Phase F: Migration Planning	Plan the implementation and migration of the baseline architecture to the target architecture by developing detailed plans.
Phase G: Implementation Governance	Oversee implementation from an architectural perspective. Draft architecture contracts and issue them. Inspect project execution for conformance to the architecture.
Phase H: Architecture Change Management	To ensure that the architecture meets the enterprise's needs and maximizes its value, the architecture should be monitored continuously, and a change management process should be established.

Preliminary phase

In this first phase, the enterprise is defining *when*, *where*, *what*, *why*, *whom*, and *how* the architecture should be done in the enterprise. The main aspects are listed as follows:

- Enterprise definition
- Key drivers and elements in the organizational context identification
- Requirements for the architecture
- Development of architecture principles

- Definition of the architecture framework
- Relations between management frameworks
- Assessment of enterprise architecture maturity

In order for executives, planners, architects, and engineers to coordinate, integrate, and conduct their activities effectively, the enterprise architecture provides a strategic, top-down view of the organization. Through the enterprise architecture framework, this team has a strategic framework that enables them to conduct their activities effectively. Therefore, enterprise architects must take into account the interoperability between their frameworks and those throughout the organization, so it is not possible to develop the enterprise architecture in a solitary manner. Aspirations and goals must be set at the strategic, interim, and tactical levels.

Enterprise

Architecture faces a number of challenges related to the scope of an organization. Enterprise architecture capability will have the most impact on stakeholders based on the enterprise's scope and whether it is federated. In order for the resultant activity to have resources and clear support from management, at this stage, it is imperative that a sponsor is appointed. There might be many organizations within the enterprise, and the sponsor is responsible for ensuring that all stakeholder groups are included in defining, establishing, and utilizing the architecture capability.

Organizational context

An enterprise must understand the context surrounding the architecture framework it plans to use before it can make informed and effective decisions. The following list of specific areas should be considered:

- When no commercial model or budget is available for enterprise architecture, it should be based on the preliminary phase
- Identifying the key issues and concerns of enterprise stakeholders across the architecture life cycle
- Describing the business principles and goals of the organization, as expressed in the directions, imperatives, and strategies set forth by the board of directors
- Focusing on technology and information portfolio management processes and methods along with current systems design and development frameworks and methods
- Based on the baseline architecture, describe how the landscape is currently portrayed in the documentation, along with the state of the enterprise
- Organizations and enterprises adopting the framework must identify their skills and capabilities.

Requirements for architecture work

The requirements and performance metrics of enterprise architecture work are driven by business imperatives. It is essential that the business outcomes and resource requirements are sufficiently clear for this phase to define the scope of the enterprise architecture work to be done and define the outline of enterprise business information requirements and associated strategies. Some examples are listed here:

- Business requirements

- Cultural aspirations

- Organizational intents

- Strategic intent

- Forecasting financial requirements

It is important to articulate the key elements of each of these. As part of the process of defining and establishing an architecture capability, it is necessary for sponsors to identify all the relevant decision-makers and stakeholders.

Principles

Prior to commencing any architecture work for enterprise approval, the preliminary phase defines the architectural principles. In order to develop an enterprise architecture, the architecture principles must be defined. In addition to architecture principles, business principles play a role in enterprise architecture. The business principles are also part of the architecture principles themselves. Normally, the architecture function is not responsible for defining business principles. These principles might be cross-referenced with other business principles, strategic business drivers, or business goals if they're formulated and promulgated within the enterprise.

Management frameworks

A TOGAF framework must coexist with other management frameworks, either formally or informally, that might exist within an organization. Most organizations develop solutions using a system, which in the majority of cases has an IT component. In business, systems are important because they include both people and processes. TOGAF is recommended to be coordinated with the following list of frameworks:

- Business capability management includes the definition of **Return on Investment** (**ROI**) and the performance measures needed to determine the business capabilities required to deliver business value

- The methods used to manage a company's change initiatives depend on the project or portfolio

- Operations management describes how a business runs its day-to-day operations, including how it manages the IT of its business

- The process of delivering business systems according to the architecture of the IT system in accordance with the methods of solution development

Relating the management frameworks

To plan, create, and deliver the architectural components specified in the project charters, the portfolio management framework employs a solution development methodology. A new building, new skills, new equipment, hiring, marketing, and more are examples of deliverables, but they are not exclusive to IT. Business processes are supported by enterprise architecture, not just IT. For the benefit of the enterprise, the management frameworks need to complement one another and work together.

At the strategy level, enterprise architecture is guided by business planning. Providing updated planning at an annual level is a method of providing a more fine-grained level of guidance. Another method popular with businesses is capability-based planning. Sometimes, enterprise architects are moved to strategic direction groups or work closely with them within some organizations. Enterprise architecture frameworks are developed using TOGAF. As displayed in the following diagram, capability planning is a complex cycle that requires an understanding of multiple aspects of the business:

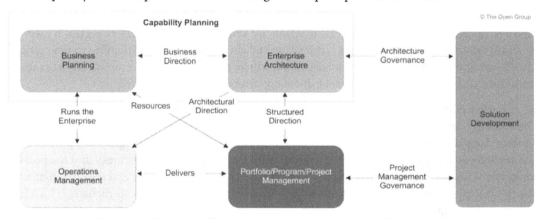

Figure 6.1 – The cycle of business development and capability planning

Business change maturity evaluation

Using capability maturity models, an organization can assess how well it can exercise its various capabilities. Typically, capability maturity models identify which factors must be present for the capability to be exercised. It is possible to identify sequential steps that will help improve a capability by measuring an organization's ability to execute specific factors. Executives can use this as a tool to improve their capabilities pragmatically.

To develop and consume enterprise architecture, an enterprise architecture maturity model must cover the features that are necessary. However, it is recommended that organizations take existing maturity models, customize them, and then determine which factors they should consider.

Phase A – the architecture vision

Starting with Phase A, the sponsoring organization sends the architecture organization a Request for Architecture Work document. Additionally, it describes what is included and what is not included in the architecture effort, along with the constraints that must be addressed.

General

ADM cycle's scope definition for architecture activity will be defined within the preliminary phase and embodied in the architecture framework for the architecture vision phase. The architecture vision phase will only address the specific objectives of the ADM cycle. Consider revisiting the preliminary phase and extending the enterprise architecture framework when the architecture framework in place does not align with the proposed architecture vision.

Creating the architecture vision

It is the sponsor's job to sell stakeholders and decision-makers in the enterprise the benefits of the proposed capability through the architecture vision. By addressing stakeholders' concerns, it meets the organization's objectives while also addressing stakeholders concerns. Adapting to emerging technologies and the impact they might have on industries and enterprises is an integral part of the architecture vision, without which many business opportunities might be missed.

One of the key parts of this activity is clarifying and agreeing on the purpose, and the purpose needs to be reflected clearly in what is created for the architecture effort. In a broader business strategy or enterprise planning process, the enterprise mission, vision, strategy, and goals are part of an organization's architecture vision. To build a bridge between the enterprise strategy and the goals and decisions underlying the architecture, it is imperative to verify and understand the documented business strategy and goals. Businesses model their benefits to customers and stakeholders, which is an important strategy artifact.

Let's examine and search for materials on fundamental business architecture concepts, such as the following:

- **Business capabilities**:

  These are specific abilities or abilities that a business might have or exchange to help it achieve a particular goal or objective. It is important that the architect determines whether the organization has a framework for representing business capabilities.

- **Value streams**:

  These are activities that contribute to an overall result for a customer, a stakeholder, or an end user.

- **Organization maps**:

  They show the relationships between the primary components of an enterprise and its partners and stakeholders.

Aside from enterprise architecture, the architecture vision also explores additional fields that are relevant to enterprise architecture. The stakeholder domains might consist of elements of the basic domains but also serve a distinct purpose. A few examples are listed as follows:

- Information
- Security
- Digital network
- Network management
- Knowledge
- Industry-specific domains
- Services
- Partnership
- Cybersecurity

Our baseline and target architectures can be described based on this architecture vision for the business, data, applications, and technology domains. Further development of this outline will follow.

Phase B – the business architecture

Throughout this report, you will be presented with a holistic overview of capabilities, end-to-end value delivery, information, and organizational structure, along with the connections among those components, products, policies, and initiatives. Taking a domain-based approach, business architecture relates business elements to business objectives and other domain elements.

General

Knowledge of business architecture is a prerequisite for all other architecture activities and should be the first step in the process, particularly when it isn't addressed in other organizational processes. Furthermore, business architecture is often needed so that key stakeholders can be convinced of the business value of subsequent architecture work and are convinced of the benefits they will receive from supporting and participating in the subsequent work.

Business strategy defines the business strategy and its objectives, although not necessarily how to achieve them. The scope of Phase B's work is primarily determined by the architecture vision of Phase A. Phase B defines, in detail, the role of the business architecture. To the greatest extent possible, existing material should be reused. There might already be existing architecture definitions in more architecturally mature environments, which might have been maintained since the last architecture development cycle.

Developing the baseline description

A baseline description should be based on existing architecture descriptions if an enterprise has them. A business capability map or a core set of value streams might have already been included in Phase A when developing the architecture vision.

These materials should be updated if a new value stream has been implemented, a business capability is missing, or a change of organizational unit has occurred that wasn't considered in the enterprise architecture project. Taking information and developing business architecture models should be carried out if architecture descriptions do not exist.

Applying business capabilities

As part of the architecture vision phase, business capability maps are developed from the perspective of a separate business, independent of organizational structures, business processes, information systems, and other products or services included within the portfolio. A map of those business capabilities must be created within the scope of the enterprise architecture project, based on organizational units, value streams, and information systems. In this way, each of those domains is aligned and optimized more efficiently.

Applying value streams

In the architecture vision phase, document the business's initial value stream models. There might be a need for new value streams within the context of a specific enterprise architecture project if the scope of the project is sufficiently broad. Through heat mapping or by developing use cases around a complete definition of the value stream, a new or existing value stream can be analyzed within the scope of the project.

Applying the organization map

Organizing an enterprise ecosystem involves identifying the key organizational units, partners, and stakeholder groups that constitute it. Organization maps are based on the business unit concept. Unlike an organizational chart that only shows hierarchical reporting relationships, the map should also show the working relationships between those entities. This map depicts the interactions and relationships between various business entities and is, typically, represented as a network or web.

Applying modeling techniques

Business capabilities, value streams, and organizational maps, as described in Phase B, are expanded and applied to the business in this phase through modeling and mapping techniques. In order to succeed in its goal, organizations must expand their operating models. The operating model is a representation of how an organization performs across various domains. There are many other modeling techniques that can be applied in addition to capability maps, value streams, and organization maps, such as the following:

- **Activity models/business process models** – These describe the functions associated with the enterprise's internal exchanges, such as business activities, the data, and/or information exchanged between activities.

- **Use case models** – These are based on the purpose of the modeling effort; they describe either the business processes or systems functions.

- **Class models** - These describe informational behaviors. Several types of granularity can also be modeled with them, as can many of the other models.

The architecture repository will be explored by the architecture team during Phase B, specifically the following list:

- Reference models for the industry for which the organization operates

- Views specific to a business enterprise such as capability maps, value stream maps, and organization maps

- Building blocks that are specific to your enterprises such as process components, business rules, and job descriptions

- Applicable standards

Phase C – key considerations for data architecture

The enterprise must address data management issues when undertaking large-scale architectural transformation. The utilization of data to capitalize on its competitive advantages is made easier by a systematic and comprehensive approach to data management.

Data management

Issues must be understood and addressed when an enterprise chooses to undergo a large-scale architectural transformation. The effective use of data can be achieved through a structured and comprehensive approach to data management. Data management considerations include the following list:

- It should be determined which of the application components in the landscape will serve as the enterprise master data system or reference

- See whether there are any enterprise-wide standards that all software packages and application components must adopt

- Understand how data entities are used in business processes, functions, and services

- Be able to clearly understand how, where, and for how long enterprise data entities are stored, transported, and reported

- In order to support information exchange between applications, what level of data transformations are required?

- In what ways will the software be required to support the integration of enterprise data with that of its customers and suppliers?

Data migration

A new application must migrate data from an existing application when it is replaced. The data architecture should include the level of data transformation, weeding, and cleaning necessary to present data in a format that meets the requirements and constraints of the target application. Data quality is the goal when populating the target application. Additionally, a common data definition needs to be developed for the transformation to be successful.

Data governance

To ensure the enterprise is able to successfully transform, data governance considerations will ensure the necessary foundation is in place, which includes the following:

- **Structure** – The data entity aspects of change can be managed by an enterprise if it has the requisite organizational structure and standard bodies to do so.

- **Management system** – In order to manage the governance aspects of data entities throughout their life cycle, enterprises should have the necessary management systems and data-related programs in place.

- **People** – This dimension identifies what skills and roles an enterprise needs to be successful in transforming its data-based business model.

It is important that businesses acquire these skills, and that existing employees are trained through well-defined learning programs if such resources and skills are lacking.

Architecture repository

Within this phase, the architecture team works on understanding the existing resources in the organization's architecture repository when it comes to data architecture. It particularly focuses on generic data models specific to the organization's industry sector:

- Energistics® – The oil and gas industry's standard for data exchange

- National Information Exchange Model (the US government)

A model for operational data and a model for a data warehouse from the Association for Retail Technology Standards.

During this phase, the architecture team will need to consider which available resources in the architecture repository are relevant with respect to application architecture. In particular, the generic business models that are relevant to the vertical sector, along with common high-level business functions, such as electronic commerce, supply chain management, and more. Please note the following:

- There are multiple vertical domain task forces within the **Object Management Group (OMG)** that develop software models for specific vertical domains, such as healthcare, transportation, and finance

- A detailed reference model for application architecture has been developed by the Open Group for the IT segment of organizations

- For organizations with IT segments, the Open Group has developed a detailed reference model for application architecture

Phase D – technology architecture

Enterprises looking for new and innovative ways to operate and improve their business are driven by the evolution of new technologies. In adopting new technology, technology architecture has the opportunity to take advantage of transformational opportunities available to the organization.

Emerging technologies

By enabling the TOGAF ADM to be flexible, technology becomes a resource and driver of change rather than the IT department. Therefore, the technology architecture might act as a driving force to deliver business capabilities and meet the information system requirements.

Architecture repository

The architecture repository is considered to identify relevant technology architecture resources, particularly the existing IT services as per the IT service catalog and the adopted technical reference model. Moreover, the technology models related to the business vertical of an organization are available in the market, for instance, The ™ forum – a comprehensive technology model has been developed related to the telecommunication industry.

Phase E – opportunities and solutions

Delivering the architecture is the focus of Phase E. All gaps between the target architecture and the baseline architecture are highlighted, and any changes are grouped into work packages within the enterprise's portfolios as needed. The primary objective is to identify a roadmap that fits the needs of stakeholders, the business transformation readiness of the enterprise, the opportunities and solutions that exist, and the available implementation constraints. In order to realize incremental business value, we must focus on the final goal.

Phase F – migration planning

Phase F consists of collaborating with the project and portfolio managers to develop an implementation and migration plan. We will complete the incomplete roadmap and implementation and migration plan in Phase F and integrate both with the rest of our change activities.

Phase F will develop the final implementation and migration plan that will include portfolio and project-level details based on the architecture roadmap, version 0.1. At that point, lessons learned from the architecture development cycle should be documented in order to promote continuous improvement.

Phase G – implementation governance

All the information that is needed for the successful implementation of the various projects can be found here. The execution of a process specific to your organization runs parallel to Phase G, where you perform the actual development. In order to minimize risk in the transformation and migration program and to enable the early realization of business value and benefits, it is advisable that you deploy the target architecture as a series of transitions. In addition to advancing the organization toward its goal, each transition generates business benefits on its own.

Phase H – architecture change management

Added business value to architecture is the goal of an architecture change management process. A cohesive, architected process is required to manage changes to the architecture. Typically, processes such as these are used to continuously monitor governance requests, technological developments, and business environment changes. Change management will decide whether a new cycle of architecture evolution needs to be launched when changes are identified.

An enterprise's architecture governance process is very closely tied to the architecture change management process. Additionally, the architecture function manages contracts between itself and the enterprise's business users. The governance body must determine in Phase H whether a change request should only be treated as an architecture update or whether a new architecture development method cycle needs to be started.

Requirements management

A flexible approach is crucial to dealing with changing requirements. By its very nature, architecture involves uncertainty and change – the *gray area* between what stakeholders want and what can be specified and planned. As a result, requirements for architecture will always change over time. Additionally, architecture encompasses many drivers and constraints beyond the control of an organization (such as changes in market conditions and new legislation), which results in unexpected changes in requirements. Requirements management processes do not deal with, decide upon, or prioritize requirements. They manage them in the relevant phases of the ADM meaning, managing requirements throughout the entire process of the ADM.

Resources

There are numerous recommendations and processes for managing requirements that are emerging in the world of requirements engineering. These processes simply stipulate what should be achieved by a successful requirements management process. The TOGAF standard does not mandate any particular processes or tools. To discover and capture business requirements, the business scenario technique is an effective and appropriate tool.

In addition to architecture definition and realization, all cloud architecture development activities follow an iterative process. The organization takes this step-by-step approach to transform its architecture along with its business goals and opportunities.

Cloud architecture development method

In the context of developing next-generation cloud-native services and applications, taking a top-down approach makes the most sense as they should be designed, architected, and constructed from the ground up. Adapting TOGAF to build cloud architectures includes specific steps.

Preliminary phase

How the enterprise does architecture will be defined during this preliminary phase. It is important to figure out the framework to use and to define the architectural principles to serve as a guide for any architecture-related work. Reusing architecture assets within an enterprise is integral to the framework and architecture principles. A mechanism has been identified and established for identifying and establishing architecture principles:

Inputs	Outputs
• TOGAF	• Enterprise architecture
• Business plans, principles and goals, and business and IT strategies	• Tailored architecture framework, including architecture principles
• Governance and legal frameworks; architecture capability	• Initial architecture repository
• Partnership and contract agreements	• Restatement of business principles, goals, and drivers
• An existing organizational enterprise architecture model	• Request for architecture work and architecture governance framework

• The enterprise architecture framework can include the following:
 	
  o Architecture method
  o Architecture content
  o Configured and deployed tools
  o Architecture principles
  o Architecture repository	

In order to establish architecture governance, once the proper methodology has been determined, the architecture principles are important.

A – the architecture phase

A high-level description of the architecture develops in Phase A to reflect cloud-based characteristics. Cloud-specific concerns related to data security, privacy, compliance, scalability, ROI, and transparency will be addressed:

Inputs	Outputs
• Architecture work request • Business principles, goals, and drivers • Enterprise architecture organizational model • Tailored architecture framework, method, content, principles, and tools • Populated architecture repository; existing architecture documentation	• Architecture work approval • Refined statements of business principles, goals, and drivers • Capability assessment • Tailored architecture framework • Architecture vision, including key stakeholder requirements • Architecture definition documents, including baseline business, data, application, and technology architecture. Also included are target business, data, application, and technology architecture. • Communications plan

B – the business architecture

There is no change in the business goals associated with a cloud-enabled application. However, in a multi-tenant scenario, the business users themselves are variable. Accordingly, this view might need to be adjusted to match the needs of different groups of users. Cloud-based applications require the management of security, privacy, and other quality attributes, and must be synchronized with an enterprise resource. Another important aspect to consider is governance, visibility, and controllability:

Inputs	Outputs

• Request for architecture work
 	
• Business principles, goals, and drivers
 	
• Capability assessment communications plan
 	
• Organizational model for enterprise architecture
 	
• Tailored architecture framework
 	
• Approved statement of architecture work
 	
• Architecture principles, including business principles, when they already-exist
 	
• Enterprise continuum architecture repository
 	
• Architecture vision, including refined key high-level stakeholder requirements
 	
• Architecture definition documents, including baseline business, data, application, and technology architectures. Also included are target business, data, application, and technology architectures.
	• The statement of architecture work updated
	
	• Validated business principles, goals, and drivers
	
	• Elaborated business architecture principles
	
	• Draft architecture definition document containing content updates:
	
	   o Baseline business architecture
	
	   o Target business architecture
	
	   o Viewpoints addressing key concerns
	
	• Draft architecture requirements specification, including content updates:
	
	   o Gap analysis results
	
	   o Technical requirements
	
	   o Updated business requirements
	
	• Business architecture components of an architecture roadmap

C – information system architecture

Cloud applications might be similar to their traditional on-premise enterprise counterparts in terms of entity relationship modeling. Nevertheless, multi-tenancy aspects of the logical data model will introduce new variations. There will be different processes for an on-premises application than those for the data security view. In addition to data integration, cloud computing might cause problems with silos of information that IT does not have direct access to. The classification of data and privacy is also important, as is prioritizing the risks associated with both data going to the cloud and data remaining on-premises:

Inputs	Outputs

• Architecture capability assessment communications
• Enterprise architecture organizational model
• Tailored architecture framework's data principles
• Statement of architecture work, architecture vision, and architecture repository
• Draft architecture definition document containing the following:
  o Baseline, target business, and data architectures.
  o Gap analysis results
  o Relevant technical requirements
• The business architecture components of an architecture roadmap
	• Statement of architecture work
	• Draft architecture definition document containing content updates:
	  o The baseline and target data architecture views
	  o Draft architecture requirements specification including content updates
	  o Gap analysis results
	  o Data interoperability
	  o Relevant technical requirements
	  o Updated business requirements
	  o Updated application requirements
	• The data architecture components of an architecture roadmap

D – technology architecture

As we assess our current capabilities and develop an environment, we will be using TOGAF to guide our efforts. Several traditional components included in the application architecture view will be abstracted by the **Platform as a Service (PaaS)**, making this view different from a traditional enterprise application. Cloud architecture will be different from on-premises architecture:

Inputs	Outputs
<ul><li>Architecture work assessment communication request</li><li>Enterprise architecture organizational model</li><li>The tailored architecture framework technology principles</li><li>Architecture work statement</li><li>Architecture vision architecture repository</li><li>Draft architecture document with the following:<ul><li>o Baseline, target, and data architectures – detailed and high-level</li></ul></li><li>Draft architecture requirements with the following:<ul><li>o Gap analysis results</li><li>o Relevant technical requirements</li></ul></li><li>The business, data, and application architecture components.</li></ul>	<ul><li>Architecture work statement</li><li>Validated technology principles</li><li>Draft architecture document containing the baseline, target, technology architecture views corresponding to the selected viewpoints</li><li>Draft architecture requirements with the following:<ul><li>o Gap analysis results</li><li>o Output from Phases B and C</li><li>o Technology requirements</li></ul></li><li>The technology architecture components of an architecture roadmap</li></ul>

E/F – migration planning

In order to deploy services in the cloud, you need to understand the cloud's available resources. Keep in mind that value can be defined in many ways, and it certainly doesn't mean the financial values associated with the total cost of ownership and ROI:

Inputs	Outputs
<ul><li>Product information</li><li>Architecture work capability assessment request</li><li>Governance models</li><li>Architecture framework statement</li><li>Architecture repository</li><li>Draft architecture document</li><li>Draft architecture requirements</li><li>Change requests for existing programs and projects</li><li>Components from Phases B, C, and D</li></ul>	<ul><li>Architecture work statement</li><li>Architecture vision</li><li>Draft architecture document with transition architecture, number, and scope</li><li>Draft architecture requirements, consolidated</li><li>Capability assessment:<ul><li>Business and IT capability</li></ul></li><li>Architecture roadmap</li><li>Work package portfolio<ul><li>Identification of transition architectures</li><li>Impact analysis</li><li>Recommended implementation</li></ul></li><li>Implementation/migration plan</li></ul>

G – implementation governance

Consider the inclusion of business processes, applications, the data and database, and technical services, along with the implementation of security and operations during the relocation. This plays a key role in Phase G of the implementation. The various implementation projects are managed here with all the information needed for success:

Input	Output
• Architecture work assessment request	• Architecture contract compliance assessments
• Enterprise architecture organizational model	• Change requests
• The tailored architecture framework statement	• Architecture-compliant solutions deployed with the following:
• The architecture repository architecture document	
• Architecture requirements	o Architecture-compliant implemented system
• Architecture roadmap	o Architecture repository
• Architecture work identified in Phases E and F request	o Architecture compliance recommendations
	o Service delivery recommendations
• Implementation/migration plan	o Performance metrics recommendations
	o **Service-level agreements (SLAs)**
	o Architecture vision
	o Updated architecture definition document
	o Business and IT operating models

H – architecture change management

As a result of Phase G, a new enterprise architecture baseline will be established, which will be managed through an architecture change management process:

Input	Output
• Architecture work request	• Architecture updates
• Enterprise architecture organizational model	• Architecture framework updates
• Tailored architecture framework	• Architecture work request
• Statement of architecture work	• Updated architecture work statement
• Architecture vision	• Updated architecture contract
• Architecture repository	• Updated compliance assessments
• Architecture definition document	
• Architecture requirements	
• Architecture roadmap	
• Change requests due to IT and business changes	
• Governance model implementation	
• Architecture contract	
• Compliance assessments and implementation/migration plan	

As a result of this, an architecture change management process is leveraged to set a new baseline for the enterprise architecture.

Cloud ecosystem reference models

This model describes how to realize and facilitate architectural capabilities in an enterprise cloud ecosystem through participation by at least one of the new or existing participants.

Business support services and ABBs of the cloud ecosystem reference model

The purpose of this section is to discuss the interoperability of an IT and business taxonomy. The following sections make up a comprehensive list of services that will simplify enterprise business operations and reduce complexity.

Accounting and billing

Bills for cloud services usage data are generated and managed based on predefined billing policies. The providers of cloud services might permit consumers to receive one bill for multiple subscriptions to qualify for volume discounts. Other accounting functions are also handled by the program.

Auditing and reporting

The audit and reporting service keeps a record of all activities for an agreed period of time, which will assist with future investigations. This helps reduce the risk of disruptive business processes and performance degradation. Reports that perform client-facing business operations activities are generated.

Availability and continuity

This service handles redundancy and workload mobility between cloud service providers. The primary objective is to ensure the selection of high availability practices and considerations in the design of cloud services.

Compliance and policies

Corporate governance and compliance with applicable laws and regulations are some of the activities that the compliance and policies service defines. The organization maintains an organizational structure, processes, tools, and business policies to ensure these services.

Consumer service

To ensure cloud service consumers receive effective care and that information about their relationships with the company is well handled, the consumer service provides an authoritative view of consumer information.

Contract and agreement

Various aspects of cloud services are offered and managed by the contract and agreement service with regard to the contract life cycle and contract life cycle management. As part of the contract, cloud service consumers are notified of applicable policies and SLAs for using cloud services.

Metering service

Cloud services and their underlying resource usage are billed/charged using the metering service. A certain level of abstraction is applicable depending on the service type provided by this metering system.

Order service

Cloud service orders are managed by the order service. In this case, cloud services are configured, service life cycle services are orchestrated, and billing and accounting are offered.

Service demand

Based on past business activity patterns and future growth projections, this service identifies the business demand for cloud services.

Subscription service

Subscription services provide cloud service providers with the option to charge for cloud services according to different subscription models. Subscribers can opt for fixed-rate, tier-based, or pay-as-you-go subscriptions. Providers monitor the allocation, consumption, and chargeback of cloud services to their subscribers.

Operational support services

Enterprise cloud ecosystems can be operated efficiently by operational support services.

Capacity and performance service

Cloud capacity and performance are optimized through the capacity and performance service. Real-time analysis and automatic workload adjustment are performed while cloud services are running.

Incident and problem handler service

In this service, problems and incidents that are related to the service are handled and the root causes are analyzed. Data is stored in a knowledge support repository for further analysis.

Inter-cloud connection service

To enable interoperability between cloud services, the inter-cloud connection service serves as a seamless bridge between different environments. Connecting with the cloud service facilitates remote access, allows users to cross different network boundaries, and improves performance.

IT asset and license service

License agreements for cloud services related to various aspects are controlled by the IT asset and license service. Additionally, some providers allow cloud service consumers to purchase licenses directly from software/solution vendors or to lease as and when needed.

Service orchestration

Cloud service orchestration allows the management of capacity and performance for cloud services on an automated basis. In this way, multi-cloud services are coordinated seamlessly.

Template service

Service templates are used to create reusable instances. The template service enables the automatic provisioning and redeploying of applications on cloud service platforms.

Cloud security services

Data, applications, and infrastructure that are stored in the cloud are protected by cloud security technologies, policies, controls, and services.

Data protection

Despite the fact that data, in today's world, is an invaluable asset, most of it remains worthless if it isn't protected. We need to protect data at every stage of the life cycle, for all data types, and at all levels of the data life cycle. To provide data protection, a variety of controls must be implemented, including data life cycle management, data leakage prevention, intellectual property protection, digital rights management, and cryptographic services.

Enterprise data management

To securely share information among enterprise cloud ecosystems, information/data is a crucial enterprise asset that must be managed. All phases of the life cycle of all categories of data must be addressed by enterprise data management. Data governance, information planning, IT architecture, record and archive provisioning, and privacy are core enterprise data management functions.

Governance risk and compliance

Compliance and governance encompass, integrate, and align various corporate governance, enterprise risk management, and regulatory compliance activities. Among these components are vendor management, audit management, IT risk management, policy management, technical awareness, and training.

Infrastructure protection services

Data security is the practice of making sure that containers and pipes of data are secure using a traditional defense-in-depth approach. Generally, infrastructure protection services are considered preventive technical controls. Most traditional or non-advanced attacks can be defended against relatively effectively.

Information security

Information security aims for the implementation of appropriate measures to eliminate threats and vulnerabilities related to data. In international enterprises, data transit and storage might differ significantly as a result of different national legislation and consequently affect information security concerns often related to privacy and confidentiality.

Policy and standards

An information security policy outlines how much security should be applied to protect the business. However, often, technical solutions are not mentioned in policies, which specify what should be done. In order for the many different components to be integrated into systems, security standards are an abstraction at the component level.

Privilege service

As part of Identity and Access Management, the privilege service ensures that users have the access that is necessary to perform duties. Examples include identity management, authentication services, authorization services, and privilege usage management. It allows access to the right resources across increasingly heterogeneous technologies and meets increasingly stringent compliance requirements.

Threat and vulnerability service

Threat and vulnerability management deals with core security matters. An enterprise must track and monitor its assets, scan for known vulnerabilities, and take action by patching the software. This is called vulnerability management. In order to identify the vulnerabilities effectively, threat modeling and security testing are also required.

Performance services

Performance services ensure SLAs are adhered to for the cloud services. It includes monitoring resource utilization, analyzing resource performance in a cloud computing environment, and assessing service performance in real time.

Resource health monitoring

In order to provide better performance, accountability, and business results, resource health monitoring generates cloud resource performance reports. This solution allows the monitoring of SLAs based on defined metrics.

Service health monitoring

Service health monitoring allows users to view the health of their cloud services, create reports on the performance of cloud services, and improve performance, accountability, and results. SLA metrics are also supported.

SLA enforcement

In order to avoid penalties, SLA enforcement ensures the SLAs are strictly enforced. As the subscription renewal process approaches, data related to SLAs can also be captured and used to make adjustments to contracts and agreements.

Interoperability and portability services

A cloud ecosystem requires effective integration with all its stakeholders through interoperability and portability services.

Data interoperability

Cloud service consumers can seamlessly manage both structured and unstructured data through interoperability. Data that is semantically consistent can be shared across multiple enterprises. A suitable semantic standard could be based on cloud-specific metadata, for instance, Open Group's **Universal Data Element Framework** (UDEF) or the US Government's **National Information Exchange Model** (NIEM). The information/data in a cloud ecosystem can be shared and reused.

Service interoperability

Data and services can be consumed across multiple cloud service providers with a unified management interface through cloud service interoperability.

Cloud service providers are able to access information related to underlying resources and provision a workload seamlessly using IaaS interoperability.

Interoperability at the PaaS level revolves around developing and deploying platform services, as well as licensing them, seamlessly. However, SaaS consumers expect their SaaS applications to have critical features supported across multiple channels.

Data portability

Data migration allows data to be transferred from one cloud environment to another or from one computer to another. On the other hand, the synchronization of data within a cloud ecosystem is the mechanism to ensure consistency across all duplicated target data storage for a single set of source data. The data is kept continuously coherent over time.

Product catalog services

An enterprise's cloud services are cataloged in the cloud ecosystem's product catalog.

Change and configuration services

Cloud services configurations are kept compliant with changes in policies and compliance by the change and configuration services. They ensure that the cloud services that are offered in the catalog are configured correctly.

Service catalog

Cloud service consumers can subscribe to services listed in the service catalog and the catalog information can be configured easily. Cloud consumers can describe and manage cloud services more easily by using a self-service cloud service provisioning portal. Alongside describing cloud service provider capabilities, the service catalog could describe how well they meet cloud performance ratings.

Resource catalog services

Cloud ecosystems manage underlying cloud services resources through resource catalog services.

Change and configuration service

Cloud services are configured in compliance with changing policies and compliance requirements through the change and configuration service.

Resource catalog

A resource catalog manages information about the resources that are needed to support the provisioning requests of cloud services. These are captured through the self-service cloud service administration.

In catalogs, metadata represents resource characteristics that can be analyzed by humans and machines for further analysis.

Enterprise architecture principles of the cloud ecosystem

Architectural Building Blocks (**ABBs**) defined in the cloud ecosystem reference model for managing the life cycle of cloud services maintain enterprise architecture principles for the use of the ABBs across the enterprise. Enterprise principles and a consensus, in terms of architectural design, should underpin these principles.

Auto-provisioned sharable system infrastructure

A cooperative infrastructure is supported by shared and auto-provisioned computing resources. The underlying computing resources of the IaaS cloud service provider utilize a multi-tenant environment in order to maximize profit. If moving workloads across IaaS is done right, the overhead can be reduced, and the SLAs can be met.

Cloud solutions are designed to address performance variance

Due to performance variances, latency fluctuations, and network failures, some cloud solutions that rely on public networks and the **Internet Protocol** (**IP**) are insecure. Cloud computing is characterized by the ability to access cloud services through standard and public internet connections. It is essential that cloud solutions address unreliable IP services and variances in latency.

Solutions for cloud computing should provide seamless connectivity and meet performance-related SLAs.

Automated ways to measure and optimize cloud solutions

The measurement and optimization of cloud services can be automated through the use of metering and cloud service solutions.

The cloud service provider and the cloud service consumer need real-time visibility of cloud services' utilization in order to minimize investment in cloud services.

Loosely-coupled cloud services

The cloud infrastructure should be loosely coupled between SaaS, PaaS, and IaaS. Dynamic and scalable cloud environments are supported by cloud services. Provide a multi-tenant deployment model with minimal customization of cloud services.

Cloud service abstraction and control

Provide a level of abstraction with cloud services that allows them to be securely exposed while hiding all of the implementation details. Providing service agility is achieved by separating the deployment details and hiding the implementation details within cloud services.

The concept of cloud services must be abstracted from the implementation details.

Multi-tenancy

Multi-tenant clouds must support tenant and solution isolation. In every case, it is critical to separate the assets of each client from the assets of other clients, regardless of the storage medium. Ensuring that their clients have secure isolation between assets is a major priority for cloud service providers. Their isolation control mechanisms do seem to succeed in controlling this capability, although they find it difficult to demonstrate.

Summary

Understanding the TOGAF architecture domains and exploring cloud ecosystems in context to AWS is what this chapter is all about. We also reviewed the reference architectures and models and shed light on how to approach each phase of TOGAF ADM in AWS cloud transformation. The aim is to understand the non-functional aspects of the system including security, reliability, operational excellence, performance efficiency, and cost optimization. Moving forward, we will talk and explain WAR alignment with TOGAF principles.

The interoperability of an IT and business taxonomy along with the comprehensive list of services that will simplify enterprise business operations and reduce complexity were also mentioned in this chapter.

Next, we will find the answer to the following questions: how do you select the IT initiative across your enterprise, and what is the strategy that drives ABBs and solution building blocks? With a deep study of multiple architectural phases and implementations, we will discuss and explain strategies for infrastructure implementation, including on-premises, cloud, and hybrid. Furthermore, we will dig deeper into SAFe and learn more about aligning enterprise architecture and SAFe for any business to determine how it caters to AWS cloud customers.

Part 3 –
SAFe in EA
and the Cloud

Moving toward the latter parts of the book, the focus is mostly on learning **Scaled Agile Framework** (**SAFe**) concepts and terminologies and understanding how SAFe principles apply to EA and the cloud in general, especially AWS. Cloud-to-cloud migration can also bring multiple challenges to unstructured organizations, such as downtime and adapting to a new cloud environment. Bringing cloud applications back to on-premises data centers involves moving them from the cloud to on-premises servers.

Company leaders and stakeholders often find it challenging to move forward after putting The Open Group Architecture Framework into action. Hence, selecting an IT initiative across your enterprise and deciding on a strategy that drives your architecture building block and solution building block are absolutely crucial. These chapters explain the strategies for infrastructure, including on-premises, cloud, and hybrid implementation and application.

One of the most difficult things is to start the journey on a productive side so much so that innovation and growth follow. This part of the book identifies whether the cloud is the right choice for you. If so, then where should you begin?

Discussing a SAFe approach, prerequisites, and implementation of successful value-added migration outcomes is one of the primary objectives of these chapters. Once implemented successfully, the benefits of cloud migration can be highly noticeable, including high scalability, better performance, and an outstanding digital experience.

Overall, you should expect to learn more about cloud adoption and migration frameworks. Ensuring successful migration can be a real game changer when it comes to an effective strategy and productivity.

This part of the book comprises the following chapters:

- *Chapter 7, Align and Scale Agile Framework with Enterprise Architecture*
- *Chapter 8, SAFe Implementation for AWS Cloud Migrations*

7
Align and Scale Agile Framework with Enterprise Architecture

Agile frameworks designed for large enterprises, such as SAFe, help companies apply lean and agile principles. Adaptive design and engineering practices are key components of enterprise architecture, according to SAFe. *These practices help teams and programs work together on a shared technical vision.* Architects provide strategic guidance, reference architectures, and technology standards to these new agile organizations. When they are combined, they facilitate the standardization of teams' work. Reworks can be avoided by aligning projects to company standards and bridging silos.

Your enterprise architecture is the collection of structures and processes that support your organization. It should be flexible, easily extended, and easily evolved over time. Enterprise architecture is all about exploring, identifying, and optimizing an organization's architectural ecosystem. Because of this, enterprise architects should have the ability to work cooperatively and in a collaborative manner, as well as collaborate closely with other teams. With the adoption of SAFe by large organizations, intentional architecture, and emergent design, the need for a better understanding of its key elements is also growing. As enterprise architects interact more frequently with development teams, their roles and practices may change as well.

The topics covered in this chapter are as follows:

- Technology choices and usage
- Architectural strategy
- Exemplifying lean-agile architecture
- Architecting for DevOps and release on demand
- Applying SAFe to Enterprise Architecture and cloud

Technology choices and usage

Gartner predicts that 60 percent of organizations will rely on EA to spearhead business strategies for digital innovation in 2023. The use of EA in plan, design, and analytics is already widely adopted by businesses today. A company's business portfolio can be expanded through EA, which enables IT and business to merge together. With EA's data management, businesses can predict future models and, as a result, increase profitability while reducing costs.

Over the past decade, the industry has developed various trends, architectures, languages, and tools. Because of that, there are many emerging JavaScript frameworks today because technology changes at such a rapid pace. It appears to be more difficult than ever for architects to choose a technology, whether it is a library, framework, programming language, or vendor product.

It is also common for enterprises to hire consultant architects when internal architects cannot reach a consensus. Technical architects are needed by companies with many products, projects, or entire lines of business. Most of the time, making a decision that affects multiple teams will prove challenging. There is a risk that it could become highly politicized, especially when selecting vendor products. An enterprise may need to even issue a **request for proposal** (**RFP**) to get vendors to respond in such a scenario. Multiple entities provide points to be considered in the selection of technologies during an exhaustive selection process. A strong understanding of why certain decisions are made, as well as why those decisions will benefit the work, is crucial for architects. In the following list, several high-level issues are discussed. Different organizations have different definitions of digital transformation. However, it generally involves the following:

- Evolving technology trends (i.e., cloud services)
- **Artificial intelligence** (**AI**) and **machine learning** (**ML**)
- Advanced analytics and big data
- **Internet of things** (**IoT**)
- **Robotic process automation** (**RPA**)

Planned strategic action has always been essential to business success. As we move further into the digital era, it has become more critical than ever to plan for this transformation. By implementing transformation, organizations become more agile and dynamic, enabling them to respond to market changes more quickly. Companies can adapt to fast growth using cloud-based offerings such as **Software as a Service** (**SaaS**) and implementing AI and RPA. As most projects need to move at a much faster pace, digital transformation offers great help in this regard to the EA facilitators.

Assigning application components to technology architecture represents the association of software/ hardware components. Assembled and configured, they form the enterprise's technological infrastructure, which is largely procured in the marketplace. By examining the technology architecture, you can see how individual application components will be realized and deployed. It is possible to study migration problems at an early stage that can develop between different stages of the Information Systems evolution path. The purpose of technology architecture is to solve logistical and location problems related to hardware and IS management. Also, a well-designed technology architecture ensures that components of the delivered application integrate seamlessly.

Adopting scaled agile in technology domains

In development value streams, specialized teams in software, hardware, electrical, electronics, and other technology areas drive the development of operational value streams. They contribute to the definition, development, testing, and deployment of solutions to internal and external customers. The right products for the right customers are created by using customer-centricity and a design thinking approach, and agility provides the flexibility to address market changes and emerging opportunities rapidly.

There is a long tradition of embracing agility in the software industry. In fact, SAFe offers practitioners the flexibility to deploy it at any level of enterprise scalability. Our advanced interests or value areas include **behavior-driven development (BDD)**, **test-driven development (TDD)**, agile testing, refactoring, and spikes. Scaled agile software architecture combines values, practices, and partnerships focused on supporting evolutionary design and architecture. DevOps embraces the philosophy of continuously updating a system's architecture over time, while simultaneously supporting the needs of its users. The **Big Up-Front Design (BUFD)** and phase-gate processes entail a high amount of rework and redesign, which results in delays.

Agile development practices are supported by an agile architecture that encourages collaboration and design simplicity. Agile architectures also enable testing, deploying, and releasing capabilities, just as Agile development practices do.

Applying SAFe to hardware

Cyber-physical system builders will be defined by hardware innovation for the next decade or more, and those who don't develop hardware quickly are at a competitive disadvantage. In order for developer changes to be verified, the larger context of the system must be taken into account. Physical parts created during hardware development have high material costs and long lead times. In this case, hardware verification often takes place later in the product development cycle.

The first step in hardware development is to develop models using design tools (e.g., electrical and mechanical CAD). Virtual models are now being used by many organizations for analysis and simulation to provide early feedback in a bigger system context. Prior to manufacturing, engineers can ensure their designs are compatible with stakeholders and validate them with stakeholders. Physical parts can only be used to verify some aspects of a design.

For early feedback, additive manufacturing and 3D printing are already widely used. As well as being used for production parts, they can be used for innovation when higher change frequencies are required and lower volume is necessary. It may also be possible to accelerate manufacturing times by reducing quality and reliability constraints. In contrast to production parts that withstand a harsh environment for years, development parts often operate in a controlled environment and are replaced after the next revision.

A vital aspect of system design is allocating functionality to various elements. With the advent of over-the-air updates enabled by growing network capacities and costs, behavior is rapidly shifting to programmable components. Small changes are tested, integrated, and validated in a context before being delivered using continuous integration. The development of hardware functions begins with virtual designs. As a result of automating continuous integration activities, developers get faster feedback on changes in these environments. In addition to building the system, developers must build a continuous integration environment.

Balance intentionality and emergence

In the early days of architecture, traditional approaches were followed, lots of documentation was generated, and unvalidated decisions were made. Combining intentionality and emergent design is another solution for aligning architecture with business needs. Developers create a system so that they can see what works before the architecture emerges.

Intentional architecture

This defines an architectural strategy and initiative that are meant to be purposeful and planned. They provide guidance for synchronizing the design and implementation of inter-team solutions, as well as improving performance and usability.

Emergent design

This implements a fully incremental and evolutionary strategy. As a system is built and deployed, developers and designers can respond to the needs of users in real time. With this balance, agile architecture can address enterprise solution complexity with a lean-agile approach. As well as supporting current users, the system has evolved to address future needs. Collectively, emergent design and intentionality provide the technical foundation for future productions of business value that continually build and extend the architectural runway.

It is impossible for an organization's value to flow through its functional silos. Most work has been structured according to functional skills. A rocket nozzle, for example, would have a mechanical structure that is made up of hardware, firmware, and software. According to the traditional method, each would be independently developed. In order to verify and validate, all components must be integrated together at the end, making adjustments very difficult. Agile development organizes cross-functional teams to increase collaboration and minimize delays:

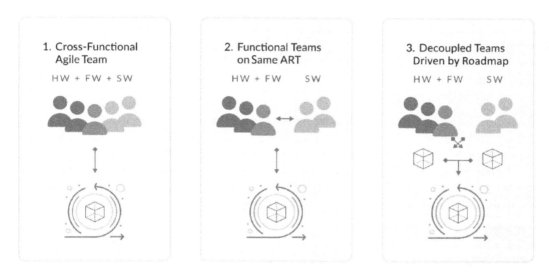

Figure 7.1 – Team structure

The acronyms in the preceding image are as follows:

- **HW – Hardware**
- **SW – Software**
- **FW – Firmware**
- **ART – Agile Release Train**

Three equally viable approaches are shown in the preceding figure, as well as the circumstances in which they are most useful. A creative environment may not require the collaboration of an entire team, and the domains may work independently. However, the teams are aligned by working together as part of the same ART and by managing dependencies and implementing SAFe practices to integrate frequently. Predictability is higher in other environments. Using a common roadmap that defines key integration points, the teams can work independently on their system components. These teams are not necessarily on the same assembly reference template, and the organization may evolve over time. Nonetheless, early product development requires more comprehensive feedback.

Agile teams utilize cross-functional skills to maximize value at every iteration. Mechanical engineers can update firmware, or software engineers can modify CAD designs and rerun analysis tests. Deep functional skills are unfortunately not rewarded in many organizations. By using Agile methods, the skills required to build innovative products are broadened while not sacrificing expertise.

Architectural strategy

Enterprise architecture involves configuring computing resources to serve a company's business objectives. Aligning the company's strategic goals with its existing business processes, the data and information it generates, and the supporting infrastructure are key components of the success of this process. By producing such a report, a company's current technology is noted, along with how future technologies will change or fit into the current technology.

In most cases, business changes are also technology changes in the age of digital transformation. Enterprise architects are also finding that the strategy and change planning process itself has a lot to gain from the enterprise architect's toolbox. A key role in the development of strategy and execution of those initiatives can be played by the enterprise architect's capability to build models and use those models to generate actionable insights. Even though conventional planning processes do not include those models, they force much greater levels of communication than conventional processes.

It's imperative for EAs to understand the source of their value if they are fortunate enough to be selected as a planner. Therefore, you should work in conjunction with the business strategy teams and the **Project Management Office** (**PMO**) teams rather than competing with them. Turning an idea into a comprehensive EA strategy takes time and a lot of conversations. As technology progresses and priorities change, the journey of the EA will evolve and mature over time.

Solutions architecture strategy

It is important for each new IT project to have a solution architecture that enables the business to implement technical solutions in line with its IT strategy, focusing on a specific set of business needs. Solution architects conceptualize the ideal solution based on a particular problem while considering all functional and non-functional requirements. Organizing and managing technical teams can be improved by establishing clear guidelines. Solution architects play a crucial role not only in collaboration with development teams but also in the broader enterprise. The EA transforms strategic visions into actionable solutions, so working with them is vital:

- Solution and EA focus on different tasks, regardless of their interdependence and ultimate goal – that is, to create more value for a business through the intelligent use of technology. EA, as its name implies, presents a comprehensive view of the enterprise, including all business entities and their relationships with technology and applications. Applications life cycles and the definition of IT strategies are key concerns for EA.

- In addition to minimizing costs, eliminating redundant technology, and managing the impact of a digital redesign, these strategies are designed to reduce risks as well. For a target architecture to be successful, it must be understood at the level of an entire organization. A company's EAs must keep an in-depth view of the organization, so their attention to detail is rather limited. The technical side of IT infrastructure is thus less significant to them.

- The EA usually handles technical questions, but the solution architect performs specific tasks as well. Neither of them is directly responsible for implementing new IT solutions. Their role is to ensure that the technical architects can properly implement them. Both solution architects and EAs share similar responsibilities. In contrast to EA, solution architecture focuses on detailed designs.

- Technical architects and EAs work together in synergy to create a successful enterprise vision. In order to maximize a company's ability to generate value through its use of technology, these two elements are essential. Despite the fact that enterprise and solution architects have overlapping responsibilities, their functions differ, and they rely on each other.

Basically, EAs develop abstract strategies that are later taken over by solution architects to be turned into actual solutions.

Infrastructure strategy

In the architecture field, infrastructure is a term that people use to describe a wide variety of things. Infrastructure architecture is a defining concept for facilitating *boundaryless communication* across an enterprise's scope. The content of e-services will expand with the progress toward e-service aggregation.

A thorough and strategic EA review is vital to the success of any system on the roadmap for core systems. Ideally, a well-designed enterprise infrastructure strategy will outline the key systems to achieve the company's business objectives and determine its success. Without careful consideration of the reality, you can get swept up in the possibilities of what could be built. Most IT and infrastructure strategies have what is called the *ivory tower* approach – when the EA introduces everything they add to the architecture review. From a practical standpoint, it fails to emphasize everything that teams should do. Enterprises reviewing systems for critical path applications benefit greatly from taking a far more pragmatic approach.

Additionally, infrastructure applications may include data that is common or shared. Business architecture also includes elements that are common across organizations, such as business principles, common business processes, and so on. TOGAF's **Architecture Development Method (ADM)** is meant to address architecture domains that are orthogonal to infrastructure architecture. Infrastructure architecture is not explicitly identified in the **ADM** description. Still, such a setup is perfectly viable with the ADM. Here is a brief overview of how the ADM was used to create an infrastructure architecture.

Implementation strategy

In order to achieve the business goals and objectives set by the EA program, the architectures created and maintained by the program must be implemented. Regardless of whether the solution is being purchased or internally developed, these architectures will be an invaluable tool for implementation teams. Both the business and technical components are involved in the implementation, and the architecture acts as a guideline to ensure that the implementations align with enterprise-wide initiatives. In addition to formal guidance, regular meetings through the PMO will likely be a regular part of the process.

A centralized repository for architecture and implementation models enables traceability between the two disciplines. It makes EA ideally positioned to provide guidance and governance. There can be an application of principles at an implementation level, demonstrating the importance and applicability of the principle. To implement the target architecture aligned with the plans and schedules defined in these offices, the architecture program must work closely with the project management offices. In addition to the oversight of implementation projects, the architectural office coordinates plans with the PM offices to schedule and carry out their architectures.

Executive support is essential for a successful EA program. In order to do so, they must understand the strategic importance of the project. A program like this can provide a lot of value to an organization. EA must have access to all divisions and the entire organization if these programs are to be effective. Creating and managing EAs can be done using an architecture framework. The architecture repository stores the content, and the architectural team is organized, including guidance on creating architectural design and governance over the construction.

EA is a powerful platform that provides all the features necessary for creating and managing architectural frameworks. A repository for architectural content is incorporated into EA and used to store architectures at multiple levels across the business domains. As a tool with powerful features designed by practitioners, it provides executives, managers, and operations managers with content and views they will appreciate. As a result, EAs can imbed content from a variety of sources, allowing architects to reuse content from other tools.

Architectures are developed according to a process or method. Many frameworks do not provide a predefined process. Organizations are responsible for creating and configuring their own processes. Through EA, processes can be specified at any level; hence, more granular aspects of the process are discussed. Input and output critical to architecture are stored in the architecture repository. Architectures, their components, standards, references, principles, governance registers, and so on are included in this activity. EA is a fully featured architecture repository regardless of the Architecture framework that is being used. Its powerful features offer a number of options for creating a program efficiently, importing content, defining viewpoints, generating publications, and so on.

Common challenges when establishing an EA strategy

Creating an EA strategy comes with a variety of risks and challenges. Technology changes so fast that even entire methodologies, systems, and applications can become obsolete in a short period of time due to how quickly technology develops. In combination with a tendency to follow the latest trends, the EA model is particularly prone to becoming outdated. This is especially true when a standard version is in place.

The EAs in this situation are constantly playing catch-up, and the strategy never delivers its full benefits. It is not uncommon for architects to be considered people out of touch with reality, as business teams often are. Developers are often not convinced that documentation is necessary. EA plays a critical role in achieving both short- and long-term business goals, so technology executives must continually promote its strategic importance. Furthermore, ensuring that documentation is operationally accountable is key.

Operationalizing the EA strategy

As a company grows, its EA strategy must translate business vision and strategy into effective business changes. To achieve this goal, we need to develop, communicate, and improve the primary requirements and the strategies that are set out for the enterprise's evolution. During the process of strategic planning, an organization defines its strategy, or direction, and then decides how to allocate capital and people to pursue that strategy. In order to accomplish goals, EA planning must be linked to strategic planning. Without strategic planning, neither will be successful. By using roadmaps, business architecture strategies address any barriers that are in the way of achieving the desired state. To implement any transformational change at any level of your organization, you need an EA strategy and business architecture strategy.

Exemplifying lean-agile architecture

Business needs and opportunities require architecture to evolve. The technology-centric approach to business execution otherwise becomes a bottleneck. As a result of changing business strategies, modified strategic themes are translated into new solutions and value streams. This process is supported by EAs who provide input and set expectations on technical feasibility. Architects collaborate with solution and systems architects to meet the new business goals once the new direction is decided. The updated strategy outlines how vision, intent, and roadmaps are changed. Additionally, EAs ensure that solutions and values streams align across the portfolio. Their role is to provide long-term guidance for the development of the portfolio solutions set's technologies and platforms. To ensure that the large shifts in technology remain aligned with business strategy, they often function as epic owners for portfolio-level enablers.

An agile architecture supports cooperative, active design and evolution of a system with a set of practices, values, and collaborations. As a result of this approach, a system's architecture can evolve continuously over time while meeting current requirements, embracing the DevOps mindset. Phase-gate processes and BUFD avoid the overhead, delays, and large-scale redesign associated with start-stop-start methodologies. In agile architecture, the design process is collaborative, emergent, and intentional, and design is streamlined. Design for testability, deployability, and release ability is an integral part of agile architecture, much like agile development practices. Decentralized innovation, rapid prototyping, and domain modeling accompany this principle.

Architecture influences the organization's ability to meet its objectives through frequent, independent releases. The architecture is optimized to enable a seamless end-to-end value stream by agile architects. Consequently, the company can continuously deliver value within the shortest possible time frame. The agile architect is motivated to ensure that the architectural runway is just enough to support a growing business. Legacy modernization initiatives are continually developed and know where to refactor to get rid of bottlenecks. Business requirements are clearly communicated through these initiatives.

Balance intentionality and emergence

Early architecture was heavily influenced by traditional architectural approaches. As a result, there was a significant amount of documentation and unsubstantiated decisions. In order to design architecture that is aligned with the business needs, architecture is created as developers experiment with the system. A balanced approach to agile architecture is as follows.

Intentional architecture

The architect defines the strategy and initiatives that are to be implemented in a planned, purposeful manner. They are instrumental in optimizing performance, usability, and design. Also provided are guidelines for synchronizing team designs and implementations.

Emergent design

Contains all of the technical bases for an evolutionary and incremental implementation approach. As systems are built and deployed, designers and developers are able to respond to immediate user needs. Agile architecture addresses the complexity of building enterprise solutions with a lean-agile approach, combining these two approaches. As a result, the system meets both current and future user needs with ease. Combined, emergent design and intentionality build the architectural runway, enabling future business value to be created.

SAFe, for example, provides a scalable agile framework for applying lean and agile principles to large organizations. EA is an element in SAFe that fosters adaptive design and engineering practices, as well as driving programs to rally around shared visions. It is the EA's job to provide technology standards, recommendations, and strategic guidance to ensure standardized development practices. In this manner, reworks can be avoided that may result from mismatches with company standards, and silos can be broken down.

A growing number of large organizations are embracing this framework, which integrates concepts such as an architectural runway, intentional architecture, and emergent design. The role of the EA will change to be able to communicate better with development teams. Further, we will look at how EA can adapt to these agile organizations.

SAFe and business architecture

A value stream is a method for satisfying customers that are incorporated into the business architecture. Organizations can create products that will generate value for customers based on a product-centric approach. As defined by SAFe, operational value streams are those that provide end-user value.

Identifying the required or missing business capabilities is determined by linking them to the stages of the value streams. A company's EAs assess business capabilities based on their value to customers, their complexity, and their alignment with strategic goals. The alignment of agile development with strategic goals is also made possible by linking business capabilities to user stories.

SAFe and the architectural runway

Architectural runways are a key component of the SAFe framework. Program increments are measured in the SAFe framework over 8 to 12 weeks. A runway can be extended by utilizing enablers in order to support future business functionalities.

Implementing infrastructure, complying with regulations, and developing architecture are enablers. Ensuring that the business features developed for the next program increment land correctly is their responsibility. Thus, the term "runway" refers to the runway on which a plane lands. An EA creates enabler epics that contain information on the application architecture, infrastructure, and technology recommendations. We put them on a kanban board so that they will be implemented by the development teams.

Intentional architecture versus emergent design

As development moves quickly, agile teams must design the architecture that will help them achieve their goals, according to *"the best architectures, requirements, and designs emerging from self-organizing teams."*

Emergent design is a result of spontaneous engineering solutions. Patterns, principles, and trade-offs shape the evolution of software. EAs, however, create intentional architectures. A high-level, plan-based architecture is intended to align cross-team roles. That is what a foundational enabler is. To follow the changes that occurred during the development process, the intentional architecture must be reconciled with the emergent design.

The evolving role of EAs – determining the best way to interact with development teams

EAs should be business partners who coordinate and integrate regulatory policies and regulatory constraints in agile environments. By collaborating closely with development teams, they build the architectural foundation for agile development. In addition to facilitating the adoption of agile practices, they determine when emergent or intentional design is most appropriate.

Evolution of the EA practice in agile environments – giving more power to local teams

The gap between the objectives of the management team and the objectives of the agile team, as described in the *The five trademarks of agile organizations* article by *McKinsey*, is the key to changing from a traditional top-down organization to an agile one.

Traditionally, managers enact what needs to be done by telling their employees what they are supposed to do. Customers must be delighted by agile organizations. In an iterative and self-organizing fashion, work is done by self-organized teams and customers are consulted directly. Transparency and continuous improvement are considered the most significant values. Under this new approach to EA, centralized management will give way to decentralized management, and local teams will have more control. Enterprise governance teams provide direction to the entire organization at the corporate level.

In addition to identifying enterprise governance objectives and regulatory constraints, the enterprise governance team assesses and plans future business capabilities. This is done in order to improve security and bring about economies of scale.

A successful agile architect should adopt these strategies and practices:

- **Define the architectural vision**: Architects work with business and strategic goals to define the architectural vision. Among the factors they consider are scope and budget, which determine the technical direction as well. A testable and adaptable architecture is designed that is appropriate for the enterprise.

  Aiming for this requires architects to understand stakeholders' goals and constraints, as well as their needs. Architects should be able to model and document architecture and designs while working closely with sprint teams.

- **Choose the right technologies and tools**: Agile enables the teams to select the right tools and technologies. In addition to assisting the team in utilizing them effectively, architects may offer guardrails, recommendations, principles, and constraints. Involving people in decisions and contributing when necessary is something the agile architect should do.

- **Plan for change**: It is fragile, not agile, to have an architecture incapable of handling change. Planning for change, managing change effectively, and understanding the associated costs are the characteristics of an agile architect.

It is not advisable for architects to be defensive of their ideas. They should embrace change and be open to feedback. A designer should, however, consider the impact and cost of a change before accepting it. If necessary, they should propose alternative solutions.

- **Socialize, collaborate, and motivate**: Building relationships with team members is imperative for the agile architect. Agile architects need to be social to be successful. Agile architects, therefore, need to be able to communicate and collaborate within and across teams. In order to understand stakeholders' expectations, requirements, and constraints, the agile architect must communicate with them. Every member of the team needs to be aware of the architecture so that it can be communicated. Having the ability to gain respect and trust from the team members is essential for the success of the agile architect. Collaboration and shared knowledge are crucial to the success of an agile team.

    You do not have to be a problem solver to be an agile architect. The agile architect should mentor, guide, and motivate people so that they can solve problems on their own rather than having the problem solved for them. The architect should collaborate with the team on design decisions. By working together with the team on the product backlog, design ideas will evolve.

- **Lead from the front**: When it comes to selecting tools and technologies, agile architects should serve as evangelists, influencing the team, communicating the design and architecture to the team, and taking the lead when it comes to providing direction to the team. The agile approach deals with uncertainty, change, stakeholder interaction, and risk management issues much more than the traditional waterfall model. Often, they play a number of roles, but they are most crucial to the team's ability to work agilely.

An architect creating architecture and design specifications has no place in the ivory tower. The architect should be involved in the agile process closely, understand the goals, requirements, and constraints of the team, and lead from the front. As an agile architect, you should be capable of delivering value to the business, maximizing stakeholder value, and managing change and complexity.

Architecting for DevOps and release on demand

In the context of continuous deployment, development and operations are becoming attractive approaches to software development. Both teams are more closely connected with each other through this approach. Putting new releases into production quickly is what CD is defined as. With DevOps/CD, architects face new challenges that impact both their design decisions and their responsibilities within their organizations. DevOps and CD adoption can have profound effects on architectural decision-making processes and their outcomes. In order to understand how this can be done, it is important to conduct sufficient research.

According to the request of customers, release on demand deploys new functionality into production and releases it without delay or in increments to them. Release on demand is supported by three primary aspects that ensure that new functionality is continuously prepared and validated in production. For an enterprise to realize the real benefits of agility, it's imperative to release the right value at the right time, when end users are operating the solution in their environment. The timing and nature of product releases are essential economic drivers that should be carefully considered. The goal of CD is to release new functionality as soon as it is developed, allowing users to exploit new capabilities right away. The actual release tends to be decoupled and on demand, occurring for particular users at specific times, when they need it or when it makes sense for the company.

A customer-centric approach is applied when determining which elements of the system to release and which end users to reach out to. Releases should be based on market rhythms and events and aligned with customer time frames. Moreover, specific customer segments should be targeted with new features or the entire system when releasing release elements.

By decoupling releases, business agility is further enhanced, especially for value streams that serve external customers. Promotional activities can be targeted at specific segments of the market. Also, the timing of the solution and the functionality of the sale can be structured with greater confidence.

The four activities of release on demand include the following:

- The release refers to the processes involved in delivering the solution to end users, either all at once or in incremental steps

- Stabilize and operate solutions describe the steps to ensure that both the functional and non-functional aspects of the project are working correctly

- Measurement is the process to determine whether newly released functionality fulfills the intended purpose

- As part of the CD pipeline, this learning module describes the steps involved in deciding what actions to take with the information collected

It is now time to open up the solution to customers once it has been put into production and has been verified as operable. The timing of the release of value is critical, as releasing too early or too late at the wrong time can have negative economic consequences. We will further explore this aspect by digging deeper into the release value to customers approach.

Release value to customers

The product management process includes policies for governing the execution of the product development process. These policies range from automatically releasing qualified code to customers to establishing a more formal review process. If the system is complex, there is a greater likelihood that a manual gate determines the answers to the previous questions (who, when, and what should be released). The release can be accomplished through the following four practices:

- Dark launches enable deployments to production environments without providing end users with the functionality

- In order to facilitate dark launches, developers have implemented feature toggles, which allow switching between old and new functionality in code

- Canary releases allow the solution to be released to a specific customer segment and measured before it is further expanded and released to more customers

- A decoupled release element is one in which the release elements have each been identified separately so that separate releases can be carried out independently

For applications to function properly, development, as well as operations, are essential. During deployment, software components or frameworks are designed, developed, and tested.

Operating a software company includes administrative tasks, services, and support. DevOps architecture can reduce the time between deployment and operation terms by combining both development and operations. This will improve the delivery of software.

Architecture for DevOps

While DevOps is viewed as a framework for building computing systems, it is not an architecture reference in modern computing. Rather than a specific technique or methodology, DevOps is a philosophy that focuses on teamwork, communication, and constantly improving the software. It will ultimately lead to producing better software as efficiently and quickly as possible. DevOps encourages an entire organization to participate in improving their software applications routinely and incrementally.

Agile is also influenced by DevOps. However, the newly developed approach is an improvement over both agile and waterfall development. This is because it requires developers to complete entire projects before handing them over to operations for testing in production. There used to be silos between developers and operations specialists. In order to run the code in production, developers write them while operators run the code as system administrators. Even so, due to breakdowns in communication and inadequate collaboration, things that are supposed to be easy can turn out to be challenging – the communication of customer requests to developers and the provision of clean code to operational personnel, for example.

Build

The total cost of the resources used to fulfill the operations was calculated based on estimates for fixed hardware allocation when DevOps was not utilized. Individual usage requirements were defined in the business strategy to make things flow smoothly. A key feature of DevOps is the use of the cloud as well as the sharing of resources. Builds can be controlled by users to ensure resources are utilized appropriately.

Code

The use of Git and many other good practices allows the code to be reused. It helps write code that meets the needs of businesses, tracks changes, and informs about the reasons regarding the differences between what is actually happening and what is expected to happen. In case of an emergency, the code can be reverted to its original state. Files, folders, and so on can be arranged appropriately to safeguard the code. Reusing them is also possible.

Test

Testing will be complete before the application moves into production. It takes more time to test manually and move code from the input to the output when using manual testing. Automated testing speeds up the deployment process because automating the scripts will remove many manual steps before the code is deployed to production. The time required to test the code will be reduced, and in turn, deployment time will be reduced as well.

Plan

Agile development is an important component of DevOps. It is easier to plan accordingly, as the development and operations teams are in sync, and thus productivity is increased.

Monitor

Any potential failure is identified by continuous monitoring. Further, it assists in tracking the application throughout so that the application is up to date with and in sync with the modern upgrades. Monitoring log data becomes easier with services such as Splunk, where multiple third-party tools enable monitoring.

Deploy

Automated deployment can be achieved by many systems through the scheduler. Cloud management platforms allow users to capture accurate insights and analyze trends through dashboards. They allow them to see the optimization scenario and trend analysis.

Operate

In contrast to traditional approaches, DevOps integrates developing and testing in one workflow. Team members actively participate throughout the entire life cycle of services in a collaborative way. As a result of the collaboration between development and operations teams, a monitoring plan that serves both business and IT requirements is created.

Release

It is possible to automate the deployment of a program to an environment. However, when deployments are made to the production environment, they are manually triggered. In an effort to minimize customer impact, there are a number of processes of release management that frequently use manual deployment for deployment in the production environment.

A DevOps approach tests software updates rigorously before they are released to users, using the appropriate people and tools. This is possible because of several DevOps principles. Cloud-hosted and large distributed applications are developed using DevOps architecture. Using agile development allows integration and delivery to be seamlessly combined as part of the DevOps architecture. Developing, testing, and deploying a product takes longer when development and operations work independently. In the event that the terms of the deal are not compatible, this may affect the delivery schedule. Therefore, DevOps streamlines the development process and allows teams to improve their productivity.

Applying SAFe to EA and the cloud

A business architecture lays out how a company will function. In a similar way to an IT architect, who determines how systems, data, integrations, and resources should be utilized to support an IT organization, business architecture defines what the organization does as well as how the business provides value, what information is needed to conduct business, and what organizations are involved. You will also find information about how the business does its work.

Enterprises can embark on a transformation of their people, processes, and technology by implementing a **scaled agile framework** (**SAFe**: `https://scaledagileframework.com/`) across the entire enterprise, going all-in with **Amazon Web Services** (**AWS**) (`https://press.aboutamazon.com/news-releases/news-release-details/cox-automotive-goes-all-aws`), and evolving to a *you build it, you run it* environment. Companies can build out small teams that use scrum, kanban, or other agile methodologies, and teams can be typically 8–10 people in size to drive ownership and autonomy, very similar to Amazon's two-pizza teams. Implementing a coordinated delivery, operations, and technology strategy allows companies to unify IT and the business by creating a team of product, engineering, architecture, and business leaders at the upper levels of SAFe, resulting in a more transparent and collaborative environment. This model provides connectivity of priorities and gives teams the context as they look to solve customer problems.

Aligning architecture with business value

Technology is an essential part of supplying value to customers in the digital age. Whenever business strategies change, the systems, applications, and technology that deliver those strategies must also adapt. Those who support applications and systems are responsible for any changes to the customer experience. It is the architects' responsibility to ensure those systems are able to achieve current and future business goals in close coordination with business owners and product managers. A portfolio vision, a portfolio canvas, and a strategic theme guide the architecture of the company. Technical investments are set into a portfolio by these constraints, which provide direction, along with an overall context.

In addition to a narrow focus on architecture, EAs should also consider the larger enterprise strategy. Essentially, an end-to-end value stream comprises all the activities that lead to the creation of a result for a client, be it the ultimate customer or an internal customer. It is crucial to identify the stakeholders who trigger and participate in the business architecture value stream. Additional incremental items that accrue as part of the path to reaching the value proposition are also included. Essentially, it illustrates the value sought and received – or, to put it another way, the purpose for which a customer deals with a company.

The operational value stream, as illustrated by the SAFe framework, explains how goods and services are provided to customers. The operational value stream contains the people and systems that did the work, in addition to the systems, flow of information, and material that delivered value to the customer.

In general, value streams align well with business architecture in SAFe. While there are a few semantic differences between the concepts of capability within the business architecture and SAFe, more consideration is necessary. Although SAFe and business architecture concepts may not be misaligned, the specific language used by the two frameworks requires practitioners of both to consider their shared vocabulary with care, especially when harnessing the power of both tools.

Developing solution vision, solution intent, and roadmaps

Using SAFe's solution intent, you can store, manage, and communicate information about the current and intended behaviors of your solutions. It provides a simple but elegant way to capture knowledge. Also, it offers a basic understanding of current and evolving requirements, designs, and intentions. This generally indicates that the solution's primary purpose has been satisfied. Business goals are more likely to be achieved when architecture is aligned with business strategy. By translating strategy into solutions, architects help businesses meet their objectives. Solution vision, context, and intent are the three characteristics of those solutions.

Solution intent is embedded storage of knowledge, providing a single point of truth for all content relevant to the architecture of the system, including requirements, design, structure, behavior, and other architectural concerns. The intent of the solution includes all the decisions, patterns, models, and other technical information required to meet minimal requirements. In addition to system constraints, the solution intent captures **Non-Functional Requirements** (**NFRs**). To ensure quality and compliance, NFRs are regularly tested via automated tests, just like all other requirements. In addition, a roadmap outlines the steps in the implementation of the project. Architects and teams explore technical options while building the architecture runway by collaboratively defining enablers in the roadmap. They provide insight into what they can achieve early in the process. Intentionality and emergence are balanced as teams implement features over the top of the architecture. Each ART is defined by its backlog, which consists of all the work to be done. Product managers and architects work together to prioritize and balance new features with technical work. In addition to predicting technical debt issues, they prioritize architectural runway needs.

Ultimately, the solution roadmap determines the backlog items to be executed and the solution intent. Solution vision defines the purpose and key capabilities of a solution, as well as its non-functional requirements. As teams create backlogs and plan their work using this knowledge and the emerging roadmap, they establish critical milestones and releases.

Preparing architecture for PI planning

The **Program Increment** (**PI**) planning sessions are regularly scheduled meetings that take place throughout the year. A shared vision and roadmap are discussed, and cross-team dependencies are identified for the ART.

PI planning includes the following essential elements:

- You will be required to attend two full-day events every 8 to 12 weeks (depending on how long your increments are)
- Prioritizing the planned features in advance is the role of the product manager
- Development teams are in charge of developing user stories and estimating their length
- **User Experience** (**UX**) and engineering teams validate the planning by testing it in the target environment
- It's all about aligning the teams with each other and the mission
- All team members should attend in person if possible
- Remote participation can be made possible through technology if required

We can never revert to the way we worked before COVID-19. It used to be standard practice to conduct PI planning in person. However, it is now evident that it may not always be feasible to group teams together. It is imperative to make sure that the teams who are doing the work are present during planning, instead of being in the same room. It is, therefore, more critical for teams to be able to plan in real time rather than face to face. PI planning may need to be adjusted in some ways: the schedule, the timing, and, of course, the technological support that is required to support this ceremony. SAFe users who are newly introduced to it should almost certainly begin by implementing PI planning. Due to its foundation, the **Scaled Agile Framework** (**SAFe**) is built upon it.

Teams develop features and enablers as part of each increment. This list of near-term work items is defined and prioritized by architects in collaboration with product management. Through their in-depth data, current features are able to be outlined and sized and their acceptance criteria defined. In addition to the current features, enablers are defined in the backlog for these future features to be explored and gives knowledge, which will ensure their viability. Technical dependencies outside an ART are also taken into account by architects, whether from a solution train or the enterprise, helping to coordinate these activities.

By collaborating with teams during PI planning, it helps reduce the number of discoveries and ensure teams are able to make effective decisions. The process of PI planning can greatly improve the efficiency of large, agile organizations. It is worthwhile to examine some numbers in order to better comprehend the implications. Depending on the size of an organization, there may be between 200 and 300 development teams. Prior to the change in work style, these teams would not have ever spoken to each other (until a critical problem forced them to share information). At first, the alignment would be at the leadership level, and then the information would be passed down by multiple levels of managers, but the team members would not communicate with one another. A constant competition would take place for the best resources, budgets, and opportunities. During this time, there have been a number of projects that clashed – one team would release something, but it would break something in another team. Most of these big businesses have never gathered their teams together to talk to one another on a call or in person before PI planning. In addition to the chance to discuss what's being done, they get a chance to discuss who is working on what. This might be important in a number of situations or circumstances:

- It is extremely crucial to consider how your changes will affect other teams when you touch a system or code repository

- If you need to work on another team's feature first or the other way round, you might have to do some work to facilitate their work

Planning PI enables you to have effective communication among and across the teams. It puts you in a better position to see the bigger picture and has visibility across the board regarding a project or a task. Collaboration comes with the package as well. This allows teams to accomplish tasks more efficiently, deliver more features within less time, and stay within budget.

Coordinating architecture through PI planning

A plan for the next increment is created by the teams during PI planning. As part of the planning agenda, the teams present the architectural briefing. While teams develop their plans during breakout sessions, architects manage the room to make sure the technical work is being planned properly. In addition, they make sure that the enabler work is being accounted for. Any questions or concerns can then be addressed. Architectural and technical issues regarding potential modifications are addressed by architects during the management review. Also, they participate in assigning value to PI objectives together with business owners. Those who support the use of enablers explain, in business terms, how they support the overall goals of their organizations and champion their importance.

Supporting CD through PI execution

A developer's responsibility for enablers is to own the technology and exploration work related to the essential and solution levels, and, as a result, guide the development progress of teams. Attending the sprint planning sessions and/or sprint demos of those teams will allow them to monitor progress, address issues, and adjust directions as needed. In addition, they provide coaching and mentoring to the teams, and respond to problems and issues as quickly as possible so that the architecture doesn't become a bottleneck. At the end of each iteration, architects ensure that enabler work includes the latest learning, runway additions, and any enhancements to the CD pipeline. Architect Sync is used for large-scale solutions to ensure alignment and progress sharing among architects.

Supporting new strategic themes and value streams

Business requirements and opportunities demand that architecture evolves. The alternative is that technology becomes an obstacle to business success. Changing business strategies results in new or redesigned strategies that are applied to the portfolio canvas and result in original or modified solutions or value streams. Business architects assist and influence this process through their input, participation in Value Stream Mapping workshops, and by setting expectations regarding technical feasibility.

Architects of systems and solutions collaborate with EAs to realize the new business direction once it is determined. They communicate how their new strategy changes the vision of the solution, its functionality, and its roadmap. In addition, EAs coordinate architecture activity across multiple business units to ensure alignment between products and processes. Technical consultants may also advise on the non-functional requirements (security, compliance, performance, and so on) of portfolio solutions in addition to provide technical guidance for the long-term evolution of technologies and platforms. In their role as enablers, these workers ensure major technological shifts are aligned with business strategy.

Leading the lean-agile transformation

The development community often respects and holds architects in high regard due to their knowledge and experience. Thus, architects play an instrumental role in any SAFe implementation. Lean-agile architects have the role of leading by example, coaching, and encouraging developers to adopt leaner ways of thinking and operating. As a result, the development community is able to expand its knowledge base and skill set due to autonomy and mastery. By becoming SAFe architects, organizations can learn how to work in a lean-agile environment, participate in developing the organization's roadmap that has been implemented, and accelerate adoption.

Summary

SAFe is among the scaled agile frameworks discussed in this chapter. These frameworks help large enterprises implement the principles of lean and agile. According to SAFe, EA fosters adaptability and engineering practices, and improves program and team coordination. EAs are instrumental in assisting developer teams to work according to standardized standards, providing strategic guidance, reference architectures, and technology standards. Rework may be avoided if the standards of the company are aligned. This also breaks down silos in the organization.

Moreover, adapting computing resources to a company's business needs is an important part of EA. It is essential to align the strategic goals of the company with its existing business processes, the information generated, and the supporting infrastructure to make this successful. Organizations achieve their objectives through frequent releases that are independent of one another. Agile architects use a customized architecture to enable seamless end-to-end value streams.

The next chapter is about cloud migration, where we will explore the journey from start to end. We will also focus on whether it is the right choice for your business needs or not and how adopting agile or SAFe helps in a cloud transformation.

8

SAFe Implementation for AWS Cloud Migrations

In this chapter, cloud migration will be discussed in detail along with other aspects including how and where to start your journey. Also, we'll be addressing whether the cloud is the right choice for you or not at certain points in your business. Additionally, we will shed some light on how adopting agile or SAFe helps in cloud transformation.

In this chapter, we will cover the following important topics:

- Reviewing the current cloud adoption and migration frameworks
- Types of cloud migration strategies
- Other cloud migration strategies
- Cloud-to-cloud migration challenges
- Migrating back from the cloud to on-premises
- AWS cloud migration tools
- Adopting an agile approach with epics
- Guidelines for a successful migration
- Waterfall or agile – which route to take

Things to consider for cloud migration

AWS **Cloud Adoption Framework** (**CAF**) provides a framework to ensure a comprehensive view of the journey to the cloud. It connects the six most important aspects, namely business, people, governance, platform, security, and operations. When attempting a migration effort for enterprises, this framework can help you understand what areas need to be improved. You can move faster and innovate effectively if you combine this framework with agile practices and streamlined cloud migrations. When it comes to large-scale migrations to the cloud, we recommend adopting an agile approach, not just as a discrete activity.

When considering cloud migration, the following three factors must be considered regardless of the type of cloud and service model you plan to use:

- What is it you plan to migrate?

- Why do you plan to migrate it?

- Which methods will you use to move it?

More specifically, what's important is figuring out how the migration process will be conducted and giving enough attention to planning. No matter how effective or efficient the process is, regardless of the high skill set of a team working with dedication toward this migration, there are certain challenges you are likely to face. The best way to deal with them is to prepare for them beforehand. Your cloud migration strategy must include anticipating potential issues. The following sections describe some of the leading challenges that might cause issues during the cloud migration process.

Cost management

Cost savings are offered by cloud computing; however, determining the exact cost can be challenging. Cloud computing expenses are more likely to be underestimated. Be sure to take into account not just the migration costs, but also migration services, potential bandwidth needs, and future recurring expenses. Efficient planning, long-term strategic decision-making, and optimal cloud costs make a world of difference.

Complexity

If you begin to introduce hybrid cloud elements, the public cloud becomes more complex and difficult to manage. The team must comprise people who know their way around cloud migration and are capable enough to manage your cloud. Additionally, they must anticipate, foresee, and understand the efforts that are essential for a successful migration.

Dependencies

Migrations are slowed down and get unnecessarily complicated when application dependencies are involved. However, you can ensure that you're keeping an eye on all the providers by using provider discovery tools.

Legacy applications

The migration of some applications to the cloud could be horrifying for many reasons, with complex setup and an inefficient team being top of the list. In these situations, the reason why you're moving what you're moving becomes of utmost importance. In these circumstances, the best approach is to consider keeping what you have, rebuilding what needs to be rebuilt, and repurchasing what might be valuable.

Database

Cloud computing can take a long time for large amounts of data. Providers can help make the process smoother and more seamless by offering their customers the option to physically copy their data to the provided hardware, which they then ship back later.

Stakeholder support

When it comes to cloud computing, it's crucial to have leaders who are willing to play the long game. As a result, establishing a **Cloud Center of Excellence (CCoE)** is very important, and it can go a long way.

Building cloud fluency

It is not feasible to scale a central cloud team. The goal of cloud fluency is for everyone within your organization to be on the same page. Hence, the need for overburdening translators is avoided.

Reviewing the current cloud adoption and migration frameworks

As per Gartner's report, AWS still holds the leading position in both **Infrastructure as a Service (IaaS)** and IaaS + **Platform as a Service (PaaS)** with a noticeable increase in revenues.

Financial and competitive advantages of the cloud

Those who are not familiar with the in-depth infrastructure of the functioning of AWS might wonder whether there are any reasons for the rapid growth of AWS. Amazon customers can expect to earn a return of 560 percent on their investment in AWS over the next 5 years according to a study based on 10 companies by IDC. A pay-as-you-go IT infrastructure not only offers financial benefits and the ability to eliminate data center costs, but it also offers many competitive advantages for companies. AWS is the main reason why Capital One moved its infrastructure to AWS, as explained by Robert Alexander, CEO of Capital One.

Cloud infrastructure management and migration to the cloud are challenges that AWS has solved by leveraging the most advanced technologies and practices. With Amazon, we can turn a cloud migration process into a digital transformation for businesses, as moving to the cloud involves more than just technology.

Main benefits of migrating to the cloud

In addition to the benefits mentioned earlier, organizations should consider moving to the public cloud for the following list of reasons:

- **Scalability**: Cloud computing scales relatively easily to support greater workloads and additional users than a traditional on-premises infrastructure. As businesses scaled up their IT infrastructure, they purchased and installed physical servers, software licenses, storage, and network equipment.

- **Cost**: Migrating to the cloud can result in significant savings as cloud providers handle maintenance and upgrades. By developing new products or improving current products, they can devote more resources to innovation.

- **Performance**: In addition to improving performance, migrating to the cloud improves the end user experience, too. In a cloud environment, applications and websites can scale easily for more users or higher performance and can be run in close geographic proximity to end users, thereby reducing latency.

- **Digital experience**: You can access data and services from anywhere, whether you're an employee or a customer. This provides modern, flexible tools for employees and contributes to digital transformation and improving customer experiences.

Cloud migration is challenging; according to the article *Almost Half of IT Migrations Doomed to Fail*, 44 percent of companies failed at migration and 66 percent delayed their migration. The CAF has been used by hundreds of companies to migrate successfully to AWS. Cloud migrations are made easier by the AWS CAF. Within the framework, there are six *perspectives* that make up the framework's focus. The focal points are listed as follows:

- **The business perspective**: Your organization's resources, missions, processes, and current state are the starting points. For example, most companies want to maximize business value by leveraging the cloud, not managing a data center.

- **The people perspective**: Cloud migration and management skills are defined within the context of this perspective. There are guidelines for updating organizational processes, training, and communication to support new business processes.

- **The governance perspective**: With consistent IT decision-making and risk management, governance brings IT and business outcomes together. This results in a technology environment that is secure, efficient, and compliant.

- **The platform perspective**: Iterative migration and the management of cloud services are the way to go. An infrastructure must be continuously optimized to stay effective. There is nothing to be scared of when trying new things; if something doesn't work, you can try something else.

- **The security perspective**: In the cloud, security is a shared responsibility. This perspective provides an overview of the skills and processes for developing or deploying resources in the cloud. Compliance requirements, security controls, and resiliency requirements must be aligned with these resources.

- **The operations perspective**: As businesses become more dependent on the cloud, operations and IT become blurred. In this way, both organizations can gain a better understanding of the skills and processes necessary to ensure the business continuity and operational health of their businesses.

The AWS CAF provides a structure to find and address skill and process gaps, allowing organizations to better understand the impact of cloud adoption on their business. The application of the CAF allows you to have a clear, actionable migration plan and fully defined workstreams to guide the process. Amazon's best practices can give you the edge in accelerating your development and your business.

Types of cloud migration strategies

The three basic types or patterns of migration to the cloud are listed next. They are listed from the easiest and fastest, with some drawbacks, to the most difficult, with greater benefits:

- Lift and shift
- Move and improve
- Rip and replace

Now, let's dive deeper into the types of cloud migration strategies, along with their pros and cons.

Lift and shift (rehosting)

One advantage of lift and shift (rehosting) is that it takes less time than traditional hosting methods. It requires very little refactoring and takes less time to implement. Nevertheless, lifting and shifting could lead to a bare minimum number of changes, so you might not see the benefits you would see by going cloud-native. In the short term, speed and ease could cost you more than a more thorough migration – especially when compared to speed and ease in the short term.

Those organizations that are still far from cloud maturity can take advantage of lift-and-shift strategies to power simple, low-impact workloads. You'll find it relatively straightforward if you already have many VMs. It is even possible to purchase products from vendors that promise to automate your migration. On the other hand, performing the migration manually is a good learning experience. If you've made a lift-and-shift strategy hastily, the good news is that once your applications are running in the cloud, they're easier to rework and optimize.

Move and improve (re-platforming)

While re-platforming, the application is shaped toward becoming cloud-native by making a few cloud optimizations. During migration, cloud load balancers can replace in-VM load balancers in order to simplify the migration process by reducing the number of VMs, configurations, and operating processes that need to be migrated without altering the application. Furthermore, this represents the first step toward cloud-native development for the application. For re-platforming, you need to know more about the cloud, the application, and what's inside the VM. In other words, you do need to have an understanding of the application, but you do not necessarily have to be a programmer. You can probably re-platform if you know how to wire things up, such as a web app to a database – this is normal system administration stuff.

In the case of re-platforming, one of the most common shaping activities is to only move your data to the cloud, not your database. Migrating using the move-and-improve or re-platforming approach involves updating your application to make it more modern, such as by introducing scaling or automating it without ripping it up completely. It might be tempting to assume that this happy-medium approach is the best option at first glance, but you will end up keeping all your technical debt and not benefiting from cloud-native architecture.

Rip and replace (refactoring)

This approach is also known as refactoring or re-architecting, which involves completely reengineering your workload to be cloud-native. The maximum benefits available in the cloud are worth the investment in time and skills development, especially for retraining and upskilling existing talent – making refactoring a positive experience. This is why, most of the time, we recommend adopting the minimum viable refactoring approach. The practice is to make low-risk, low-cost, and high-value changes to an app prior to migration. It enables migration to occur more quickly while taking full advantage of the opportunity.

Cloud-based testbeds can be used to accelerate these improvements before migrating your production apps. A development and test environment can be spun up in seconds, and the environment can be shut down just as easily. In addition, cloud computing allows for greater flexibility in terms of work. Through PaaS and **Software-as-a-Service (SaaS)** solutions, you can connect with powerful solutions with just a few lines of code.

High impact and low effort with AWS-offered refactoring

The five most important minimum viable refactoring activities at AWS are listed next. Despite the differences between apps, these actions typically deliver big rewards with little risk.

Updating the operating system (OS)

Do you receive security updates and patches for your **operating system (OS)**? Unless you do, you should consider upgrading as part of the migration process. As a result of upgrading on-premises, you must purchase new licenses, provision capacity through complex IT procurement processes, test the application, and then perform the migration. There are numerous steps, and the process can be both time-consuming and costly. Because of this, businesses often delay OS upgrades, especially when there are time-sensitive applications that must always run. Performance and security can both be compromised by running on a legacy OS.

An ideal opportunity to upgrade is through cloud migration. It is easy to begin testing your application by spinning up a small instance quickly and cheaply. **Amazon Machine Images (AMIs)** come with many of the Linux and Windows Server OSes already preinstalled, along with dozens of other options. You can test it by connecting Amazon CloudWatch-managed monitoring services and uploading your code. Often, it is not necessary to change the app to move to a supported version. The system can be kept running and tested at a low cost before migration.

With a small team and without a formal procurement process, most application owners can handle this themselves. By compressing the feedback loop, the upgrade process is made quicker and less expensive. There are times when this is not so easy. Usually, there are some applications in a large company that are running on an older platform. That long-running software can be obscure and fragile due to documentation gaps. Here, a cloud-based experimentation environment would be even more valuable. To get it to the cloud faster, you can run it in a container, and then you can continue improving it in a sandbox environment.

Upgrading your framework

Usually, framework versions, such as .NET and Node.js, have an expiration date after which they are no longer supported, and patches are no longer available. This is for logical reasons, as companies need to maintain frameworks for a considerable length of time. Upgrading in-house often involves app surgery and is prohibitively expensive. Experimenting with framework updates is much easier in the cloud. The entire stack can be licensed and deployed without the need for additional data center capacity, as demonstrated in the OS scenario.

The cloud makes it possible to run two versions of the same framework side-by-side in parallel and analyze results to determine what works best. Security groups empower you to ensure that your production network is not affected by the application. By separating your application, you can test it under pressure and figure out how to upgrade your framework in the most economical way. Some older versions of Windows are still supported, and you can upgrade to them. In any case, this approach provides you with quick, inexpensive feedback to identify what requirements need to be met.

Improving security

Having your own data center behind a firewall gives you a false sense of security. Taking your DNS or IP address into the cloud, a local address or DNS that seemed safe in 2004 might become a hacker's entry point in 2020. It is routinely discovered during migrations that there are significant security gaps; in many cases, these are *one-time* exceptions that never get taken care of. Before your app moves to the public cloud, take advantage of this opportunity to ensure adequate security.

Will the data be encrypted in transit and when it is stored on the server? Does the API use modern security measures? Does the DevOps process include security testing? Understand what elements of security your vendor takes care of, what you share responsibility for, and what you must handle yourself. What is the culture of your organization like when it comes to managing security in the cloud? The conversation about the minimum viable security needs to be in-depth before migration, even though you will not be able to address everything.

Optimizing access rights

Security is closely related to identity and access. Technical debt can easily accumulate in these areas, too. In most cases, an application starts in a pristine state, where only a small number of privileged users have access to it.

You will know who has access to your data when you are ready to migrate, so you can choose whom to grant access to. You will have the advantage of no direct access to your data when you use AWS. We manage every access request through a command line or an automation process due to our change management process. Standing privileges do not exist. Permissions are granted or denied in accordance with roles. Additionally, a separate layer of protection is provided by IP masking, between the admin and the instance.

Exploring your database options

A wide range of difficulty levels is associated with moving to a new database on this list. It is also true that the cloud can be an ideal platform for experiments and incremental improvements. It is relatively easy for most organizations to upgrade to **Amazon Relational Database Service** (**Amazon RDS**) with little or no change. Using Amazon RDS, you'll be able to reduce your costs and resize your capacity, while automating a number of administrative tasks such as database setups, patching, backups, and hardware provisioning.

Among the many versions of PostgreSQL, MySQL, MariaDB, Oracle, SQL Server, and Amazon Aurora available, your application should be able to use it. Migrating or replicating data is surprisingly quick and easy with AWS Database Migration Service. When it comes to commercially available applications, vendor support might be the limiting factor. You might see Amazon RDS listed as an option, but Amazon Aurora isn't yet supported. Upgrades to a different database option are much simpler in the cloud than on-premises when your vendor allows it. Cloud-native design principles should be adopted when moving to the cloud if your purpose is to benefit from its benefits and capabilities. While every organization and workload is different, embracing a cloud-native design should be your approach. By making the right move, you can ensure your people possess the necessary skills.

Other cloud migration strategies

Some other cloud migration strategies include repurchasing, driving factors, limitations, and risks.

Do you have a legacy application that you can't move to the cloud? Consider buying a cloud-based product. The following is a list of examples of repurchasing that can facilitate the whole process and provide guiding principles:

- Switch from a self-managed email system to one that provides email as a service.
- An appliance built by the Marketplace vendor replaces a self-built VPN server.
- Use web application firewalls instead of the Marketplace offering provided by the cloud provider.

In fact, building and operating your own email system is becoming increasingly rare. If an email service is currently running internally as part of the discovery assessment, then a recommendation for a SaaS email offering is likely to be the best value.

AWS repurchasing is continuously evolving, and the number of migrations to AWS is likely to increase significantly from the current 5% since this development is opening many new paths to repurchasing. There has always been the option to repurchase applications in AWS Marketplace rather than migrating fragile on-premises products. It is similar to an upgrade process, where old configurations and data are transferred to the repurchased platform.

Now that AWS Marketplace and Service Catalog have been developed, there is the option of renting both appliances and SaaS products. Additionally, you can bring your own license and even work with AWS and the vendor to negotiate complex private offers.

Drivers of repurchasing

It's important to note that the cloud computing revolution is being driven by several important influences.

Consumption-based procurement model

Consumption-based procurement is the preferred model for technology consumers. As a result, they prefer monthly, no-obligation payment plans that effectively link their spending to their personal income rather than three-year capital expenditure contracts.

Retiring legacy "enterprise" software

Enterprise software has lost its status as the gold standard of technology. Due to open source, innovation in software, and its rapid pace, enterprise software is now viewed as outdated, unattractive, and difficult to use. As a result, customers are changing their software stacks more frequently to stay competitive. Enterprises can refresh their application stack in a frictionless manner by purchasing software through cloud procurement frameworks such as AWS Marketplace, which is beneficial to enterprises. By eliminating lengthy, complicated, and expensive software procurement cycles, such as multistage **requests for information (RFIs)** and **requests for proposals (RFPs)**, this process reduces costs.

AWS Marketplace is an effective way to test software and turn it off if it doesn't meet your needs. As a result of migration to AWS, organizations opt to prune down the number of self-designed, self-built, and self-operated applications to reduce costs and improve bottom-line net income.

Benefits of repurchasing

Apart from a few that have already been mentioned earlier, we have jotted down a few more benefits of repurchasing that can transform the organization structure for good:

- **Future-centric**: Modern appliances and cloud-based software should replace antiquated systems.

- **Simplified procurement**: Through one procurement mechanism, customers can purchase appliances, **Bring-Your-Own-License** (**BYOL**) products, SaaS, and private offers.

- **Reduced in-house skills requirements**: It is possible to purchase systems built by specialists with no need for you to hire them. In addition, SaaS applications are run by people you do not have to hire.

- **Reduced effort/faster migration**: When less has to be migrated, the migration program will be cheaper, faster, and less risky.

The risks of repurchasing

There are risks associated with repurchasing. By failing to consider and manage these risks, migrations can be made worse:

- **Integrations and dependencies**: What clients and applications must you reconfigure to use the new cloud service if you replace your on-premises Active Directory system with a cloud version?

- **Procurement friction**: This new way of buying applications might be incompatible with your procurement team and procedures. It is crucial for them to learn four methods: appliance licenses (rented), BYOL products, SaaS, and private offers.

- **Incompatible financial models, culture, and processes**: Are the finances capable of handling future costs that are unpredictable and pay-as-you-go?

- **Incompatible operational models, culture, and processes**: What if operations would like to administer the purchased system? Data and applications are rarely the only factors affecting migrations. People and processes often play an equally important role.

In case of avoiding or ignoring these risks, mismatches might occur when the shiny, new system purchased does not perform as expected.

How to repurchase

A common approach to repurchasing can be summarized in the following steps. AWS Marketplace is a standard approach, but it might need to be modified for different applications:

- Use AWS Marketplace to compare the discovered and known applications.

- Acquire a thorough understanding of current and upcoming licensing and purchasing options.

- Consider the payment, operation, and consumption of the repurchased application.

- Identify any blockers early on as you configure and migrate to the new application.

- Repurchasing the application into a well-designed AWS account using AWS Marketplace is the best option.

- The migration of data and configuration of the application.

- The transition between tests and transition.

Although the AWS platform is a widely adopted solution, sometimes, it needs to be tweaked to suit various projects, applications, and requirements.

What you need to repurchase

Repurchasing is quite different from rehosting and re-platforming. Migrating configurations and data become the only migration activity now. On systems with import capabilities, data migration should be simple.

To make repurchasing successful, you need to have the following capabilities:

- The operation, finance, and procurement on the inside.

- You should involve the in-house application expert when replacing an existing application.

- Hire a partner with extensive AWS Marketplace and AWS Service Catalog knowledge, or train someone internally. Proper navigation and execution require experts.

- There is an organized migration program with repurchasing as a work package, which has a supporting business case, resource allocation, and a timeline.

- There are no standard timelines or budgets when it comes to repurchasing. This is the easiest, fastest method to migrate information, but it varies greatly depending on the software.

When you repurchase, you drop your current system and look for a new one. It's likely you'll discover there are things in your environment that you can do without having to worry about the consequences. Hence, consider the following:

- **Retiring**: Take action. You'll save money, increase security, and reduce the amount of new software your employees must learn.

- **Retaining**: Are you unsure whether you are ready to retire or move to the cloud for something you're not quite ready for? Take a look again later. Sometimes, it might be a wise idea to simply keep things as they are. As we have seen, moving to the cloud just for moving's sake might prevent you from realizing all the benefits that come along with it.

- **Cloud-to-cloud migration**: As an example, moving from AWS to Azure requires moving from one cloud to another. Often, companies fail to consider all the factors that determine a good cloud fit when selecting their first provider. Additionally, a company might only take into account those factors that are essential in the short-to-medium term. However, needs will change over time.

The following are some reasons why companies might wish to migrate to another cloud provider:

- Reduced costs

- Enhanced reliability

- Secure environment

- Greater scalability

- Performance enhancements

- Business changes in which extra cloud features are required

- The current platform is not able to meet business needs

- Integration improvements

When this occurs, a migration from cloud to cloud is the best solution. Even for companies that have previously migrated to the cloud, often, it can be much more challenging. You can prevent these problems from ever becoming problems by solving them before they arise.

Cloud-to-cloud migration challenges

Among the most common challenges that a company might face with cloud computing, some of the leading ones that can be avoided using the right methods are listed as follows:

- **Migrating workloads**: Data, applications, and servers must be moved between cloud providers with precise planning and process. Workloads need to be moved securely between clouds, just as they are when transferring from on-premises to the cloud. Downloading data at a fast enough pace can be a challenge, which can cost more.

- **Downtime**: The risk of downtime during cloud migration is significant. The migration should be completed with data consistency, an examination of the network connection, and preparation for the possibility of downtime during internal applications.

- **Adapting to the new cloud environment**: The majority of the time, a company will build its own applications for a specific cloud provider. There might be some difficulties when migrating to another provider because these customizations might not be compatible with the new cloud. To leverage the new platform's advantages, a company must plan ahead for the time required to reconfigure apps.

- **Budgeting and timing**: Migrations from a server to the cloud, as well as from one cloud to another, should take into account these two factors. During this stage, companies should consider partnering with a migration company because they can ensure a smooth and affordable migration.

Cloud repatriation is the process of migrating applications from the cloud to on-site data centers. De-clouding is also known as reverse cloud migration. A cloud environment differs from an on-premises environment in that the user owns and manages the technology. A cloud solution and an on-premises solution could both use the same technology. However, the way the solutions are consumed is different. On the other hand, cloud users need to rely on generic tools since cloud providers are unlikely to offer specialist equipment.

In addition, some governments require sensitive information to be stored and operated on-site. Cloud providers cannot ensure compliance with security regulations for only organizations in the government, health, and financial sectors. Conversely, cloud infrastructures distributed across many large, dispersed networks provide a greater level of redundancy while allowing organizations to access more computing resources than they otherwise could. Typically, in-house environments are more expensive upfront and more complicated to maintain.

Migrating back from the cloud to on-premises

When it comes to a cloud provider, your options might be limited if they begin charging higher prices. Therefore, including any other factors, this sets the foundation for migrating back to on-premises storage.

Planning your exit strategy

To successfully exit the cloud, planning is essential. Your applications will be secure when they are transferred if you have an adequate plan in place. Make sure you are prepared in advance if you have to leave the room quickly. To build an exit strategy, the following list factors should be considered:

- **Make an inventory**: Make a list of all the assets you own so you don't forget anything. Determine how all the dependencies of your application are distributed within the cloud infrastructure, and where your data is located.

- **Know your SLAs**: When de-clouding or switching vendors, you need to abide by your **service-level agreements** (**SLAs**). Make sure you understand your obligations under the contract.

- **Start small**: Move small applications first and then move onto whole systems.

- **Testing**: The best way to choose your deployment model is to test and retest potential solutions. Perform tests prior to migrating to avoid disruptions.

- **Reallocate resources**: Assess whether you require more resources, an allocation of assets, or a realignment of priorities. Ensure that potential solutions are operationally viable, secure, and long-lasting. In order to migrate to AWS at scale, organizations must travel a path along the stages of adoption. Projects, foundations, migrations, and reinventions are the four stages:

- **Project**: This project evaluates whether or not the AWS cloud meets the organization's specific needs and determines a course of action. It does not require any AWS experience.

- **Foundation**: The organization extends its data centers to AWS. In particular, the organization implements AWS compliance and security models. It creates the initial landing zone framework with the help of AWS migration specialists. Employees receive AWS skills training and cloud-focused training. Applications are transferred to AWS from within the enterprise.

- **Migration**: Organizations prepare for long-term cloud operations at this stage by defining roles in the IT department. Additionally, the CCoE creates a multi-disciplinary team within a company that helps drive cloud adoption efforts across the company and migrates data centers and production applications.

- **Reinvention**: As a result, all projects are now using the cloud. New business models are explored in the cloud, and the organization becomes more comfortable with cloud operations than it is with on-premises operations.

An assessment of the readiness of the organization to move onto the next stage of adoption is the purpose of a readiness assessment. Before you begin the preparation and planning phases of migration, you must complete the readiness assessment. You review your readiness assessment results to understand your current state as part of the agile program described in this guide.

AWS cloud migration tools

How does AWS support cloud migration? Well, the answer lies in the fact that AWS has a wide range of solutions that you can use for cloud migration – many of them free – to get you rolling. Some of the leading ones are mentioned next.

AWS Migration Hub

AWS Migration Hub gives you the tools to accelerate and simplify your journey with AWS by bringing your cloud migration and modernization needs together under one roof. It might be that you're developing a data-driven inventory of existing IT assets or making the case for the cloud within your organization. If so, maybe you're migrating applications to AWS and managing them. Or perhaps you're upgrading previous AWS applications. Migration Hub can assist you with all of these complex cloud transformation projects. With AWS Migration Hub, IT asset inventory data can be stored in one place while migrations to any AWS region can be tracked. If you have already migrated, use Migration Hub to accelerate the transformation of your applications to native AWS functionality. Utilizing Refactor Spaces, you are only charged for the resources you use. Migration Hub allows you to follow the migration progress across AWS solutions, selecting the right tools, tracking metrics, and more.

AWS Application Delivery Service

Enterprise customers can plan migration projects using AWS Application Discovery Service, which gathers information about on-premises data centers. Often, it is necessary to consider thousands of workloads that are extremely interdependent when planning a data center migration. Initial steps in migration include gathering server utilization data and mapping dependencies. AWS Application Discovery Service provides you with information about your server configurations, usage, and behavior to help you better understand them.

AWS Application Discovery Service stores collected data in an encrypted form. This data can be exported as a CSV file that can be used to estimate your **Total Cost of Ownership** (**TCO**) and plan your migration to AWS. Additionally, the discovered servers can be migrated to AWS Migration Hub from which you can track their progress as they migrate to AWS. Get AWS to review your data setup on-premises to plan your migration. All data collected through Migration Hub is encrypted.

AWS Server Migration Service

Migrations to AWS should be done using AWS Application Migration Service. Application Migration Service is recommended for customers currently using **Server Migration Service** (**SMS**). Cloud migration is simplified and expedited by AWS Application Migration Service. By migrating applications without changes and with minimal downtime to the cloud, you can quickly achieve the benefits of cloud computing. When moving large-scale server migrations to AWS, this service will make the process as simple and quick as possible.

AWS Database Migration Service

Database migrations to AWS are made easy with **AWS Database Migration Service (AWS DMS)**. In this way, applications that rely on the source database do not experience any downtime during migration. Data can be migrated from and to the most popular commercial and open source databases using AWS Database Migration Service.

In addition to homogeneous migrations, which include MySQL to MySQL, AWS Database Migration Service also supports migrations between different databases such as Oracle and Microsoft SQL Server to Amazon Aurora. AWS Database Migration Service works with any supported source and any supported target to continually replicate your data with low latency. **Amazon Simple Storage Service (Amazon S3)** allows you to replicate data from multiple sources to build an agile data lake solution that is highly available and scalable. Data can be streamed into Amazon Redshift to create a petabyte-scale data warehouse. Transfer your databases safely and securely to AWS. There is no downtime during the migration, as the source database is functional throughout.

CloudEndure migration

A 90-day free trial of this lifting and shifting solution is available. With CloudEndure Migration, your applications are rehosted on AWS using an agent-based tool. Lift-and-shift migrations can be done without disrupting the business with self-service capabilities and automated processes. The CloudEndure Agent should be installed on the source machine. Applications and data are replicated to AWS's staging area by the Agent. The CloudEndure Agent performs asynchronous, block-level data replication of your source and target environments, so changes from your source environment to the target staging areas can be tracked and migrated without causing any downtime or performance issues.

A self-service web-based console is available on CloudEndure's website for configuring your target environment, checking for compatibility issues, and validating that your apps run smoothly on AWS before you move over. You can rewrite, re-architect, and restructure your applications after you host them on AWS and use the services. Other tools for migrating data include AWS Snowball, AWS Snowball Edge, AWS Snowmobile, AWS DataSync, and AWS Transfer for SFTP.

Adopting an agile approach with epics

The concept of an epic refers to a large body of work that can be broken down into smaller stories, which Jira sometimes refers to as *issues*. Multiple teams can work together on multiple projects, and multiple boards can be used to track multiple epics at once. Usually, a set of sprints precedes an epic. The user stories of an epic will be added and removed as the team learns more about it through development and customer feedback. Essentially, agile epics adopt a flexible scope based on customer feedback and team cadence.

A good epic should provide all the resources a development team needs to succeed. As far as their work hierarchy is concerned, it is the top tier. While understanding how an epic fits into other agile structures is critical for directing the daily developer work, it also provides important context for evaluating epics.

The act of breaking down an epic into smaller pieces makes it easier to understand and maintain momentum, but for a novice, it might seem intimidating. There is no perfect way to create storylines from epics, but we can consider several options:

- **User role or persona**: Every user persona should have its own story. New visitors will be able to log in more quickly, returning customers will be able to log in more quickly, and more.

- **Ordered steps**: Define each step and provide a story behind it.

- **Culture**: Let the team's norms determine whether a story is quick to complete or takes a week to complete.

- **Time**: Set realistic deadlines. Design stories that should be finished in one print.

Neither a big story nor an epic has a universal definition. Generally, it is best to break down any work that is estimated to take weeks or even months, into smaller stories. A project's initial epics are rarely determined by enterprises; however, their definition is necessary. Let us learn how to create your first epic by following these simple steps.

Definitions of an *epic* should be outlined first. Epics are solution development initiatives in SAFe that measure potential **return on investment** (**ROI**) before launching. Additionally, each epic in SAFe can be outlined in an organization's business case.

A similar concept can be found in software projects and programs. To secure funding, both must be economically feasible and evaluated for ROI. A major difference between SAFe epics and other project-based methodologies is that the company creates a new team for a funded project. **ART** (**Resource Tagging API**) can handle epics, with a team of 50 to 125 dedicated to this task.

Portfolio epics and software epics

Software or program epics are derived from portfolio epics, but this is a common misconception. Portfolio epics are actually composed of multiple agile releases (ARTs), whereas program epics are composed of a single ART. The complexity is compounded by the fact that both software epics and portfolio epics are typically collected in one repository called a *portfolio*. The portfolio management team is responsible for creating epics.

Similar to the project conveyor, both kinds of epics go through a Kanban portfolio for flawless execution. According to the ART model, every software epic is an epic. However, only a few can be traced to portfolio epics.

Business epics and architectural epics

Epics in business and architecture are clearly different. Architectural epics add quality to your portfolio and accelerate its value delivery. Business epics improve your customers' experience.

Defining your initial epic

Some of the companies we've worked with did not have clear processes for advancing projects that were yet to be funded. Upon receiving funding, an idea or proposal becomes a project. The fastest proven method for designing an initial set of epics is by converting existing proposals, initiatives, projects, and programs into epics.

In the same way, you can also determine possible ARTs based on this initial process. Rather than creating new teams, consider using existing ones. Your team already has a number of specialists who can serve as your primary resource at the outset of your program or project. In the next section, we will discuss how to apply agile principles to cloud migrations, including preparing, implementing, and tracking outcomes.

Approach

The agile approach to epic management involves starting small: iterating, measuring, managing, and scaling. Large cloud migrations can be prepared and implemented using an agile methodology. This method includes the following:

- Using epics and stories as a way to organize your work allows you to adapt quickly to changes.
- Produce a backlog with clearly defined priorities.
- Your progress should be reported.
- Build a roadmap for connectivity between the stakeholder needs and the technology initiatives to improve efficiency and effectiveness.

Preparation

Here are the steps involved in preparation for migration:

1. Set up two scrum teams of two-pizza-team sizes each. As part of readiness and planning, these teams are comprised of internal resources from different workstreams. The teams are grouped according to their underlying functional/technical roles. The teams work together to drive adoption, enable initial migrations, and set up the organization for enterprise-scale migration:

    I.   Two-pizza team 1 structure and resources: Business case analysis, program governance, people skills, and **center of excellence** (**CoE**)

II.   Two-pizza team 2 structure and resources: App discovery and migrations, landing zone, and integration of security and operations

2. Review the migration readiness assessment results with both scrum teams.

3. Wave 1 migration should involve between 10 and 30 on-premises applications moving to AWS.

4. A backlog should be set up. All workstreams that already have migration patterns should be used to create *pre-baked* epics. Some of the most relevant examples are shown in the following figure:

Summary	Issue Type	Description
App Migration - Wave 1	Epic	As the Migration Program Leader I want to migrate all the identified application for MRP in waves with customers
OI - License Mgmt	Epic	As the Head of Cloud services, I want to manage the licenses of the software effectively so that there are no licen
OI - Problem Mgmt	Epic	As the Head of Cloud services, I want to ensure a problem management mechanism and process in place so that r
OCM - Make it Stick	Epic	As the Cloud Executive Sponsor, I want to ensure key activities outlined in the Mitigation Strategy & Plan are execu
OCM - Enable Capacity	Epic	As the Cloud Executive Sponsor, I want to drive a new organizational culture that produces a return on reward, in c
OCM - Engage the Organization	Epic	As the Cloud Executive Sponsor, I want to ensure alignment and commitment across leadership and key stakehold
OCM - Envision the Future	Epic	As the Cloud Executive Sponsor, I want to ensure Change Strategy, Communication, Engagement Strategy, Training
OCM - Align Leaders	Epic	As the Cloud Program Sponsor, I want to secure alignment of key global and regional/local business stakeholders t
OCM - Mobilize Team	Epic	As the Executive Cloud Program Sponsor, I want a thoughtful, structured, documented approach to delivering cloud
OI - Patch Management	Epic	As a head of security, I need to provide a mechanism as well as ensure that all the application services and the inf
Security - Incident Management	Epic	As an incident response manager, I want to develop and implement an incident response plan/methodology so tha
Security - Data Management	Epic	As a data protection manager, I want to establish and implement an encryption at rest and in transit methodology
Security - Infrastructure Management	Epic	As a infrastructure security manager, I want to implement security and compliance infrastructure so I can have a r
Security - Logging and Monitoring Management	Epic	As a logging and monitoring manager, I want to implement logging and monitoring framework so that I can moni
Security - Access Management	Epic	As the identity and access manager, I want to securely control access to my AWS services and resources for my us
Migration-at-scale Planning	Epic	As the Migration Program Leader, I want to ensure that all prerequisites have been baselined so that the applicati
Landing Zone Setup	Epic	As a CIO, I want to a build a scalable and resilient virtual data center in the cloud so that we can support business
Program Management Setup & Execution	Epic	As the Executive Sponsor (CIO), I want to lay down the foundation for mobilizing my teams so that they are prepa
Business case and TCO	Epic	As an Executive Sponsor, I want to know the migration and run costs in AWS, so that I can generate a business cas
Baseline Discovery	Epic	As an IT Director, I want to discover all my infrastructure assets so that I have a complete picture of my current sta
MRA	Epic	As a CIO, I want to a assess my current organizational capabilities so that I can decide if my team is ready for Clou

Figure 8.1 – Prebaked epics to set up a backlog

5. A product owner and scrum leader should be assigned to manage the backlog.

6. Migrate applications in eight two-week sprints.

7. You should prepare a migration plan encompassing resources, a backlog, a risk/mitigation log, and a roles and responsibilities matrix such as the responsibility assignment matrix.

Using the following plan, you can identify the resources that are responsible for each risk that occurs throughout the plan.

Implementation

This is what the migration implementation stage looks like:

1. Plan the sprint schedules with the teams and set the sprint objectives together.

2. Organize sprints 1–8 by dividing epics into stories with acceptance criteria and reviewing epics.

3. Both two-pizza teams should have a daily meeting. Consistent workflows and quick responses depend on this meeting. By facilitating daily stand-up meetings, the scrum leader keeps the scrum team informed about progress in resolving blockers and reports on deliverables.

4. Organize implementation oversight meetings by establishing communications and reporting protocols.

5. Align, enable, and mobilize resources and teams during sprints. Start slowly, create early successes, and work up to your full migration capacity.

6. Build your migration at scale around outputs, best practices, and lessons learned.

7. Use Wave 1 to create agile blueprints for scaling migrations. This will provide a foundation to prepare for and plan migrations.

As you work through Wave 1 migrations, you gain experience and confidence. Additionally, you must choose a migration plan based on your organization's needs, along with the patterns and tools that will be used. This ensures that operational and security procedures are tested. A list of application groupings based on common patterns is also created, using patterns (such as architectures and technology stacks) within the portfolio. Group migrations are then handled in a standardized way.

Value-add outcomes

You can accelerate operations at scale by using this agile model. This agile approach leads to the following value-added business outcomes:

- **Application selection**: Evaluate applications using a 7 Rs migration analysis.
- **Migration wave plan and migration tools**: Prioritize the move groups and determine which tools are available.
- **Landing zone**: Test and deploy various landing zone components.
- **DevOps**: Using DevOps, provide frequent features, fixes, and updates.
- **Automation**: Implement migration tools offered by vendors.
- **Migration patterns**: Refer to the Prescriptive Guidance catalog for the available patterns.
- **Design architectures**: Plan, design, and create migration targets for the servers, data, and applications.
- **Training tools**: Provide resources with hands-on training on AWS.
- **Operational runbook**: If you're running applications on AWS, monitor and report on them.

Lastly, establishing plans and schedules for migrations are essential along with coordination and resource allocation, identifying issues and risks, and communicating them.

Guidelines for a successful migration

In this section, there are guidelines that are divided into multiple parts to help you plan your migration and to conduct migration sprints.

Planning

In order to migrate resources to AWS, you must figure out how you will migrate them, the tools you will use, and the operating model you will use to maintain, govern, and secure them. Prepare for the migration by following these best practices:

- Identify the key assumptions for a comprehensive wave plan. The number, dependencies, and tools used in each sprint, along with the owner of each sprint, should be identified.
- Integrate account structures, security, networking, automation, and pipelines.
- Preparing the landing zone is essential.
- The migration tools must be selected and obtained.
- Define the processes for change management and impact assessment.
- Decide how you will communicate.
- Establish the production processes and operating models.
- Resources, including partners, must be selected and committed.

Activities

All sprint weeks should be planned in advance. Members of the team should be involved in every sprint week! Bear in mind the following:

- To monitor progress and guide team members, create key metrics. Define what and how each objective should be measured.
- Plan for risks by conducting a premortem.
- Decide how everyone will be kept informed and set a schedule.
- Identify and improve sprint activities by holding an inception retrospective.
- The backlog of products should be reprioritized.
- Plan how you will continue to practice each day.
- Organize a retrospective to identify areas for improvement.
- Stay on schedule at all times.

The sprint, planning, and retrospective meetings should also be set up on a shorter cadence. A two- to three-week sprint offers rapid feedback, allows you to pivot, and creates urgency. The Wave 1 migrations consisted of developing blueprints and building blocks and testing specific migration patterns. Developing a migration factory process and expanding agile models for your entire application portfolio is now your next step as you build a team to support your initial wave of migrations.

Migration factories enable large-scale moves to AWS by paving the way. An efficient migration workflow combines the technical, business, and human elements of cloud migration. Cloud migrations have been disappointing in several cases for their teams. Despite their failures, they stuck with it and improved their results with follow-up attempts. When you're planning to migrate mission-critical applications to the cloud as part of your organization's modernization, you can't afford to repeat mistakes made by others. To maximize your chances of successful cloud migration, this post uses those learnings to craft a 10-step checklist of the most important factors you need to consider. The following sections are the components of the cloud migration checklist.

Step 1 – establishing the migration-architect role

You should establish the role of the migration architect before you begin your cloud migration. Migrating architects play a pivotal role in planning, implementing, and closing out all aspects of migrations; their primary responsibilities include defining the refactoring strategies necessary to facilitate migration success, developing the migration strategies for data migration, defining the cloud-solution requirements, and determining the migration priorities and switchover mechanisms.

When a migration project is large, there are many technical decisions to make, and the presence of a migration architect who can address all of the aspects of the project is essential to the success of the project.

Step 2 – choosing your level of cloud integration

A shallow cloud integration or a deep cloud integration can be used when moving an application from a data center to the cloud. When you use shallow cloud integration, you move the on-premises application to the cloud without changing anything about the servers you use to run the application in the cloud. It just takes a few changes to make the application run in the new environment. The services are not unique to the cloud. Lift-and-shift is another term for this model, in which the application is transferred to the cloud intact.

You modify your application to take advantage of key cloud capabilities during the migration process for deep cloud integration. A serverless computing capability such as AWS Lambda for portions of the application might be as sophisticated as auto-scaling and dynamic load balancing. Using a cloud-based data store such as Amazon S3 or DynamoDB might be another option.

Step 3 – choosing a single cloud or going multi-cloud

If you plan to migrate your application to the cloud, you should ask yourself the following question: are you planning to run your application on a single cloud provider, or are you planning to run it on multiple providers? Cloud provider-specific application optimization is relatively straightforward. You only have to learn one set of cloud APIs, and your application will be able to take advantage of all the features the cloud provider has to offer. This approach has the downside of vendor lock-in. Your application might require just as much effort to migrate to another cloud provider when you have already updated it to work with that one provider. Furthermore, you might not be able to negotiate key terms with your cloud providers, such as pricing and SLAs, if you have one cloud provider.

A cloud contains one application, and another cloud contains another application. Using multiple clouds might seem straightforward at first; one set of applications runs in one provider and another set in another. The advantage of this method is that you can leverage multiple providers to increase business leverage and flexibility when it comes to where to put new applications. Additionally, the applications can be optimized for the provider on which they run. Using multiple cloud providers can help you scale your application. Several companies choose to run parts of their applications with one cloud provider but others with another. It allows you to take advantage of the key advantages that each provider offers. In this situation, your application might be impacted by either provider's performance, and any issues with either provider could affect the customer experience.

Cloud-agnostic development is crucial to your application's success. Those who do not adopt cloud-agnostic development risk losing their customers. Your application could be run simultaneously across several providers, or the load could be shared among them. The model makes it easy for you to easily switch the load between different cloud providers, giving you the best flexibility when negotiating with vendors.

Step 4 – establishing cloud KPIs

An application's **key performance indicators** (**KPIs**) relate to how the application or service performs relative to the expectations you have for it. Your applications and services might have already been assigned KPIs, but are they still the right ones when they are cloud-based? KPIs are the most useful for understanding the progress of your cloud migration, highlighting any problems that you might not have noticed. A cloud migration KPI can determine when migration is complete and successful, which is perhaps the most important factor. Cloud migration KPIs can be divided into several categories:

Category	Sample KPI
User experience	Page load time
	Lag
	Response time
	Session duration
Application/component performance	Error rates
	Throughput
	Availability
	Apdex
Infrastructure	CPU usage %
	Disk performance
	Memory usage
	Network throughput
Business engagement	Cart adds
	Conversions and conversion %
	Engagement rates

Assess the importance of each category to your business and determine which metrics will be affected the most by the cloud migration. Using tools such as infrastructure monitoring, you can then track what is happening.

Step 5 – establishing performance baselines

Baselining involves measuring the current performance of your service or application and determining if its future performance is acceptable. Based on your baselines, you can determine when your migration is complete and how much you can improve your performance post-migration. As you migrate to the cloud, you can also use baselines to diagnose any problems that occur.

Each key performance indicator should have a baseline metric. Set the timeframe for collecting data to establish the baseline. Short baseline periods allow you to move more quickly, but they do not give you a representative sample of your performance. In terms of time, a longer baseline period results in more representative data, but it takes more time.

Additionally, you should decide whether you will only collect average or representative baseline data, or if you will include data collected during critical or peak periods. Would you like to collect information over a day with a big news event if you're a news site, or would you prefer to avoid such days? You should clearly define what types and duration of data you're going to collect, regardless of which data-collection model is appropriate for your industry.

Step 6 – prioritizing migration components

Aside from migrating your entire application to the cloud at once, you must also decide whether to migrate the application component by component or service by service. Determine which services are dependent upon which other services, and which services are connected to which others. Consider using an application performance monitoring tool that can create dependency diagrams from service maps for larger, more complex applications.

Determining which components and in what order to migrate requires the use of the dependency diagram. Usually, the services with the fewest dependencies are the best to start with. As a result, you would migrate your innermost services first, and then the outermost, which are usually the ones your customers have access to. As an alternative, you might want to begin with the most critical outside services closest to your customers, so you can control any effect on them.

Step 7 – performing any necessary refactoring

If you want your cloud-based applications and services to work as effectively and efficiently as possible, you might need to make some other changes to your applications and services beforehand. If so, you should refactor your application:

- This allows you to dynamically scale your service using a variable number of running instances, potentially saving you money.

- By doing so, you will be able to take greater advantage of cloud technologies, such as dynamic allocation and de-allocation of resources as needed, instead of static allocation in advance.

- Consider moving to a service-oriented architecture before moving individual services to the cloud so that the migration is easier.

Step 8 – creating a data migration plan

Cloud migration is notoriously complicated, especially when it comes to migrating data. It's important to understand how data location impacts your application's performance. Adding cloud-based data access when the primary access method is still on-premises can affect performance tremendously. Additionally, data can reside on-premises or in the cloud, depending on which service is accessed.

You can migrate your data using the following options:

- Integrating your on-premises and cloud databases with a bi-directional synchronization mechanism. The on-premises database should be removed after all consumers of the data have been moved to the cloud.

- Implement one-way synchronization between an on-premises database and a cloud-based database and allow consumers to only access the on-premises version. Enable cloud-based consumers to access the new database when you are ready to disable access to the on-premises version.

- Data migration services, such as AWS', can be used to move data to the cloud.

Plan your data migration well, and don't underestimate its complexity. It is very easy to fail a cloud migration if you do not follow your data migration plan closely before you begin. In the data migration planning process, your migration architect should play a central role.

Step 9 – switching overproduction

So, how do you move the old on-premises system over to the new cloud-based version, and when? Your answer will depend on the complexity and architecture of your application, as well as how your data and datastores are built.

You can choose either of the following approaches:

- **All at one time**: Ensure that the on-premises stack is running properly before switching traffic over to the cloud stack.

- **Gradually migrate traffic**: Start with a few customers, test to make sure everything works, and then move a few more. Continue moving your clients to the cloud-based application until you have transferred all your customers.

Step 10 – reviewing application resource allocation

There are a few things to consider after you've migrated everything to the cloud. Your top priority should be optimizing resources. In the cloud, resource allocation can be dynamic, so you shouldn't allocate resources statically to utilize the cloud's advantages. Prepare your teams for distributing resources to your application as you move to the cloud. Often, cloud vendors offer additional resources in virtually any quantity at a moment's notice when extra resources are needed for an application in the cloud. Assuming your teams have the application architecture in place to accommodate dynamic scaling, you can usually rely on your ability to scale as needed to meet user demands.

Other considerations for your cloud migration

There are certainly other things to consider during a cloud migration besides the steps mentioned in this checklist. For example, an essential part of any cloud migration is ensuring that the environment is secure and safe. You can build and maintain a secure system using the tools and resources offered by most cloud providers.

Two rules of thumb stand out when it comes to cloud pricing: cloud computing is cheaper than on-premises computing, and cloud computing is more expensive than on-premises computing. Depending on the situation, either rule could hold true. Indeed, cloud computing can increase your infrastructure bill in comparison to your physical data center if you start using it as opposed to using the former. This could be due to a few reasons.

As noted earlier, all infrastructure systems have hidden costs, and you might not be considering all the expenses of running your own data center, whereas cloud providers clearly outline all expenses. There are times when you compare apples to oranges, making the cloud seem more expensive than on-premises.

A cloud-based infrastructure is typically financed by **operating expenses** (**OpEx**), whereas an on-premises infrastructure is primarily financed by **capital expenditures** (**CapEx**). Capital expenditures may be easier to obtain than operating expenses, depending on how your business manages its books. Making sure that your financial models reflect the differences between cloud and on-premises infrastructure is key to being able to recognize cloud cost improvements.

Waterfall or agile – which route to take

There have been significant changes in the industry throughout the years, and in particular, the industries have seen massive progress with endless resources that have been ineffective. A plethora of tools, methods, and experiences have been documented, but the needle hasn't moved significantly. So, how is that possible? With all the tools and methodologies at our disposal, shouldn't we be smarter about managing programs?

Changes ahead

On paper and in principle, yes, but when it comes to large-scale projects, particularly data center migrations and consolidation programs, the outcome has barely changed despite the latest tools and methodologies.

Regardless of all the research and indicators, this is what seems to be the case. In addition, it is well-known that portfolio, program, and project management can work, since certain industries – usually, outside IT – successfully manage projects using best practices, construction, for instance. Developing a plan whose aim is appropriate, practical, and that meets key program constraints such as time and resources is essential to the creation of a skyscraper from scratch.

Planning is everything, the plan is nothing

Here is where things can easily start to go wrong. It becomes difficult for most organizations who wish to work in an agile format to develop a plan with enough detail that represents the actual tasks to be done. However, how can this dilemma be resolved? Creating a master plan, establishing a set of key milestones and deliverables as a governance framework, but letting sub-projects work agile within their scope, is the answer.

Practical application

By the end of the year, the deal was out of control. Many migration plans of different quality levels were available, but no high-level plan matched them up. Essentially, there was no high-level plan, which meant that nothing was clearly understood about what needed to be done, the timeline for completing it, and the dependencies that existed around it.

Our conclusion was that we needed to develop highly standardized migration template plans that cover the phases of preparation and the execution of migrations. Our kick-off session was held after each team was invited, and we explained the concept and determined binding delivery dates based on the template plan. More than 1,400+ applications have been successfully migrated, and we have tracked their progress against the high-level migration plan. For simplicity's sake, we haven't paid attention to how teams track their individual progress; this is so that we can avoid unnecessary paperwork.

One plan to rule them all

As far as the consolidation of data centers and migration programs are concerned, this approach is very similar to what AWS has implemented as part of its migration best practices:

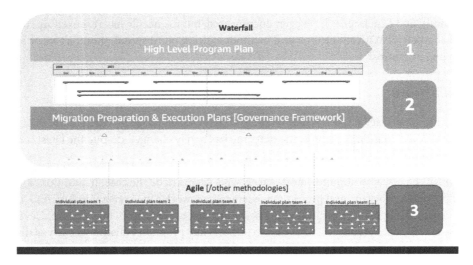

Figure 8.2 – Cloud migration best practices, strategy, and workflow

Overkill

You will face fewer issues during migration phases if you plan ahead and think about potential risks and mitigations beforehand. Of course, it's not an option for businesses to fail during migrations.

Summary

Transforming technology is not the only benefit of adopting the cloud. This framework provides a comprehensive view of the journey to the cloud with the AWS CAF. With the business, people, governance, platform, security, and operations, it connects the six most important aspects of the software. The following framework can be helpful when attempting a migration effort for enterprises. However, it is not without challenges, such as financial constraints, database problems, and dependencies.

Once implemented successfully, the benefits of cloud migration can be highly noticeable, and this includes high scalability, better performance, and an outstanding digital experience. Cloud migration strategies among many others based on the team and organization infrastructure include repurchasing, various driving factors, limitations, risks, and more.

Additionally, cloud-to-cloud migration can bring multiple challenges for unstructured organizations such as downtime, adapting to the new cloud environment, and budgeting. Repatriation of cloud applications to on-premises data centers is the process of moving them from a cloud to on-premises servers. Bringing cloud applications back to on-premises data centers is the process of moving them from the cloud to on-premises servers. De-clouding is also referred to as reverse cloud migration.

In the next chapter, we will dig deeper into the EA enablement readiness. We will focus on understanding the process and flow to establish EA practices, identify owners, and the workflow for each of the owners along with their roles and responsibilities.

Part 4 – Setting Up an EA

Toward the end of this book, we will put all our focus on EA enablement and readiness. Once the need for this cloud migration and a slight but subtle shift in the strategy has been determined, the next step is to understand the process and flow to establish EA practices. We will explain EA modeling languages, which will prepare you to learn about ArchiMate.

This last part will give you a better insight into the basics of EA practices and the way they align with the EA Center of Excellence. At this point, you might wonder whether or not the architectural tools and modeling languages are necessary for EA. Hence, the book talks in detail about architectural tooling with ArchiMate.

We will take a deeper look into challenges and risks related to operations, customer experiences, and the ability to grow, which can help improve the transformation process. Enterprise architects need to keep a streamlined and agile IT environment so that the IT department can run upcoming business transformation projects. In light of that, these chapters impart information on how crucial EA enablement readiness is and what steps organizations can take to facilitate it.

EA promotes consistency across an organization's systems by allowing development teams to work with proven approaches and product lines. Hence, we will establish and determine a foundation that assists in understanding the process and flow by which to establish an EA practice. Further discussed is the importance of EA enablement readiness and the steps that organizations can take to enhance it.

Overall, the primary focus of this last part of the book is on explaining EA modeling languages in more detail.

This part of the book comprises the following chapters:

- *Chapter 9, Setting Up an Enterprise Architecture Practice*
- *Chapter 10, Conclusion*

9

Setting Up an Enterprise Architecture Practice

The success of a company's growth prospects depend on its digital transformation. To make themselves more competitive and relevant to their customers, large companies, in particular, must complete their business transformation through technological change. While more technology-savvy competitors seize market share and customers, they want to seize digital growth opportunities. An enterprise architect's role in transformation is crucial since they have visibility into the entire business process and are aware of how the IT landscape affects business outcomes.

As business changes constantly, enterprises need to easily assess the impact of these changes on the IT landscape, and how they will affect their operations, customer experiences, and their ability to grow. An overview of these issues can boost the transformation process. Enterprise architects ensure that IT is ready to run upcoming business transformational projects by maintaining a streamlined and agile IT landscape.

This chapter will cover the following topics:

- Enterprise architecture practice and the Center of Excellence
- The enterprise architecture approach
- The process and workflow within enterprise architecture practices
- Goals of enterprise architecture
- Benefits of enterprise architecture
- Enterprise architect role
- Enterprise architecture tools and software

- Enterprise architecture practices with roles
- Enterprise architecture practices with responsibilities
- Setting up the Architecture Board
- Operation of the Architecture Board
- Characterization in terms of enterprise segmentation
- Architectural tools and modeling languages
- Full collaboration between IT and business stakeholders
- Recommended steps for adopting an Enterprise Architect Management tool
- Initiating and evolving an **enterprise architectures** (**EA**) practice in organizations
- Developing digital skills

Enterprise architecture practice and the Center of Excellence

By creating an infrastructure used throughout the company, enterprise architects can map the current IT environment. Multiple perspectives can be used when performing the application inventory, such as the application life cycle, costs, deployments, exchange flows, and how they support the business. We add information to the inventory via the data collection and crowdsourcing process in addition to roles, processes, locations, and vendors. The outcome of these steps is capability maps that help fill operational gaps by reflecting the organization's business capabilities. To conduct objective analysis, enterprise architects use the collected data, including **key performance indicators** (**KPIs**) such as life cycle, cost, risk, enabling technology, and vendor dependency.

Additionally, they are going to perform subjective analyses by giving stakeholders automated questionnaires to determine whether the applications they use are efficient, effective, and meet their business needs. Based on importance and value, enterprise architects consolidate scores and cross-reference KPIs. Getting the most critical applications first is imperative to ensuring that the most important resources and investments are invested into those applications.

The enterprise architecture approach

IT portfolios can be standardized so that enterprise architects can avoid obsolescence by using technology architecture management. Technologies are inventoried with vendor and life cycle information (release date, end of life, and so on) that's been obtained from existing Customer Managed Databases and cleansed. A normalization tool can streamline technology names when there are multiple sources of information. A technology life cycle database and technology inventory may also be compiled from external libraries.

After that, they conduct the following procedures:

- Pick the technologies that will be evaluated as standards, based on feedback from developers, architects, and risk managers.

- Decide whether to rate the vendor based on its ability to support applications, its business capabilities, or its vendor dependency.

- Throughout the various stages of a technology's life cycle, its status can be updated:

  - **Envisioning**: Currently, potential applications for the technology are being assessed.

  - **Emerging**: The technology is still under development. The technology has not been widely deployed yet.

  - **Confirmed**: The organization understands the technology and has full access to it.

  - **Obsolete**: Obsolete technology may pose risks. Once the technology has been evaluated, we can determine whether it is compliant with the company's standards and put it in one of two categories:

    - **Approved**: Technologies that meet company policy and are considered standard

    - **Permitted**: Technologies approved by the company

    - **Prohibited**: Technologies prohibited by the company.

The first step to achieving business objectives is to establish clear goals. With support from business teams, enterprise architects can map current business capabilities and analyze how they may change. This helps you understand how a capability should develop in the future or whether it can address a new customer segment or align with the business strategy. Business architects use enterprise roadmaps and timetables to capture and measure current and future business needs. After that, the enterprise architects ensure that the future IT architecture supports business capabilities. By defining business capabilities based on a map of the current IT environment, they can develop a new IT architecture. When a company evolves to meet new challenges, capability maps identify what IT resources are required.

The keys to successful data governance are to define standard data governance processes, share best practices, and document data usage throughout the entire business process chain. Data that's been collected, processed, and managed by a business is clarified and made easier with EAs. Business glossaries and semantic representations of an organization are developed by data architects or data stewards through the EA process. It is possible to create a data dictionary and model existing databases logically. In this process, the consultants discover data from existing sources or data lakes and extract metadata from them to rationalize it. Data dictionaries are then able to connect with business data. Architects can use this information to analyze the impact of a potential change by automating the linkage of data, which allows for business data lineage. Having a consistent representation of their business and technical data helps the company anticipate and manage continuous market changes. Additionally, companies can increase compliance with the following revised regulations by consolidating **general data protection regulation (GDPR)** requirements with EA, such as the California Consumer Privacy Act:

- EAs need to describe how personal data is processed in their applications so that GDPR impacts can be documented.

- Reusing applications developed by EAs support GDPR compliance officers (Data Protection Office) in documenting GDPR processing activities more easily.

- The DPO can access detailed information concerning existing GDPR processing activities by accessing business processes and applications. This information is often presented in the form of diagrams, flowcharts, or detailed descriptions.

There is a common belief that enterprise architects live in an ivory tower and that they are disconnected from reality and are unable to demonstrate the business value produced by EA. Nonetheless, enterprise architects play an important role in facilitating digital business transformation in today's highly disruptive and agile environments.

As a business partner

The benefit of working with agile teams and being a true business partner is that the business partner can highlight trends and provide valuable insight for digital transformation. The enterprise architect makes strategic recommendations as a business partner. Assessing the potential of emerging technologies, assessing the impact of implementing business changes on IT systems, and setting up an entirely customized ecosystem are some of the tasks they perform. They demonstrate the value derived from the connections between people, processes, applications, and infrastructure in their role as a business partner.

The role of enterprise architects today includes doing the following:

- Often, organizations work in silos and lack an overall view as a result of organizational silos. They must bring a strategic vision to these organizations.

- Participate in business discussions to refine its needs, giving examples of how a business capability should evolve over the next 3 years, or whether the company is capable of addressing new customer segments.

- Contribute to a better IT roadmap that improves business effectiveness and efficiency while planning future IT investments in the enterprise.

As a technology trendspotter

Investing heavily in emerging technologies is one of the key indicators of a company's competitiveness. In 2017, Forrester surveyed 105 international technology executives online. According to the survey, 86% of leading companies saw technology as the most influential factor in business strategy. As companies attempt to understand and analyze the impact of emerging and strategic technologies, enterprise architects play a key role. Digital business platforms are defined as a way to deliver value to the modern enterprise by these leaders, who take a hands-on approach.

Trendspotters are enterprise architects since they can see market trends and potential value in upcoming technologies. They primarily deal with new or emerging technologies or those that may disrupt the market. By using the technologies that will move their company ahead of competitors, they help business leaders and IT teams make better decisions. By combining IT capabilities and business strategies, enterprise architects also serve as pacesetters for business transformation.

As an active member of agile dev teams

In agile environments, development happens quickly, and the eleventh principle of the Agile Manifesto empowers agile teams to design whatever architecture is needed. It is known as *emergent design* in the SAFe framework. In addition, some development teams do not have an understanding of organizational business objectives, technical standards, or other architectural projects that are in progress. Using architectures designed by development teams can drive reworks and affect time to market.

An enterprise architect's role as a member of an agile team includes doing the following:

- Sharing the intentional architecture with the development teams and identifying its limitations. Developing teams can then assist in correcting the intentional architecture.

- Using the SAFe framework, an *architectural runway* is created by combining emergent design and intentional architecture. As new epics are developed, enterprise architects must not only keep the architecture up to date but also support new epics.

As an influencer and leader

One of the most influential leaders in an organization is the enterprise architect. As change leaders, they leverage enterprise assets, explore new business opportunities, and leverage emerging technologies. Traditionally, EA has been viewed as a cost center that creates architecture just for the sake of architecture, resulting in a lot of wasteful spending. To move from being perceived as noisy to being truly influential, enterprise architects can take multiple steps to accelerate and elevate their value.

All companies need to approach digital transformation from a new perspective, absorbing best practices that have proven successful over the last few years. Furthermore, it prioritizes EA as a critical component of the business transformation and innovation process. To ensure the success of an organization's digital transformation initiative, an enterprise architect must be employed. Enterprise architects analyze the impact of constant business changes to offer an integrated view of the impact of business digitization, IT strategic planning, data governance, and more.

Digital twin technology and **artificial intelligence** (**AI**) will provide new challenges for enterprise architects since both are expected to accelerate the process of digital transformation. Within this context, EA models will be enhanced (by data mining) by incorporating real data at the business and application levels. By analyzing the data, architects can identify the gaps between theoretical models and the real world and determine the most critical areas where systems can be improved or failed. To accelerate digital transformation, enterprise architects play a crucial role. These experts assist decision-makers in implementing strategic business planning, adopting emerging technologies, improving customer experience, and safeguarding data.

To build digital twins, you must start with a workspace that represents a single work site. A workspace holds all the resources (such as models and visual assets) needed to create the digital twin. Inside the workspace, you can create entities that represent digital replicas of their real-world systems. You can also specify custom relationships between the entities that will form a digital twin graph. Then, you must connect to data from various data stores and add equipment context to the stored data. AWS IoT TwinMaker makes it simple for you to bring this data together without creating another data store and without requiring you to reenter the schema information that already exists in your data stores. To provide context to the data present in the data stores, you can associate entities with built-in connectors to these diverse data stores, such as time-series sensor data in AWS IoT SiteWise, video data in Amazon Kinesis Video Streams, and document data in Amazon S3.

The process and workflow within enterprise architecture practices

The practice of enterprise architect is to analyze, design, plan, and implement enterprise strategies in a way that facilitates business success. Using architecture principles and practices, enterprise architects help companies structure their IT projects and policies to achieve business outcomes and stay current with market trends. This process is also referred to as enterprise architectural planning. EA emerged from various architectural manuscripts and business systems planning in the 1960s, according to the

Enterprise Architecture Book of Knowledge (EABOK). During the 1980s, when the first computers were introduced into the workplace, the EA framework emerged to respond to the increase in business technology. Technology has grown rapidly, and companies have realized that they need a long-term strategy to support that growth.

A modern-day EA strategy encompasses the entire organization, not just IT, to make sure the business is aligned with digital transformation strategies and technology growth. It is especially beneficial for businesses with legacy processes and applications to implement a digital transformation program such as EA since it merges them seamlessly.

Goals of enterprise architecture

Business requirements guide the organization's EA. Among other things, they determine how information, business, and technology flow within the organization. Cloud computing, IoT, **machine learning (ML)**, and other emerging trends such as these have become priorities for businesses attempting to stay on top of the latest technologies.

As per the EABOK, a comprehensive understanding of the interrelationships within an IT organization is gained by combining people, data, and technology. From the perspectives of the owner, designer, and builder, the process takes a comprehensive view of the entire enterprise. This framework does not rely on formal documentation; instead, it is designed to offer an enterprise view from a holistic perspective.

EAP strategies must take into account the latest developments in business processes, organizational structures, information systems, and technology. Standard language and best practices will also be covered, as well as how to integrate or eliminate processes in various parts of the organization. Business information should be reliable, timely, and as efficient as possible.

Benefits of enterprise architecture

In redesigning and reorganizing activities, especially in mergers or acquisitions, EA can help. Additionally, standardization and consolidation of processes promote more consistency within an organization. The most important benefits of EA, according to CompTIA, are as follows:

- Allowing IT and business units to collaborate more easily
- Making investments easier for businesses
- Facilitating long-term evaluation goals by evaluating existing architectures
- Setting up processes for evaluating and procuring technologies
- Increasing the level of understanding of the IT architecture outside of IT by giving all business units a comprehensive view
- Setting up benchmarks for benchmarking against other organizations or industry standards

A result of EA is a reduction of errors, system failures, and security breaches, as well as IT management. The technology can also make IT more accessible to other business units or enable businesses to navigate complex IT structures.

Enterprise architect role

A company's architect typically reports to the **chief information officer** (**CIO**) or another IT manager. The job of a business analyst is to assess the alignment of business structures and processes to the company's goals. An enterprise architect must also ensure structures and processes are agile and robust so that they can quickly adapt to changes and withstand major disruptions.

Data from PayScale indicates that the average salary for this role is $128,600 per year, with a salary range of $93,000 to $190,000 per year. CTOs, developers, software engineering directors, and CIOs are often acquired from enterprise architects. An enterprise architect needs at least 10 years of experience in IT or a related field, as well as an undergraduate degree in computer science, information technology, or a related field. PayScale reports that IT enterprise architects require the following hard skills:

- **Service-oriented architecture** (**SOA**)
- Enterprise application integration
- Cloud computing
- Software and systems architecture
- Enterprise solutions
- Strategy development
- IT and project management

Furthermore, you need to have a thorough understanding of computer systems, hard drives, mainframes, and other architecture technology. Communication, teamwork, problem-solving, critical thinking, and leadership are all soft skills enterprise architects need to possess.

Enterprise architecture tools and software

To plan EA, you'll mostly use Excel and PowerPoint. Several popular options currently available on the market are based on Gartner Peer Insights:

- Orbus Software
- Sparx Systems
- Software AG

- Avolution

- Mega

- Erwin

- BiZZdesign

- Planview

- BOC Group

However, there is another set of tools and software suites that can help your business develop advanced EA strategies.

Enterprise architecture practices with roles

In architecture, architectural artifacts are documents that describe the state of an enterprise, a system, or a solution. System *environments* are the factors that determine all the external influences that have an impact on a system. The environmental factors that can affect a system include developmental, technological, economic, legal, governmental, ecological, and societal factors. A *system*, however, refers to a set of interconnected components that perform one or more predetermined functions.

Architects define architecture as the fundamental concepts or characteristics of a system. Architectural descriptions are work products that are used to convey information about an architecture; they consist of views and models that, together, describe the architecture. *Stakeholders*, on the other hand, consist of individuals, teams, or organizations that have an interest in a given system.

The term *concerns* refers to one or more stakeholders who are interested in a system. Any aspect of a system's development, operation, or functioning, including performance, reliability, security, distribution, and evolvability, may be considered a concern or a determinant of its acceptability. Taking a *system architecture view* is like representing a system from the view of a specific set of concerns. A system architecture model represents what a system is like. *Architecture models* represent subjects of interest. As a simplified representation of a subject, a model presents the subject matter at a smaller scale.

One or more architecture models may be created by an architect as part of capturing or representing the design of system architecture. As a result, an architecture view will consist of elements of one or more models, chosen in such a way as to demonstrate that the concerns of one or more stakeholders are being appropriately addressed in the design of the system architecture. Generally, an architecture view is an architecture specification of conventions for an architectural view to be implemented. This kind of architectural view can be referred to as a definition or schema. To address a particular concern (or set of concerns) about a *system of interest*, it establishes conventions for constructing, interpreting, and using an architecture view.

Model kinds establish a type of modeling convention. Models may be viewed through an architecture viewpoint; an architecture view may include several models. The Reference Library portion of the Architecture Repository contains a collection of specifications for architecture viewpoints:

- Viewpoints that determine what you see, from what vantage point or perspective
- An architecture view is always specific to the architecture that it depicts and can be stored in libraries for reuse; a viewpoint is generic and can be stored in libraries for reuse
- It's at least implicitly described by an architecture viewpoint associated with every architecture view

Be aware that *concern* and *requirement* are not synonymous. They describe different things. Some stakeholders may have a concern/an interest in system reliability. Architecture viewpoints should be associated with concerns to ensure that these concerns will be addressed in some way by the architectural models. Architects who only select a structural architecture viewpoint, for example, are almost certainly not considering reliability issues, because a structural model cannot represent these problems. There may be many different stakeholder requirements within that concern; there may be different requirements of different classes of users in terms of the system's capabilities.

An Architecture Board overseeing the implementation of the strategy is essential to a successful Architecture Governance strategy. Typically, this group comprises executives responsible for reviewing and maintaining the overall architecture, as well as a representative of all the key stakeholders. The majority of architecture boards in larger organizations are made up of representatives at least two tiers deep – that is, local (domain experts' line responsibility) and global (organization-wide responsibility). A board will be established in such situations with identifiable and articulated duties:

- Responsibility and ability to make decisions
- Limitations on authority and remit

Enterprise architecture practices with responsibilities

The following goals are typically entrusted to the Architecture Board:

- Establishing the basis for all architecture-related decisions
- Maintaining consistency across sub-architectures
- Setting targets for reusing components
- Creating a flexible EA to leverage new technologies and meet changing business requirements
- Ensuring that compliance with the architecture is enforced

- Initiating a maturity level improvement of the architecture discipline in the organization
- Ensuring that architecture-based development is implemented
- Enhancing the visibility of escalation capabilities for out-of-bounds decisions

The following responsibilities should be addressed from an operational standpoint:

- Monitoring and controlling all aspects of the Architecture Contract
- Holding regular meetings
- Managing and implementing the architectures in an effective and consistent manner
- Resolving escalated ambiguities, issues, or disputes
- Assisting with information, advice, and guidance
- Implementing a technology strategy and objectives, ensuring compliance with architectures, and granting dispensations as necessary
- Considering changes in policies that are requested and granted for similar dispensations, such as new service types
- Obliging with the Architecture Contract implementation team to publish all information relevant to implementation under controlled conditions and make it available to authorized parties
- Verifying the reported service levels and cost savings

Moreover, the Architecture Board is responsible for the following from a governance perspective:

- Developing usable materials and activities for governance
- Establishing a formal system for the acceptance and approval of architectures through consensus and the authorized publication of architectures
- Ensuring effective implementation of the architecture by providing a fundamental control mechanism
- Implementing EA and linking it to the strategic objectives of the business, based on the architectural strategy and objectives embodied therein
- Dispensations or policy updates may be needed to realign the architecture and planning activities

In the process of detailing requirements, concerns are the starting point. The requirements are what represent concerns in the architecture. It is a good idea to have SMART requirements (that is, specific metrics).

Setting up the Architecture Board

The CIO (or another senior executive) is often the executive sponsor of the initial architecture effort in most companies. Sponsoring bodies have more influence, however, when it comes to garnering corporate support. An Architecture Board is the sponsoring body here, but the title isn't important. The strategic architecture and all of its sub-architectures are reviewed and maintained by this executive-level group.

Triggers

Typically, an Architecture Board is established in response to one or more of the following:

- The new CIO
- Acquisitions or mergers
- Considering switching to a more advanced form of computing
- Recognizing the lack of alignment of IT with the business
- Technology as a means of achieving a competitive advantage
- Implementation of the EA program
- Rapid growth or significant business changes
- Cross-functional requirements for complex solutions

Within the enterprise, the Architecture Board sponsors the architecture, but the Architecture Board itself requires an executive sponsor at the highest levels of the corporation. Architecture projects must be committed to during the planning process and through maintenance. In some companies, architecture planning fails because executive participation and encouragement are lacking.

In many cases, the Board of Directors of a company is overlooked as a potential source of Architecture Board members. Such individuals are often knowledgeable about a business's operations and competitors. They are an important part of validating the alignment of IT strategies to business objectives since they influence the business vision and objectives.

Size of the Architecture Board

We recommend that an Architecture Board includes four to five permanent members (10 at the most). It may be possible for the Architecture Board to rotate its membership over time, with decision-making privileges and responsibilities transferring from one senior manager to another, to keep the Architecture Board to a reasonable size. Some members of the Architecture Board may find that time constraints prevent them from participating actively for a prolonged period.

The Architecture Board must, however, maintain continuity to prevent the corporate architecture from diverging from one idea to the next. Rotation can be ensured by setting a term for each member and having the term expire at different times. An Architecture Board may need to be re-chartered during the ongoing architecture effort following the initial effort. If needed, the architecture compliance review process is updated or changed by the executive sponsor after reviewing the work of the Architecture Board.

Board structure

A generic organizational framework provided by the TOGAF Architecture Governance Framework positions the Architecture Board in the context of the broader enterprise governance structure. In addition to identifying the major organizational groups and responsibilities, it also outlines their relationships with each other. Adaptations of this model may be necessary, depending on the structure and form of the organization.

Taking into account the size and form of the organization, as well as the IT function implementation, is essential. By taking the overall governance environment into account, you can form the basis of designing the Architecture Board structure. An important concept to consider is worldwide ownership and local implementation, and the integration of new technologies and concepts from various areas.

As an organization, the Architecture Board should be structured according to its structure. There may be more complex architecture governance structures needed than the TOGAF Architecture Governance Framework outlines. An organization would need to put an IT governance process in place that combines the corporate structure and capabilities already in place. It typically includes a global governance board, local governance board, design authorities, and working parties.

Operation of the Architecture Board

In this section, we will describe the Architecture Board primarily from the perspective of governance.

General

Meetings regarding the Architecture Board need to have clear objectives, topics, and actions. The **Control Objectives for Information and Related Technologies (COBIT)** framework, as an example, explains best practices for board meetings. During these meetings, key decisions will be made regarding the following:

- Producing quality governance materials and activities
- Providing a formal mechanism for acceptance through consensus and authorization
- Implementing a control mechanism that ensures the architectures are implemented successfully

- Linking architecture implementations with organizational strategy and objectives (business and IT) and maintaining this link

- Dispensations or policy updates may be needed to realign with the contract in the event of divergence from it

Moreover, the agenda of a meeting regarding the Architecture Board contains clearly defined topics and the required actions.

Preparation

Each participant should be familiar with the contents of the agenda and all supporting paperwork, such as dispensation requests, performance management reports, and more. Individuals who have assigned actions are responsible for reporting on progress against those actions. Attendance and availability at Architecture Board meetings must be confirmed by each individual.

Agenda

Agendas for Architecture Board meetings are outlined in this section. The items on the agenda are all described based on their contents.

Minutes of the previous meetings

The minutes of previous Architecture Board meetings are a standard organizational protocol that provides details about past meetings.

Requests for change

Change requests under this heading typically relate to architecture and principle amendments. The business control may also include blocking voice traffic to premium members, such as weather reports, and controlling access to certain websites. The Architecture Contract defines authority levels and parameters within which changes can be requested.

Dispensations

As a mechanism for requesting changes to existing contracts, principles, and structures, dispensations are used. The agency also operates outside of normal operating parameters, such as having a subsidiary excluded from service provisioning, requesting unusual service levels for special business reasons, or deploying non-standard technology or products to support specific business initiatives.

Dispensations are granted for a set period and must comply with certain operational criteria and a set of identified services. Compensations are not granted indefinitely but serve as an alternative way of ensuring that levels of service are met, as well as allowing for flexibility in the implementation and timing of payments. Time-bound dispensations will trigger architecture compliance because of their time-bound nature.

Compliance assessments

The organization assesses compliance against **service-level agreements (SLAs)**, **operational-level agreements (OLAs)**, and the required architecture refreshes. Based on the criteria specified in the TOGAF Architecture Governance Framework, the assessments will either be accepted or rejected. Assessment reports will contain detailed information about the architecture.

Dispute resolution

In the Architectural Compliance assessments and dispensation, disputes that have not been resolved through Architecture Compliance and dispensation processes are documented.

Architecture strategy and direction documentation

Only the global Architecture Board will formulate the architecture strategies, directions, and priorities. Standard architectural documentation should be produced.

Actions assigned

An overview of actions assigned at previous Architecture Board meetings is provided in this report. During Architecture Board meetings, actions are assigned to a tracker, which is used to keep tabs on their status and document how they are progressing:

- Reference
- Priority
- Action description
- Action owner
- Action details
- Date raised
- Due date
- Status
- Type
- Resolution date

Contract documentation management

The architecture documentation is formally accepted here for subsequent publication, updated, and changed.

Any other business (AOB)

This includes issues that fall outside of any of the aforementioned stages. They should be raised at the beginning of the meeting, regardless of whether they are included in the agenda. It is the responsibility of Architecture Governance to manage supporting documentation.

Scheduling meetings

Dates for all meetings should be published in detail. The enterprise architect is a visionary, coach, team leader, liaison between tech and business, and an expert in their field.

Enterprise architect job description

Achieving a complete architecture requires the architect to adequately respond to all the pertinent concerns of its stakeholders. They must ensure that all perspectives are connected, reconcile the conflicting interests of key stakeholders, and indicate the trade-offs made to do so. A key component of the enterprise architect's role is to decide which architectural views to develop. It is imperative to limit the choice to practical factors, as well as to the principle of fitness-for-purpose. As an enterprise architect, your role is more similar to a city planner than a building architect. Rather than defining the enterprise architect's work as a well-designed building or set of buildings, it is more appropriate to describe the community architect's work as a planned community.

An enterprise architect does not create the technical vision of an enterprise, but rather develops and articulates the technical vision in consultation with executives of the enterprise and formulates the strategy to realize that vision. Business plans are always connected to this plan, and design decisions also follow the business plans. This ensures design decisions are not circumvented for tactical convenience since the enterprise architect's strategic plan is linked to the Enterprise Architecture Governance process.

For implementation teams and application development teams, enterprise architects document design decisions.

Throughout the entire process, an architect assists the customer in understanding their needs versus what they want, translating those needs into capabilities that are verified to meet their requirements. In addition, the architect may present each customer with different models that demonstrate how those needs could be met, thus making them indispensable to the consultative sales process. An architect cannot be a builder, and they must remain abstract enough to not hinder implementation.

Hence, the architect's role may be summarized as follows:

- **Understand and interpret requirements**

  This involves information gathering, listening, influencing, consensus building, synthesizing ideas into actionable requirements, speaking those ideas to others, identifying use or purpose, constraints, risks, and so on. In addition to discovering and documenting the customer's business scenarios that drive the solution, the architect contributes to the solution's concept design process.

- **Create a useful model**

    This involves taking the requirements and formulating effective models of the solutions, augmenting the models as needed to address all of the circumstances, and communicating the ideas in multiple ways through the models.

    In terms of architecture, the architect is responsible for maintaining the vision of the offering and preserving architectural integrity. Additionally, the architect ensures that leverage opportunities are identified and that they are realized by leveraging building blocks as a liaison between the functional groups. Architects build and maintain these models to guide work within or outside the organization and to understand the domain of development work. An architect must understand all the business components to represent the organization's architecture.

- **Validate, refine, and expand the model**

    The model should be revised and further defined, using subject matter experts if needed, to increase flexibility and to ensure it is based closely on current and expected requirements. Architects should also consider the value of any enhancements that arise from fieldwork and include them in architecture models where appropriate.

- **Manage the architecture**

    The models should be regularly updated to display changes, additions, and alterations as necessary. They must assist with discussions and decisions about the program's architecture. Architects represent change as an agent for implementing the architecture. Through this process, the architect ensures that information about the customer, architecture, and technical aspects among organizations is shared continuously.

Characterization in terms of enterprise segmentation

In certain scenarios, additional architects may be required to support the architecture effort due to the complexity of a solution. All categories of architects do the tasks outlined previously as well. An enterprise, enterprise solution, and solution architect team can come together to accomplish the task. Depending on the phases of the development process, each member may have a specific focus, if not a specific role and responsibility. If it is deemed necessary to organize an architectural team, a lead enterprise architect must be assigned to manage and lead the team, as follows:

- The enterprise architect is responsible for applying architecture design and documentation to both the technical and landscape reference models. In most cases, the enterprise architect leads a team of segment architects and/or solutions architects to implement a particular program. The focus of the enterprise architect is on the enterprise-level business functions required.

- The segment architect documents and designs specific business problems of organizations. They combine detailed technical solutions with the overall architectural landscape, relying on the output from all other architects. The segment architect is responsible for scoping enterprise-level business solutions across multiple domains, including finance, human resources, and sales.

- Solutions architects are responsible for designing and documenting systems at various levels, such as management and security. By shielding the enterprise/segment architect from unnecessary details of systems, technology, and products, solutions architects might benefit enterprise/segment architects. The solution architect deals with system technologies. For example, a component of an enterprise data warehousing solution would fall under this focus.

Skills and experience in producing designs

Designing complex systems requires the skills of enterprise architects. In addition to discovering and analyzing requirements, it involves identifying and assessing solution alternatives, selecting technologies, and configuring designs.

Extensive technical breadth with technical depth in one or more disciplines

Having experience in the IT industry is an important qualification for an enterprise architect. In addition, the team will be able to develop and deploy applications, as well as design and maintain the infrastructure for complex application environments. In today's IT environment, heterogeneity is the norm, which means experienced enterprise architects must be able to work across multiple platforms, from traditional mainframes to distributed systems. At the end of their careers, enterprise architects will possess expertise in at least one field that they are considered to be subject matter experts in.

Method-driven approach to execution

The TOGAF **Architecture Development Method** (**ADM**) is among the most recognized design methods used by enterprise architects. Enterprise architects should be knowledgeable about more than one design method and should be able to accurately adapt parts of those methods to the circumstances in which they find themselves. An enterprise architect demonstrates this in their repeated use of more than one design method when they're creating their design work. To use methodologies proficiently, you must know which parts of methods to use and which not to use in a given situation.

Full project scope experience

The role of the enterprise architect is to design the project and hand it off to the implementation team, but it is vital to have experience with developing, testing, implementing, and supporting all stages of the project. Enterprise architects will benefit from this range of experience as it will help them use the notion of system implementation that is practical and fit for purpose. As an enterprise architect, experience with full project scope should lead to greater design decisions, and ultimately, better-informed decisions regarding tradeoffs.

Leadership

For an enterprise architect to succeed, communication and teamwork are essential. To be successful at this job, you need both good technical skills and leadership qualities. IT management and clients should regard enterprise architects as leaders in the enterprise.

Personal and professional skills

Communication and relationship skills are essential for the enterprise architect. The enterprise architect is responsible for communicating complex technical information, including those without technical training, to all stakeholders of the project. The role also requires excellent communication and negotiation skills. To keep projects on track, enterprise architects must work closely with project managers to make timely decisions.

Skills and experience in one or more industries

The enterprise architect can gather requirements more easily and more effectively if they have expertise in the industry. A good enterprise architect should understand how a company's business processes interact with the processes of peers in the same industry. As well as spotting key trends and identifying flawed processes, they should be able to provide IT groups with the capability to lead enterprises, not just to respond to requests. A business architect's role is to be a strategic technology leader.

Architectural tools and modeling languages

Enterprise architecture tools aimed at helping organizations thrive in the future are designed to help them succeed. The following enterprise architecture tool features will help your business goals align with IT when selecting the best solution for your team and company.

Fast time-to-value

Enterprise Asset Management (**EAM**) tool adoption, and how quickly it produces value for an organization, determines the success of an EA strategy. An organization has to wait 3 to 6 months for results when using legacy tools, as well as have a lot of customizations made to them. Although modern EAM software is more intuitive and yields much faster results, it has a learning curve. There are several features of EAM tools that set them apart from legacy products:

- In today's EAM world, out-of-the-box and ready-to-use products provide strong data models based on industry best practices and they are easy to understand.

- Intuitive user interfaces require little training and customization, and they're ideal for launching products across organizational silos.

- Costs are based on how many applications are stored in the repository, rather than how many users use the service. Multi-user access and cross-institutional collaboration are the benefits of this concept.

Best practices and a flexible data model enable them to be easily configured without requiring extensive initial configuration. Also, the model can be adapted as they go, allowing them to gain valuable insights early on.

Full collaboration between IT and business stakeholders

Legacy EAM tools typically require a background in IT and are thus out of reach for those who do not possess a computer science degree. However, modern EAM tools are designed for a variety of users, have an intuitive interface, and let anyone understand the data models. Also, this means that enterprise architects aren't isolated in an ivory tower, but are part of the daily activities of all business functions. By making modern EAM tools more user-friendly, a broader range of users can access them, thereby increasing data diversity.

Here are the characteristics that matter most:

- Using application owners and subject matter experts as crowdsource EA resources
- Optimizing the impact of IT on business outcomes through a unified language
- Providing easy access to information relevant to business needs by customizing information displayed for individual stakeholders

However, there are certain challenges that companies face in their EA efforts. The biggest one is to initially locate and gather meaningful data and find a way to keep it up to date.

Automated data discovery and report generation

Automated synchronization and seamless integration are built into EAM tools. Low-code integration capabilities allow them to integrate seamlessly into the modern IT4IT ecosystem. Due to the explosive growth of SaaS applications and vendors, it is not at all surprising that enterprises, and specifically their IT departments, rely on automated **Software-as-a-Service** (**SaaS**) discovery to assure full visibility of all applications. To optimize usage, keep proper entitlements, eliminate waste, and control cloud costs, this transparency is essential.

Additionally, many EAM vendors offer a marketplace where technology partners and users can exchange custom-made reports. EAM tools provide three distinct advantages in terms of automation and integration, as follows:

- API integrations that are low-code and seamlessly integrated into the IT4IT ecosystem

- Discovering SaaS, **Platform-as-a-Service (PaaS)**, and **Infrastructure-as-a-Service (IaaS)** automatically

- Through online ecosystems, EAM enables automatic reports and diagrams

Integrated platform for corporate IT and product IT

A modern EAM tool is built with complementary links to other products so that it functions as an integrated platform and helps increase visibility in a dynamic work environment. As a result, EAM tools do not rely on legacy EA systems but are compatible with SaaS and value stream management solutions; they meet the needs of both corporate IT and product IT through their convergence.

EAM tools can be viewed differently within each tool to help organizations predict, plan, and execute transformation initiatives that give companies a competitive edge. The following are three final traits of an EAM tool:

- An understanding of the present state of the IT architecture and the capacity for road mapping the desired future state

- Collaboration across functional lines and repurposing IT assets

- Flexibility to keep up with new technologies and maintain control

Recommended steps for adopting an Enterprise Architect Management tool

It takes various steps to ensure successful integration and maximum benefit for EA tools and EAM tools in general. Here, we have outlined five steps that you and your team should follow before, during, and after the adoption of EA:

1. **Understand the benefits of EAM tools**: Aside from reducing your cloud spending and potential security risks for sensitive data, EAM tools can help find and eliminate unmanaged IT applications. You can find the right solution to fit your EA strategy once you understand the benefits modern EAM tools have to offer.

2. **Choose an EAM tool based on your EA program**: You need to ensure that the EAM tool you opt for helps you achieve your IT and business objectives. An application portfolio management program, technology risk management program, or a business transformation program could be a part of these efforts.

3. **Assess the needs of stakeholders**: You should evaluate how EA can bridge knowledge gaps between stakeholders since you do not want to create another IT silo. The tool is intended to improve workflows and foster cross-departmental collaboration. Access to data and independent analysis should be available to stakeholders. In addition, quality assurance mechanisms will make the data more accurate.

4. **Review the data model of prospective EAM tools**: You should examine the data models of your prospective EAM tools. Adapting it to fit your current terminology and attributes and assigning authorization roles should be straightforward.

5. **Measure the onboarding process against goals**: After selecting an EAM solution that meets your current as well as foreseeable needs, onboarding can begin. To make progress, set goals and measure your progress as you go.

Moreover, you can use these tools to measure your onboarding success using the desired method and keep track of the progress through data mapping, imports, workspace reviews, and KPIs.

Initiating and evolving an EA practice in organizations

To manage the complexity of constant change and to align organizations toward a single goal, EA is widely applied as a planning and governance technique.

EA for the enterprise, not just the architects

When it comes to convincing business leaders that EA is valuable, there is no big secret. Demonstrate how stakeholder decisions are impacted by greater availability and quality of data. Think of your stakeholders' questions as you plan your EA capabilities.

Start with real business problems

Traditional EA has a reputation for being too expensive and technical, causing widespread perceptions that it hinders business growth. Business challenges must be addressed by your EA initiatives to succeed. We must consider how we frame the EA's value in terms of business performance.

Build decisions on data, not opinion

In addition to traditional, complex tools that only a few can understand, EA still depends on traditional tools that only a few can interpret. Ensure that your data is accurate, then prioritize which metrics are most important, and develop data visualizations that can aid your stakeholders in understanding it.

Governance is good, collaboration is better

Collaboration and alignment between stakeholders are encouraged by open data. Retrospective governance can also be reduced due to open data. To achieve our EA strategic goals, we must address the question of stakeholder engagement.

Turn data into insight into action

Data insights play a major role, but action is most significant. You can make sense of disparate information by constructing metrics based on EA data. Smart business decisions can be made as a result. To move forward, address this question of whether or not a digital twin of your organization using current tools can be created or other options need to be considered.

The future is a work in progress

It is impossible to predict the future. Consequently, your EA functionality must assist in rapidly and accurately adopting the strategy within your business. Here, automation is essential – by automating your future models, you can build many more quickly.

Here's what you need to know: is your mindset flexible enough to encourage flexibility?

Build scalability in EA

Data estates can grow exponentially – and that's one thing you can count on. Scalable EAs, processes, and services are essential. This is the key question you will need to answer: does your EA tool automatically scale as your estate grows?

Embrace collaboration and demonstrate value for the EA's efforts to succeed. It is important that stakeholders from all parts of the enterprise participate in your efforts – and that they benefit from them. Inform stakeholders about the expectations they should have and how to use the data to make strategic decisions more effectively.

To achieve a goal or to deliver the desired outcome, today's EA focuses on customizing and optimizing business capabilities. As enterprise architects, we can transform organizations to invest in the right capabilities, which can be viewed as a portfolio of business capabilities. With the advent of outcome-based architecture, organizations have become more aware of the effects of digital transformation and have created novel ways of keeping ahead of the digital curve to keep competitive. This shift from traditional to digital EA has been accomplished through the use of these novel approaches.

It seems that EA trends are also shifting in favor of creating communities of domain experts, as opposed to a designated EA team. A platform that allows multiple businesses and IT teams in an organization to collaborate, have discussions, and consider different architectural views and approaches is crucial for achieving EA. The role of EA has changed as people are becoming more agile, and governance has grown to be an increasingly significant aspect of EA. Traditionally, the EA would have only been used for project teams and solutions and would have been governed by an EA board. Because EA has become a central part of a company's culture, a digital EA promotes collaboration through a flexible governance model.

Static documentation in the traditional form of EA deliverables was difficult to maintain and update due to its instability. Digital EA has evolved to become a live repository that can be updated and maintained over time as a central point of truth that can lead to enterprise agility. Innovation management also plays a crucial role in fostering an organization's innovation culture through digital EA. The focus here is on changes that are disruptive or iterative. Digital EA must have a well-managed innovation process for it to become a digital change driver.

Developing digital skills

According to organizations, the development of the digital skills of employees is one of the most pressing issues of the current era. When organizations decide to implement EA, they typically just relocate their people from one area to another without understanding that not everyone can act and think like an architect. EA is social by nature, not merely an intellectual endeavor. Architectures are difficult to understand from a purely abstract perspective. Even though EA is not new and is in its nascent stage, it still brings several concepts that are difficult for stakeholders to comprehend. Toward achieving trust, the EA effort must be understood by both organizations. People will doubt the value of EA if they have become tech-savvy because their ability to deliver value is already limited.

Poor communication in traditional EA today can also lead to strong resistance to new initiatives in an organization. The EA message must be communicated clearly and concisely for all stakeholders to understand and eventually expand the discussion. To manage the artifact life cycle and relationships among all entities within an organization, organizations approaching digital EA adoption should consider investing in digital EA tools and repositories. EA through a digital EA acknowledges the impact of digital transformation and strives to maintain the organization at the forefront of the digital era. In addition to differences in technology, digital teams differ fundamentally from traditional teams in terms of culture, practices, platforms, and domains.

Summary

Business is constantly evolving, and businesses must be able to assess the impact of these changes on the IT landscape, as well as how these changes will impact their operations, customer experiences, and ability to grow. Taking a closer look at these issues can help improve the transformation process. Additionally, enterprise architects keep a streamlined and agile IT environment so that IT can run upcoming business transformation projects. In light of that, this chapter shed light on how crucial EA enablement readiness is and what steps organizations can take to facilitate it. Along the way, we also determined and provided a base that helps us understand the process and flow of establishing EA practice. Identifying owners and the workflow for each of the owners, along with roles and responsibilities, were covered in this chapter. Our primary focus remains on explaining EA modeling languages in more detail.

In the next chapter, we will review and summarize all nine chapters of this book and provide use cases as well.

10
Conclusion

As your organization's systems become more interconnected, enterprise architecture promotes consistency across them by allowing development teams to work with a standard set of clear, proven approaches, and even product lines, for their application architectures. The common mechanisms and compatible semantics across systems enable reuse, as well as system integration. By looking beyond the current technology needs and laying the groundwork for future initiatives, these teams can go beyond single applications and assess architectural impacts on the entire enterprise.

The task of formulating, verifying, and then supporting architectural frameworks falls in the enterprise architects' bucket. Data, security, networking, and hardware infrastructure are built out by your enterprise administrators. Also, your application project teams will be in charge of implementing your enterprise architecture. This is an effort that your enterprise architects should actively participate in, as well as support.

It is the scope of enterprise architecture that distinguishes it from application architecture. Enterprise architects guide application architects to understand and apply enterprise architecture, just as application architects guide application designers and implementers on their way to understanding and applying application architecture. In a similar manner to application architects, enterprise architects take a much broader, but generally shallower, view than designers and implementers of systems. Your application development teams and enterprise administrators are responsible for actually implementing your enterprise architecture, even though it is established by your enterprise architect.

Architecture governance

To maintain a smooth and seamless workflow, enterprise architecture leaders must be ahead of certain elements of the organization. At the top of the list is the size of the team, the infrastructure, and the organizational structure. Nevertheless, digital industry leaders must consider the challenges and complications that come along with this transformation. Only a well-structured and thoughtful business agility model is capable of adapting to continuous advancements within a system. Choosing to change constantly comes with a great deal of risk and unpredictability, which can be exhausting for some stakeholders.

Levels of governance within the enterprise

It is not uncommon for architecture governance to operate within a hierarchy of governance structures, which, for large enterprises in particular, may include all of the following distinct domains with their disciplines and processes:

- Corporate governance
- Technology governance
- IT governance
- Architecture governance

Within the enterprise, these governance domains can occur at multiple geographical levels, such as global, regional, and local. An enterprise architecture framework such as **The Open Group Architecture Framework (TOGAF)** does not cover the entire topic of corporate governance. As explained previously, this section and the related subsections describe architecture governance from the standpoint of enterprise-wide governance due to the hierarchical structure within which it typically operates.

The nature of governance

It is the responsibility of the government to ensure that business is properly conducted. An organization's strategic objectives are more likely to be achieved with guidelines and equitable and effective use of resources rather than overt control and strict adherence to rules.

Governance – a generic perspective

The **Organisation for Economic Co-operation and Development (OECD)** has identified the following as the basic principles of corporate governance:

- An examination of shareholders' rights, roles, and equitability
- Ensures the organization's strategy is well-guided, the board monitors management effectively, and the board is held accountable for the company's success
- Board members oversee management's achievement of corporate objectives by reviewing and guiding the corporate strategy

As part of the corporate governance structure, the board of directors sets out who is responsible for what and how, as well as what the rules and procedures are for deciding what to do with the corporation.

Characteristics of governance

Adapted from corporate governance, the following characteristics of governance are shown to emphasize both the value and necessity of adopting governance within businesses and their interactions with other parties:

- **Discipline**

  Throughout the process, all parties involved must follow the organization's policies, procedures, and authority structures.

- **Transparency**

  An authorized organization or service provider can inspect all implemented actions and their decision support.

- **Independence**

  Efforts will be made to minimize or avoid potential conflicts of interest in all processes, decision-making, and mechanisms used.

- **Accountability**

  Several distinct groups are authorized and accountable for their actions and decisions within an organization; for example, governance boards.

- **Responsibility**

  The organization and its stakeholders expect that each contracted party will act responsibly.

- **Fairness**

  There will be no unfair advantage given to one party through any decision taken, the process used, or the process's implementation.

These characteristics help the company's objectives to be established, offer the means for achieving them, and help with monitoring the company's performance.

Technology governance

Using technology for developing, producing, and marketing an organization's products and services is the responsibility of technology governance. Technology governance involves more than just IT governance. As a result of the prevalence of technology across the entire spectrum of organizations, technology governance is a key capability, requirement, and resource.

In addition to their operations and profitability, organizations increasingly depend on IT for their brand and reputation, which ultimately affects the value of their assets.

IT governance

Managing IT resources and information in line with enterprise goals and strategies is known as IT governance. To ensure that an enterprise's IT assets support its business objectives, IT governance institutionalizes best practices for planning, procuring, implementing, and monitoring IT performance. As a result of increasing reports of information system disasters and electronic fraud, regulators are increasingly mandating tighter company controls over information. In today's enterprise governance framework, managing the risks associated with IT is widely accepted as a critical component.

In conclusion, a strategy for IT governance, backed by top management, with a clear definition of who owns the IT resources of the enterprise and who has ultimate responsibility for their integration, is needed.

Architecture governance framework

This section explains architecture governance conceptually and organizationally. Among the many aspects of architecture governance, implementation governance is just one. Its purpose is to manage and control all processes in an organization. The enterprise architecture and other architectural designs are also taken into consideration by the enterprise architect.

With traditional IT silos still in place, moving to the cloud is not standardized, and no centralized management or compliance measures are in place. The difference in standards between enterprise workloads may result in competing interests and inconsistency within an organization when parties are not aligned. Often, IT organizations are unaware of where or how workloads are deployed, what metrics are available for monitoring, or which workloads are vulnerable to security threats. The lack of controls and an audit trail makes this a major compliance risk. Developers may not even follow industry standards in terms of security. Centralized management is nonexistent. This needs to be controlled. **Amazon Web Services** (**AWS**) enables customers to provision and control their environments to achieve business agility. Cloud computing as a service, along with AWS Management and Governance services, offers builders preventive and detective controls to build a robust infrastructure and reduce vulnerabilities.

Basic principles of corporate governance

Rather than enforcing rules rigidly, strategic planning is more about providing direction, as well as ensuring a fair and equitable allocation of resources to sustainably achieve goals. Governance essentially speaks to the proper management of business affairs.

A company's board, management, shareholders, and other stakeholders are assigned different rights and responsibilities, and rules and procedures are in place for corporate decisions. A business plan serves as a way to set and measure company goals, as well as monitor how well they are being achieved.

Amazon services and organizational structure

At Amazon, the product team thinks about every reason a certain product may be developed and why anyone would want it. To convince the target customer to choose the product, a compelling press release is drafted. Your life would be incomplete if not for this announcement. Only by doing so can you be influential.

A service from Amazon is much more than just software; it represents an organization as well. This can be achieved by working backward for your customers. With a strong ownership model, small teams are assigned to a particular product to maximize productivity. An individual's needs and wants are taken into account, as well as their individual and undivided attention. Work backward is the process we use to ensure that a service meets a customer's needs.

As digitalization accelerates quickly, many companies are rethinking their architecture. To meet their constantly increasing expectations, companies should make their products available on as many digital channels as possible. Multinational corporations have developed very complex structures over time, which makes it difficult to make timely changes to their structures. Rather than scaling individual parts of the application, scaling should be applied to the whole. Microservices architecture can reduce software throughput times when integrated into software development. In addition to enhancing productivity and flexibility, microservices are also robust and resilient since they can be constructed and deployed independently.

TOGAF and its objectives

A large part of TOGAF is derived from the TAFIM framework developed by the United States Department of Defense. TOGAF, as well as other IT management frameworks, emphasizes cross-departmental coordination and alignment of IT initiatives with business objectives. Defining and organizing requirements in TOGAF before a project begins keeps the project moving smoothly with few errors. It is designed to assist enterprises with organizing and addressing commercial and strategic needs through four objectives:

- All stakeholders and team members must use a common language
- Don't rely on proprietary solutions for your enterprise architecture
- Time and money can be saved, and resources can be utilized more efficiently
- A measurable **return on investment (ROI)** is required

Despite adding new titles for enterprise architecture artifacts to TOGAF's dictionary, its approach to planning remains unchanged. The overlap between current TOGAF prescriptions and industry best practices appears to have been minimized as a result of recent changes. According to TOGAF, it is a reference library that contains guidelines, templates, patterns, and other types of reference material to accelerate the creation of enterprise architecture.

Cloud transformation

Moving your data, applications, networks, and infrastructure into a cloud environment is known as cloud transformation. The cloud in all its forms, including on-demand computing, smart development, and artificial intelligence, must be harnessed. If you are having problems gaining a competitive advantage due to legacy technology, processes, and infrastructure, the cloud may seem like the perfect solution. Google it and you'll find that several big consulting firms can help you plan your cloud transformation strategy. In the end, you need to move your applications to the virtual world. Although many guides and steps are provided to help you, it all comes down to moving your applications. As part of enterprise architecture, which ensures organizations are aligned with their goals, the changes made toward achieving those goals are defined and analyzed. Cloud computing has created new business models that are centered around services. Cloud computing offers numerous benefits, including cost savings, improved efficiency, shorter development cycles, and quicker time-to-market. A move to the cloud can help companies drastically cut costs because it can improve asset utilization, reduce operational costs, and redefine the relationship between IT staff and management.

A well-architected enterprise architecture

Developing best practices on AWS has been a result of our experience running internet-scale systems. Experts such as principal engineers play a key role in identifying the best practices, which are usually driven by data. As new best practices emerge from community work, principal engineers ensure teams follow them. These best practices will be incorporated as time passes, ensuring compliance. We present our customer-friendly implementation of the Well-Architected Framework as a result of our internal review process. Architects, internal engineers, and others from the field have been incorporated into it. This information can be utilized on a scalable basis using the Well-Architected Framework.

By using a principal engineering community with distributed ownership, a well-architected enterprise architecture can emerge based on the needs of customers. Having a holistic view of risks across the entire portfolio is crucial for CTOs and other technology leaders. As a result, your organization can identify themes across teams that could be addressed through training, lunchtime discussions, or other mechanisms where your principal engineers can share their thoughts on specific topics across teams.

As part of AWS' internal review process, well-architected systems and services are reviewed. A root cause analysis focuses on design principles that influence how architectural approaches are implemented; it also asks questions to ensure that individuals do not overlook factors that are present in many RCAs. Our review process is reviewed whenever there is a technical problem with an internal system or service, or when a customer contacts us, to see whether it can be improved. Reviewing products should occur at key milestones throughout the product life cycle, such as early on in the design phase to avoid one-way doors, and before the initial launch of the service. You will continue to have more work to do after you go into production if you add new features and implement new technologies. Workloads change when they grow. Maintaining good hygiene practices is essential if you want its architectural characteristics to remain intact as they age. It is recommended that a Well-Architected review is performed before significant architectural changes take place.

To use the review as a one-time snapshot or for independent measurement, you must ensure that the right people are involved in the conversation. During review sessions, teams can assess the quality of their work for the first time. When reviewing the workload of another team, it is helpful to have informal discussions about the architecture of another team. To gain clarity or dig deeper, you can hold a second or third meeting to clarify or address the ambiguity. The business context should help you decide what your priorities are after reviewing the issues. Additionally, you will need to consider how those issues may impact your team's regular work. It would be possible to solve recurring problems earlier, allowing you to invest more time into creating value for the company. As issues are addressed and the architecture improves, your review will be updated.

The benefits of a review will become evident after it has been conducted, but a new team may first express resistance. You can address objections with education about why a review will benefit the team:

- The team is too busy! (The term used before launching a big program.)

  - Before launching a big product, make sure it is prepared well. You can determine whether any mistakes were made through a review.

  - To develop mitigation plans early in a product's life cycle, it's very important to conduct reviews early.

- Before a major event such as the Super Bowl, it is often said, *There is no time to act on the results!*

  - There is no way to change the events mentioned previously. Is it your wish to experience this risk without understanding how it relates to your architecture? Even if you don't address all of them, playbooks will still be needed if they arise.

- It's not our intention for others to know how we implemented our solution:

  - When pointing the Well-Architected Framework team at the questions, it is obvious that none of the questions reveal any technical or commercial proprietary information.

A series of reviews by different teams within your organization may lead to thematic issues being identified. The problem may lie in a particular pillar or topic if you examine a group of teams. You will need to identify any mechanisms, training, or engineer-led discussions that could help you address these thematic issues as part of your comprehensive review. In many sectors, change is happening faster due to the proliferation of digital technologies. Companies are being increasingly forced to reinvent themselves every few years as it becomes harder and harder to earn competitive advantages. Government agencies are also improving how they provision digital services in response to citizens' expectations and behaviors. Businesses that use digital technologies to adapt to market changes, delight customers, and accelerate their business outcomes are more successful.

Cloud migration strategy

There are millions of customers using AWS, from startups to government agencies. Business processes must be digitalized and optimized, legacy workloads must be migrated and modernized, and business models must be reinvented. A cloud-powered transformation makes their operations more efficient, reduces risks, and lowers their costs. Additionally, they improve employee morale and customer satisfaction, as well as their agility. The cloud can be effectively leveraged for digital transformation, but only if you have a set of foundational organizational capabilities (your cloud-readiness). By identifying these capabilities and offering prescriptive guidance, the AWS Cloud Transformation Accelerator helps thousands of organizations across the globe accelerate their cloud transformation endeavors.

Once you understand the reasons for migrating to a cloud environment, you can develop a cloud migration strategy. In cloud computing, data centers don't need to be maintained, scalability is improved, resilience is improved, and teams can collaborate remotely. When you use AWS, you can modernize your technology, as well as access end-to-end support for mobile capabilities, cloud architecture, design, and development. A Well-Architected Framework for AWS allows you to optimize how your applications are developed, maintained, and upgraded.

By facilitating communication among principal engineers about specific topics through training sessions, lunchtime discussions, or other mechanisms, your organization can address topics across teams. You can identify and prioritize opportunities for transformation using the Amazon Cloud Architecture Framework. Assessing and improving your cloud readiness, and iteratively improving your roadmap as you transform your organization, will ultimately increase your organization's agility.

Phases of the architecture development method

As TOGAF is mostly used by VLEs, an ADM will suffice for smaller firms. Iteration during requirements phases is common in agile projects. In most cases, business requirements are elicited and clarified beforehand without you having to define them and understand them clearly. ADM has 10 phases, as outlined here. The TOGAF documentation on Open Group's website provides a complete overview of TOGAF's approach and descriptions of each phase, identifying its objectives, inputs, steps, and outcomes.

Preliminary phase – framework and principles

An organization's preliminary phase is concerned with defining where, what, why, who, and how the architecture is done within that particular enterprise. It addresses the enterprise definition and helps you identify key drivers and elements. It also allows you to determine the requirements for the architecture and define the architectural principles that will perform any architecture work. Defining the framework and the relationships between management frameworks, as well as determining the maturity of the enterprise architecture, are also covered.

Phase A – architecture vision

Requests for architecture work are sent to the architecture organization by the sponsoring organization. This phase consists of defining the scope of the architecture, developing the vision, and applying for approvals.

Phase B – business architecture

It is imperative to start with the business architecture if it hasn't been addressed in other processes already. You could, for instance, re-engineer business processes through enterprise planning or strategic business planning.

Phase C – information systems architecture

In this phase, you develop the data architecture, the application architecture, and the information systems architecture. For each architecture domain, you are given details separately for the data architecture and applications architecture, for example.

Phase D – technology architecture

Technology architecture consists of the following steps:

- Tools, viewpoints, and reference models
- It will be developed as part of the baseline technology architecture description
- Develop the target technology architecture description
- Assess gaps
- Develop roadmap components
- Resolve impacts across the architecture landscape
- Conduct a formal stakeholder review
- Finalize the technology architecture
- Create the architecture definition document

Phase E – opportunities and solutions

When you identify the parameters of change, you are in the opportunities and solutions phase. Also identified are the major phases to be undertaken on the way to the target and the top-level projects to be executed to accomplish that.

Phase F – migration planning

Prioritizing implementation projects is part of migration planning. Assessing the costs, benefits, and dependencies of migration projects are included in this activity.

Phase G – implementation governance

During this phase, you gather all the information you need to manage the various implementation projects.

Phase H – architecture change management

In this phase, you establish a process for handling architecture change management for your new enterprise architecture baseline.

ADM architecture requirements management

Through the architecture requirements management process, ADM is continuously driven. Developers working in technology expertise areas such as software, hardware, electrical, electronics, and others develop operational value streams. Those involved in this role define, develop, test, and deploy solutions both internally and to external customers. Customer-centricity and design thinking enable companies to develop products that are right for their customers, and agility allows them to address market changes and emerging opportunities rapidly.

The software industry has embraced agility for many years. The SAFe process is flexible enough to be deployed at a variety of enterprise scalability levels. **Behavior-driven development (BDD)**, **test-driven development (TDD)**, agile testing, refactoring, and spikes are some of our advanced interests. The scaled agile software architecture supports evolutionary design and architecture by combining practices, values, and partnerships. The DevOps philosophy stresses the importance of continually enhancing a system's architecture while supporting the requirements of its users. A high level of rework and redesign goes into BUFD and phase-gate processes, resulting in delays. Just as Agile development practices provide testing, deployment, and release capabilities, Agile architectures do too. In agile development practices, collaboration and design simplicity are encouraged by an agile architecture.

ADM architecture requirements management

Configuring computing resources for a company's business goals is a prerequisite for enterprise architecture. To achieve success, the company's operations, data, and information, as well as the supporting infrastructure, must be aligned with its strategic goals. An organization can produce a technology analysis report that shows how technology is changing and how future technology will fit into its present technology. A digital transformation era has brought about a variety of business and technology changes. It has been observed that enterprise architects have been gaining a lot from the toolbox of change management as well. An EA's ability to build models and use those models to produce actionable insights plays a crucial role in developing a strategy and executing these initiatives. Even though conventional planning processes do not include those models, they force much greater levels of communication than their conventional counterparts.

If they are fortunate enough to be selected for the role of an enterprise architect, enterprise architects must understand where their value comes from. Hence, rather than competing with business strategy teams and PMO teams, you should work together. It takes a lot of conversations and time to turn an idea into a comprehensive enterprise architecture. Over time, the EA's responsibilities and the journey will evolve and mature as technology advances and priorities change. Risks and challenges come with developing an enterprise architecture strategy. Due to the fast pace of technological advances, even entire methodologies, systems, and applications can become outdated in a very short period. EA models tend to become outdated fast when combined with the tendency to follow the latest trends. Standard versions are more susceptible to this.

It is a never-ending game of catch-up for enterprise architects in this situation, and the strategy never fully delivers its intended benefit. A common perception of architects is that they are out of touch with reality, as many business teams are. Developers are often skeptical about the benefits of documentation. Technology executives must continually emphasize the strategic importance of enterprise architecture for achieving short and long-term business goals. The enterprise governance team also assesses and plans future business capabilities, in addition to identifying enterprise governance objectives and regulatory constraints. These efforts are carried out to increase security and achieve economies of scale.

These practices and strategies are essential for an agile architect to succeed.

A digital era is one in which technology is essential to providing value to customers. The systems, applications, and technologies that deliver business strategies must also change when business strategies change. All changes to the customer experience are the responsibility of the team that supports applications and systems. Business owners and product managers should coordinate closely with architects so that these systems can achieve current and future business objectives. To develop a company's architecture, a portfolio vision, a portfolio canvas, and a strategic theme are drafted. These constraints provide direction, as well as context, to technology investments in a portfolio.

Enterprise architects should also consider the larger strategy of the organization in addition to narrowing their focus on architecture. The definition of an end-to-end value stream includes all the activities that ensure the desired result, be it an internal client or an external client. To identify stakeholders who trigger the business architecture value stream and who participate in it, it is crucial to identify their identities. Additionally, incremental items accumulated through achieving the value proposition are included. This represents the value sought and received by the customer, or, to put it another way, the purpose for which they do business with a business.

The operational value stream explains the process of delivering goods and services to customers from the SAFe framework. In addition to the people and systems doing the work, the operational value stream includes the information flow, systems, and materials that deliver value to the customer.

SAFe and scaled agile frameworks

This chapter discusses SAFe, one of the scaled agile frameworks. These frameworks are designed to help large organizations adopt lean and agile practices. Based on SAFe, enterprise architecture promotes innovation and engineering practices and helps teams coordinate. In addition to providing strategic guidance and reference architectures, enterprise architects are instrumental in helping developers implement standardized standards. When the standards of a company do not align, rework may be necessary. Additionally, silos within an organization can be broken down.

In addition, enterprise architecture emphasizes the importance of matching computing resources to business needs. Getting a company's strategies in line with the information produced, its support infrastructure, and its current processes is critical to success. Organizations obtain success by releasing separate information at regular intervals. To create seamless end-to-end value streams, agile architects use a customized architecture.

It may seem miraculous that AWS is growing so rapidly if you don't know about the in-depth infrastructure of how it operates. The **International Data Corporation** (**IDC**) study, based on the experience of 10 companies, results in an ROI of 560% for Amazon customers based on AWS. Pay-as-you-go IT infrastructures offer many advantages for companies, including financial benefits and the ability to eliminate data center costs. Robert Alexander, CEO of *Capital One*, explained that a major reason for moving Capital One's infrastructure to AWS was because of AWS. In Alexander's opinion, the company needs to focus its efforts on high-performance software engineering. Furthermore, he added that firms with impressive technology in the banking industry will win, and companies utilizing AWS can run their businesses with greater security than they can with their private data centers.

Utilizing the most advanced technologies and practices, AWS has solved challenges related to managing cloud infrastructure and migrating to the cloud. We can help companies move to the cloud and transform their business into a digital enterprise by collaborating with Amazon because migrating to the cloud involves more than just technology. Repurchase opportunities are determined during the discovery process for the organization. Nowadays, it is becoming increasingly difficult to build and maintain your email system. The most cost-effective email solution would be a **Software-as-a-Service** (**SaaS**) offering if an email service is currently run internally and is part of the discovery assessment.

Since this development is opening many new paths for AWS repurchasing, we expect to see migrations to AWS increase significantly from 5% to 15% in the next few years. In the AWS Marketplace, buyers have always had the option to repurchase applications instead of migrating fragile on-premises products. The process is similar to an upgrade, in which the data and configuration from the old platform are transferred to the repurchased platform.

Due to the development of the AWS Marketplace and Service Catalog, it is now possible to rent both appliances and SaaS software. The seller can negotiate a complex private offer with AWS, and you can even bring your own license. The rapid growth of AWS may make those unfamiliar with its intricate infrastructure wonder whether there are any underlying reasons. According to a study based on data from 10 companies, Amazon customers can predict their investment in AWS will return 560% over the next 5 years. Companies can reap financial benefits from pay-as-you-go IT infrastructures, as well as eliminate the need to invest in data centers, which can also provide many competitive advantages. Capital One's CEO, Robert Alexander, explained that one of the main reasons it made the move to AWS was to take advantage of the cloud computing platform. Alexander believes that the company needs to transform into an organization that specializes in high-performance software engineering. He stated that "*a banking industry's company with great technology will win and for companies like ours, AWS makes it much easier for us to run our business more securely in the public cloud versus in a private data center.*"

Utilizing the most advanced technologies and practices, AWS has solved challenges related to managing cloud infrastructure and migrating to the cloud. We can help companies move to the cloud and transform their business into a digital enterprise by collaborating with Amazon because migrating to the cloud involves more than just technology. Due to the development of the AWS Marketplace and Service Catalog, it is now possible to rent both appliances and SaaS software. The seller can negotiate a complex private offer with AWS, and you can even bring your own license. The rapid growth of AWS might make those unfamiliar with its intricate infrastructure wonder if there are any underlying reasons. According to a study based on data from 10 companies, Amazon customers can predict their investment in AWS will return 560% over the next 5 years. Companies can reap financial benefits from pay-as-you-go IT infrastructures, as well as eliminate the need to invest in data centers, which can also provide many competitive advantages. Capital One's CEO, Robert Alexander, explained that one of the main reasons it made the move to AWS was to take advantage of the cloud computing platform. Alexander believes that the company needs to transform into an organization that specializes in high-performance software engineering. The banking industry's company with great technology will win, he said, and for companies like ours, AWS makes it much easier for us to run our business more securely in the public cloud versus in a private data center.

Utilizing the most advanced technologies and practices, AWS has solved challenges related to managing cloud infrastructure and migrating to the cloud. We can help companies move to the cloud and transform their business into a digital enterprise by collaborating with Amazon because migrating to the cloud involves more than just technology.

Cloud computing challenges

Some of the leading challenges that companies may encounter with cloud computing can be avoided using appropriate methods. The following are a few such examples:

- **Migrating workloads**: The migration of data, applications, and servers between cloud providers should be planned and executed with precision. The same considerations apply when transferring on-premises workloads to the cloud as they do when transferring between clouds. It is sometimes difficult to download data quickly enough, causing higher fees.

- **Downtime**: Migration to the cloud entails a significant risk of downtime. In addition to data consistency, network connections, and preparing for downtime during internal applications, the migration process should be completed with consistency.

- **Learning how to adapt to the cloud environment**: A company is more likely to build its own applications for a particular cloud provider than to use existing ones. When moving to another cloud provider, there may be some problems since custom settings may not work with the new cloud provider. A company must allow time for app reconfiguration to take advantage of the new platform's advantages.

- **Budgeting and timing**: These two factors should be considered when migrating from one cloud to another or from one server to the cloud. Businesses should consider investing in a migration company during this stage since they can ensure a seamless migration at a competitive price.

Repatriating applications from the cloud to an on-premises data center is called cloud repatriation. It is called reverse cloud migration to repatriate applications from the cloud to an on-premises data center. Cloud environments differ from on-premises environments in that the technology is owned and managed by the users. It is possible to use the same technology for both an on-premises and cloud-based solution. Their consumption models are different, however. Users of cloud services, on the other hand, must use generic tools since providers don't usually provide specialized equipment.

Moreover, some governments mandate on-site storage and operating on sensitive information. Companies in the government, health, and financial sectors cannot use cloud services and ensure compliance with security regulations. Deploying cloud infrastructures across multiple large, dispersed networks, on the other hand, provides a greater level of redundancy, while allowing businesses to access more computing power than they would otherwise be able to. The cost and complexity of maintaining an in-house environment are typically greater in the beginning.

The migration back to on-premises storage is prompted for several reasons. In particular, the following reasons justify repatriation:

- **Cost**: While they offer high scalability and cheap computation power for short-term surges, public clouds are not always cost-effective for long-term deployment.

- **Control over data and security**: Using public cloud services involves a security risk associated with distributed configuration management. Public cloud services involve high levels of security risks related to distributed configuration management. This is because distributed configuration management affects public clouds. Security vulnerabilities are frequently caused by misconfigured buckets. In contrast, on-premises solutions tend to provide greater control, handle security in a consolidated manner, and have a clear security perimeter.

- **Performance**: As a result of WAN bandwidth and cloud provider workloads, public clouds differ greatly in how quickly you can move data to and from the cloud.

- **Vendor lock-in**: You may become dependent on your cloud provider if you become locked in. If your systems have all been developed using the tools of a single vendor, changing vendors may be difficult.

If they begin charging higher prices, your cloud provider options could be limited. The foundation is set for migrating back to on-premises storage based on these factors, as well as any others. Epics are an organized body of work that can be divided into a collection of smaller stories called issues, which Jira uses to refer to these smaller narratives. Multiple projects can be handled by several teams working together, and multiple boards can be used to manage multiple epics simultaneously. Epics are usually preceded by a set of sprints. As the team learns more about an epic from development and customer feedback, the user stories will be added and removed.

Based on customer feedback and team cadence, agile epics have a flexible scope and use customer feedback.

For a development team to succeed, an epic should include all the resources it needs. When it comes to their work hierarchy, they are at the top. In addition to providing context for evaluating epics, it is also important to understand how each epic fits into other agile structures.

A beginner may find it intimidating to break down an epic into smaller pieces, but it makes understanding easier and maintains momentum. AWS' rapid growth may raise the question of whether there is a reason for it.

By leveraging the most advanced technologies and practices, AWS has been able to solve the challenges of managing cloud infrastructure and migrating to the cloud. Getting to the cloud involves more than just technology, so with Amazon, you can transform your business via a cloud migration. Rehosting is a faster method than lift and shift or traditional hosting methods since it requires less time. In addition, it is less time-consuming to implement and requires minimal refactoring. Lifting and shifting, however, may only result in the bare minimum of changes, so you may not realize the same benefits as you would from having a fully cloud-based system. If speed and ease are the only factors they consider, you could end up paying more for a more thorough migration in the short term.

Even organizations that do not have a fully cloud-ready, simple, low-impact workload can benefit from lift and shift. So long as you already have many **virtual machines** (**VMs**), this should be fairly straightforward. You can even buy products from vendors who provide migration automation. There are even vendors who offer products that promise to automate your migration. Manually performing the migration, on the other hand, is an excellent learning experience. In addition, if you make a lift-and-shift decision hastily, once your apps are running in the cloud, they can be reworked and optimized easily. In addition to transforming technology, cloud computing offers other benefits. The **AWS Cloud Adoption Framework** (**AWS CAF**) offers a comprehensive perspective on cloud adoption. Furthermore, it connects six of the most important features of a software system – business, people, governance, platform, security, and operations. When an enterprise attempts to migrate, it can be helpful to use the framework provided as follows. Despite this, it faces challenges such as financial limitations, database issues, and a variety of other factors.

After a successful migration to the cloud, several benefits can be realized, including high scalability, superior performance, and an exceptional digital experience. Several cloud migration strategies may be applied, depending on the team infrastructure and organization, such as repurchasing, which has its own set of driving factors, limitations, and risks.

As well as multiple challenges posed by migrating to the cloud, unstructured organizations will deal with budgeting, adjusting to the new cloud environment, and downtime. In the repatriation of cloud-based services from the cloud to on-premises data centers, these services are transferred from the cloud to on-premises servers. When cloud applications are repatriated from a cloud to an on-premises server, they have been transferred from the cloud. Cloud applications that are moved from the cloud to on-premises servers are called to bring them back to the data center. De-clouding, also known as reverse cloud migration, is a process that removes the public cloud from a system.

An organization's growth prospects determine its success in digital transformation. In particular, large companies must complete business transformation through technological advancement to remain competitive and relevant. Competitors who are more technological savvy take market share and customers, but many companies are looking for opportunities for digital growth. An enterprise architect's role in transformation is not only crucial since they have a thorough understanding of the business processes, but because they also understand the impact that the IT landscape has on business results.

Constant business changes impact the IT landscape

Enterprises must easily assess how changes in the business landscape are affecting the IT landscape, and how these changes affect their operations, customer experiences, and the ability to grow. An understanding of these implications can help propel the transformation process forward. IT architects play a vital role in making sure IT infrastructure is streamlined and agile to handle upcoming business transformation projects.

The organization's enterprise architecture is guided by its business requirements. They are responsible for defining how information, business, and technology flow within the organization, among other things. To stay competitive, companies have become more focused on emerging technologies such as cloud computing, IoT, and **machine learning** (**ML**).

People, data, and technology can be combined to provide IT organizations with a comprehensive understanding of their interrelationships. Owners, designers, and builders take a comprehensive look at the organization as a whole during the design process. It is designed to provide an enterprise view from a holistic perspective, rather than rely on formal documentation.

To effectively implement EAP strategies, it is crucial to take the most recent changes in business processes, organizational structures, and information technology into account. Various aspects of the organization will be discussed, such as standard language and best practices, as well as how to integrate or eliminate processes. It is crucial to have reliable, timely, and efficient business information.

One thing you can rely on is that data estates will grow exponentially. Scalable enterprise architectures, processes, and services will become increasingly important. The key question to answer is whether or not our estate management tool automatically scales with our estate.

To succeed in enterprise architecture, embrace collaboration and highlight the value of your efforts. Including stakeholders from every part of the organization in your efforts is vital – and ensuring that they benefit from them as well. The data should be used by stakeholders to make more effective strategic decisions. Provide them with information about what they should expect. EAs, in today's world, concentrate on optimizing and customizing business capabilities to achieve a goal or deliver the desired result. By addressing business capabilities as a portfolio, we can assist organizations in investing in the right capabilities. This digital transformation has caused organizations to come up with new ways to keep up with the digital curve to remain competitive. By using an outcome-based architecture, these organizations have been able to address the effects of digital transformation. The shift from traditional to digital EA has been made possible by utilizing these novel approaches.

Also, it appears that the trend of creating communities of domain experts, rather than one single EA team, is shifting. For enterprise architecture to succeed, it must be possible for several businesses and the IT team inside an organization to collaborate, have discussions, and consider different architectural approaches and views. Due to the growing number of Agile workers, EA has taken on a more significant role, even when it comes to governance. It has traditionally only been used for project teams and solutions, and it has been governed by an enterprise architecture board. An enterprise architecture that incorporates a flexible governance model promotes collaboration so that the enterprise architecture can be integrated into a company's culture. In the traditional EA deliverables form, static documentation was difficult to maintain and update because it was unstable. As a result of the evolution of the digital enterprise architecture, a central repository can be updated and maintained over time as a point of truth that drives enterprise agility. The digital enterprise architecture plays a vital role in fostering an organization's innovation culture through innovation management. Disruptive or incremental changes are emphasized here. If digital EA wants to become a digital change engine, it must have a well-managed innovation process.

In today's business world, changes are constant, and businesses must assess the impact of these changes on their IT landscapes, and how these changes will impact their operations, customer experiences, and ability to grow. This can help improve the transformation process if the issues are examined closely. Architects ensure that IT can run upcoming business transformation projects by ensuring that the IT environment is streamlined and agile. As such, we have discussed the importance of EA enablement readiness, and the steps organizations can take to enhance it in this chapter. During the process, we also establish and determine a foundation that assists in understanding the process and flow by which to establish the EA practice.

Writing a book was harder than I could have imagined but equally rewarding as well. I am hopeful that this book offered you enlightenment and in-depth knowledge on the matter. I am eternally grateful to everyone who was involved in making this book what it is – my editors, researchers, and publishing team.

Index

Packt.com

Subscribe to our online digital library for full access to over 7,000 books and videos, as well as industry leading tools to help you plan your personal development and advance your career. For more information, please visit our website.

Why subscribe?

- Spend less time learning and more time coding with practical eBooks and Videos from over 4,000 industry professionals

- Improve your learning with Skill Plans built especially for you

- Get a free eBook or video every month

- Fully searchable for easy access to vital information

- Copy and paste, print, and bookmark content

Did you know that Packt offers eBook versions of every book published, with PDF and ePub files available? You can upgrade to the eBook version at packt.com and as a print book customer, you are entitled to a discount on the eBook copy. Get in touch with us at customercare@packtpub.com for more details.

At www.packt.com, you can also read a collection of free technical articles, sign up for a range of free newsletters, and receive exclusive discounts and offers on Packt books and eBooks.

Other Books You May Enjoy

If you enjoyed this book, you may be interested in these other books by Packt:

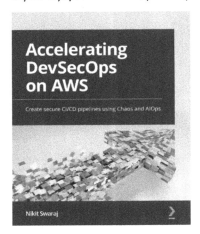

Accelerating DevSecOps on AWS

Nikit Swaraj

ISBN: 9781803248608

- Use AWS Codestar to design and implement a full branching strategy
- Enforce Policy as Code using CloudFormation Guard and HashiCorp Sentinel
- Master app and infrastructure deployment at scale using AWS Proton and review app code using CodeGuru
- Deploy and manage production-grade clusters using AWS EKS, App Mesh, and X-Ray
- Harness AWS Fault Injection Simulator to test the resiliency of your app
- Wield the full arsenal of AWS Security Hub and Systems Manager for infrastructure security automation
- Enhance CI/CD pipelines with the AI-powered DevOps Guru service

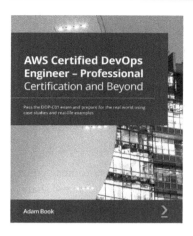

AWS Certified DevOps Engineer - Professional Certification and Beyond

Adam Book

ISBN: 9781801074452

- Automate your pipelines, build phases, and deployments with AWS-native tooling
- Discover how to implement logging and monitoring using AWS-native tooling
- Gain a solid understanding of the services included in the AWS DevOps Professional exam
- Reinforce security practices on the AWS platform from an exam point of view
- Find out how to automatically enforce standards and policies in AWS environments
- Explore AWS best practices and anti-patterns
- Enhance your core AWS skills with the help of exercises and practice tests

Packt is searching for authors like you

If you're interested in becoming an author for Packt, please visit authors.packtpub.com and apply today. We have worked with thousands of developers and tech professionals, just like you, to help them share their insight with the global tech community. You can make a general application, apply for a specific hot topic that we are recruiting an author for, or submit your own idea.

Share Your Thoughts

Now you've finished *Realize Enterprise Architecture with AWS and SAFe*, we'd love to hear your thoughts! Scan the QR code below to go straight to the Amazon review page for this book and share your feedback or leave a review on the site that you purchased it from.

https://packt.link/r/1801812071

Your review is important to us and the tech community and will help us make sure we're delivering excellent quality content.

www.ingramcontent.com/pod-product-compliance
Lightning Source LLC
Chambersburg PA
CBHW062111050326
40690CB00016B/3284